THE CROSS
IN THE SAND

A Discovery Quincentenary Edition
1492-1992

THE CROSS
IN THE SAND

he Early Catholic Church in Florida

1513-1870

MICHAEL V. GANNON

University of Florida Book   University Presses of Florida
Gainesville

Published under the sponsorship of the St. Augustine Foundation
Printed in the U.S.A. on acid-free paper

04   03   02   01   00   99   8   7   6   5   4

Library of Congress Cataloging-in-Publication Data
Gannon, Michael V.
The cross in the sand.
Bibliography: p.
Includes index.
1. Catholic Church–Florida–History. 2. Missions–Florida–History. 3. Florida–Church history.
I. Title.
BX1415.F55G3   1983   282'.759   83–10498
ISBN 0-8130-0776-3

The engraving on the cover, reprinted courtesy of the P. K. Yonge Library of Florida History at the University of Florida, is from *Historia general de los hechos de los Castellanos en las islas y tierra firme del mar oceano* (Madrid, 1726), by Antonio Herrera y Tordesillas.

The University Press of Florida is the scholarly publishing agency for the State University System of Florida, comprising Florida A & M University, Florida Atlantic University, Florida International University, Florida State University, University of Central Florida, University of Florida, University of North Florida, University of South Florida, and University of West Florida.

University Press of Florida
15 Northwest 15th Street
Gainesville, FL 32611
http://www.upf.com

TO
THE
MEMORY
OF MY
FATHER

CONTENTS

INTRODUCTION

to the Second Edition

I T IS A PLEASURE after eighteen years to offer a second edition of *The Cross in the Sand*. The book was written to observe the 400th anniversary of the permanent beginning of Christianity in the United States, an event that we date from September 8, 1565, at the city of St. Augustine in Florida. It seems to have found a congenial place on the bookshelf for early American religious history, and in response to continued demand the University of Florida Press has favored the writer with a new edition.

Though written with the general reader in mind, this history of the early Catholic Church in Florida has been found useful as a textbook in colleges and as the major source for the earliest period of American Christianity in general histories by Robert T. Handy and James Hennesy, S.J. That the book has had such apparent broad appeal gladdens the heart of its author, who makes bold to hope for eighteen more years in reprint.

It is important to acknowledge that this new printing is not a revised edition. A rereading of the text persuades that the narrative has stood well the test of time and that the many intervening discoveries in manuscript and archeological sources have not altered substantially the tale that is told in these pages. The most significant of these, one which does require emendation of the text (pages 20–21), is that the original commission to Pedro Menéndez de Avilés to settle Florida was not issued in direct response to the French military encroachment at Fort Caroline. Historian Eugene Lyon discovered in research at the Archivo General de Indias in Seville that Menéndez received his *asiento* from Philip II on March 15 (not March 20), 1565, eleven days before the Court learned of the existence of the French colony. One other change that seems appropriate is to withdraw the word "savages" on page 9 and to replace it with "aborigines" or "natives." The original Florida inhabitants were remarkable peoples of rich and diverse cultures, and while much of their behavior did not suit the taste of Spanish Christians, it would be wrong to suggest that they alone were experienced in what today is commonly called savagery.

An updating of the bibliography would include the writer's own "Church Influence in Louisiana and Florida in the Eighteenth Century," in *Cardinales de Dos Independencias: Noreste de México-Sureste de los Estados Unidos* (México City, 1978); "Mitres and Flags: Colonial Religion in the British and Second Spanish Periods," in *Eighteenth-Century Florida: The Impact of the American Revolution*, ed. Samuel Proctor (Gainesville, 1978); and "El Conflicto entre la iglesia y el estado en la Florida española: la administración del gobernador Juan Márquez Cabrera, 1680-1687," in *Congreso de La Rábida: Impacto de España en La Florida, El Caribe y La Luisiana, 1500-1800* (Madrid, 1983). Other new titles on or related to Florida religious life in the early centuries include Robert Allen Matter, "The Spanish Missions of Florida: The Friars Versus the Governors in the Golden Age, 1606-1690" (Ph. D. dissertation, University of Washington, 1972); and Jerald T. Milanich and William C. Sturtevant, eds., *Francisco Pareja's 1613 Confessionario* (Tallahassee, 1972).

MICHAEL V. GANNON
University of Florida
1983

Addendum: Since the foregoing introduction to the second edition, it has become appropriate to acknowledge that the writer altered his view of the "Golden Age," in an article written by him under the name of Charles W. Spellman, "The 'Golden Age' of the Florida Missions, 1632-1674," *Catholic Historical Review*, LI, 3 (October, 1965), 354-372. The following recent works on the mission period should also be acknowledged: David J. Weber, *The Spanish Frontier in North America* (New Haven, 1992); three volumes by John H. Hann, *Apalachee: The Land Between the Rivers* (Gainesville, 1988), *Missions to the Calusa* (Gainesville, 1991), and *History of the Timucua Indians and Missions* (Gainesville, 1996); and John E. Worth, *The Timucuan Chiefdoms of Spanish Florida*, 2 vols. (Gainesville, 1998).

MICHAEL V. GANNON
1999

INTRODUCTION

to the First Edition

THIS IS THE STORY of the early Catholic Church in Florida, the oldest establishment of the Christian Faith in the United States of America. It is a story told from original sources, as far as that was possible, and from the best secondary accounts of this century and of the centuries past. It makes no pretense at being the complete story, for many more volumes than this one would be needed to pursue three centuries in all of their detail. Still, the essential facts and episodes are here, and the writer hopes that they have been related in a manner likely to commend the tale to the general reader. An attempt has been made to keep the events moving at a good pace, and to tell as much as possible of what happened in the words of the participants themselves.

This book appears in a year when the Church of Florida is observing the 400th Anniversary of its founding. That founding occurred at Nombre de Dios, the venerable mission ground at St. Augustine, where on September 8, 1565, Pedro Menéndez de Avilés landed with his famous band of settlers and Father Francisco López de Mendoza Grajales celebrated the First Mass in America's First City. Yet just as the name Florida was once used in Spanish times to designate far more continental territory than the present peninsula of that name, so also the presence of the Church in Florida extended many years, half a century in fact, beyond that September day when she was permanently planted in the sands of St. Augustine. Catholic priests sailed with Ponce de León in 1521 on his second voyage to the land that Ponce had discovered and named; and on six subsequent Spanish explorations to the Florida shoreline from 1521 to 1565, priests of the Church were here to raise the Cross in the sand, and to offer unnumbered Masses on wilderness altars. In the striking phrase of the nineteenth-century historian John Gilmary Shea, "The altar was older than the hearth." Wherever the historian's eye is cast, there stands the altar with its surmounting Cross—*Stat crux cum volvitur orbis*. Around that altar there gathered, at one date or another, all the great names that made up our state's early history, when La Florida was an outpost of empire and a curve on the rim of Christendom. With but one brief interruption, from 1763 to 1768, the practice of the Catholic Faith was a distinguishing feature of our state's early culture, and the proudly worn badge of many of her people: priests and friars, conquistadors and hidalgos, soldiers and statesmen, Indians from the swamps and shoreland, Spaniards and Minorcans, rich and poor, the innocent and the repentant—they were a long line of stout men, and if there was some evil in them, there was also much good; and if at times they stooped to small and mean things, they also rose to heights of courage and generosity and sacrifice which are the real patents of nobility and the expected fruits of Christian life.

Florida's story began with a positive contribution: the founding of missions for the Indians. If in later English colonies to the north the only good Indian was a dead Indian, as Herbert E. Bolton concluded ("The Mission as a Frontier Institution in the Spanish American Colonies," *American Historical Review*, XXIII, October, 1917), in the Spanish colonies it was considered a Christian duty to improve the native for this life and to prepare him for the next. Before the House of Burgesses met at Jamestown and well before the Pilgrims set foot on Plymouth Rock, the Indians of Florida were being taught the elements of Christianity and the arts of reading, writing, and singing. A century and a half before Fray Junípero Serra's friars could count 26,000 settled Christian Indians along the *camino real* of California, an equal number lived under the sound of mission bells between St. Augustine and Tallahassee, and along a second line northward from St. Augustine to Saint Catherines Island. Their villages bore such names as Name of God,

XII

Holy Faith, St. Joseph, St. Francis, Holy Cross, Ascension, St. Michael, and Our Lady of the Rosary. And the mission chains survived until 1702-1704, when the Spanish Indian system, based upon religion and agriculture, came at last into fatal collision with the English system, based upon trade and aggrandizement.

The thoroughness and cruelty with which Colonel James Moore of Carolina annihilated the missions of Florida has few parallels in American history. Only in comparatively recent years, thanks to careful research conducted at the two oldest universities in the state, the veil drawn over that incident by English-oriented writers of our national adventure has been lifted from the borderland proscenium, and the cause for the temporary collapse of Catholic life in early eighteenth-century Florida has become apparent. By 1763 when Florida was ceded to England, the Indian missions belonged to history, and after the retrocession in 1783 they were never successfully revived.

The large influx of English-speaking Protestant planters and yeomen into Florida after the peninsula became a United States territory in 1821 assured the gradual diminution of Catholicism as a religious or cultural force, and the influence, as well as the members, of the Church tended afterwards to contract around the two ancient parishes of St. Augustine and Pensacola. Indeed, after the mission era was wiped out, until the time of the Civil War, the story of the Catholic Church in Florida was almost solely the story of St. Augustine and, to a lesser degree, of Pensacola. With the coming of Bishop Augustin Verot as Vicar Apostolic of Florida in 1858, the Church began again to do what she had labored so hard to do three centuries before: to break out of the coastal parishes into the Florida interior. By 1870, when our account closes, she had succeeded to an extent that may be called remarkable, and even amazing, when one remembers that during the intervening years several of her buildings had been destroyed and many of her people demoralized by the Civil War. Prewar figures showed that the Church in Florida east of the Apalachicola River possessed six churches and chapels, four schools, three priests, and a Catholic population of perhaps 3,000. By 1870 within the same area there were nineteen churches and chapels, seven schools, twelve priests,

XIII

and about 10,000 Catholics. So promising again was the Church in Florida, that the Holy See, three hundred and one years after Pope (St.) Pius V sent his commendations to Pedro Menéndez at St. Augustine, erected Florida east of the Apalachicola into the Diocese of St. Augustine. As a diocese the Church in Florida enjoyed thereafter a continuous advance in numbers, prosperity, and fervor. But that is another story, and, God willing, another book.

For the benefit of readers who may be unacquainted with some of the ecclesiastical terms that appear in this narrative, it may be well in this place to explain the important difference between "secular" and "regular" priests. "Secular," or "diocesan," priests work in geographically defined parishes under the direct supervision of a bishop. Their mode of life dates from the beginning of Christianity. The term "secular," which was the more common designation in Florida's Spanish days, refers to the fact that secular priests work "in the world"—the Latin *saecularis*. They are called "diocesan" because their parishes make up a larger geographic unity called a "diocese," over which the bishop presides. (A diocese is also called a "see," from the Latin *sedes*, seat. A "see city" is the city in which a bishop has his cathedral, from the Latin *cathedra*, chair. A group of dioceses forms an ecclesiastical "province," over which an "archbishop" presides. An archbishop is also styled a "metropolitan," because his see is usually the most important city of the province.) "Regular," or "religious," priests, on the other hand, are members of "religious orders" (e.g. Franciscans, Jesuits, Dominicans) committed to special tasks, such as charity, education, or the missions. Regular priests take vows of poverty, chastity, and obedience. The older orders, including those that worked in Florida, are exempt in great part from the jurisdiction of the local bishop. The noun form "religious" is often used to signify the. regular clergy.

The writer is indebted to many persons for assistance given in the preparation of this book. In the first instance, he thanks his ordinary, the Most Rev. Joseph P. Hurley, D.D., Archbishop, Bishop of St. Augustine, whose deep sense of history and never-failing encouragement underlie much of what was accomplished in these pages. Special thanks are owed also to Dr. Rembert W. Patrick, Graduate Research Professor of Florida History in the University of Florida, who read most of the manuscript and made valuable suggestions for its improvement; Rev. Father Thomas R. Gross, pastor of St. Patrick's Church, Gainesville, the writer's gracious host during several extended visits to the University of Florida Library; the late Rev. Father Charles W. Spellman, priest of the Diocese of St. Augustine, who was one of the nation's foremost authorities on the Spanish missions of Florida; Albert C. Manucy and Luis R. Arana, National Park Service historians at the Castillo de San Marcos National Monument in St. Augustine; Mrs. Doris C. Wiles, the capable and always helpful Librarian of the St. Augustine Historical Society; Rev. Fathers Vincent E. Smith and David Page, editors of the *Florida Catholic* in whose pages some of this material originally appeared; Dr. Samuel Proctor, editor of the *Florida Historical Quarterly,* who kindly gave permission to reprint material in Chapters I and II which originally appeared in that publication (Vol. XLIV, Nos. 1 and 2, October, 1965); Mr. Eugene P. Willging, Director of the Mullen Library, The Catholic University of America; Miss Elizabeth Alexander and her fine staff at the P. K. Yonge Library of Florida History, the University of Florida; Dr. James R. Anderson, Head, and Mr. David E. Boyd, of the Department of Geography in the same institution; Rev. Father Oscar H. Lipscomb, Archivist of the Diocese of Mobile-Birmingham; Rt. Rev. Msgr. Richard C. Madden, pastor of St. Andrew's Church, Myrtle Beach, South Carolina; and the Sisters of St. Joseph, St. Augustine.

Finally, the writer expresses his gratitude to Dr. and Mrs. Lewis F. Haines of the University of Florida Press; to Mr. Paul Chalker, his editor at the Press; to Mrs. Ethel Reidy, his typist; and to Mr. Gabriel Rebaf, whose helping hand was never far from the writer's side.

Responsibility for any errors of fact or judgment is, of course, the writer's own.

MICHAEL V. GANNON

Mission Nombre de Dios
Feast of Saint Augustine, 1965

PONCE DE LEÓN (from *Florida under Five Flags*, University of Florida Press)

DE SOTO LANDING AT TAMPA BAY

Hernando de Soto, by Enrique Pérez Comendador. The heroic-sized statue, commissioned by the St. Augustine Foundation and unveiled at the New York World's Fair in 1965, stands in Bradenton to commemorate De Soto's march through Florida in 1539–40.

I

The Rim of Christendom

1513-1565

Thanks be to Thee, O Lord, Who hast permitted me to see something new." So spoke Juan Ponce de León on first sighting the "island." The year was 1513, and the land was fragrant with tropical flowers. It was Easter time —*Pasqua florida*, Easter of the flowers—and a name for this land came naturally to the Spaniard's mind. During the next one hundred years the name "La Florida" would identify for Spaniards not only the present peninsula of Florida, but the entire American continental territory extending north to Newfoundland and westward indefinitely from the Atlantic.

Ponce's voyage of discovery in 1513 was not a chapter in Catholic history. It was more like a preface. Dispossessed of a governor's office in Puerto Rico, he had set out to find wealth and power—and, some say, a fabled fountain—in islands that he thought lay to the northwest. According to the best estimates, Ponce made his landfall on the upper east coast of the present state of Florida sometime between the second and the eighth of April.

Of the ceremonies of landing there is no record. In any event, there could have been no offering of Mass, because no priest was with the party. Some historians conjecture that on landing Ponce may have solemnly recited the simple prayer said to have been used by Christopher Columbus, from whom personally Ponce may have learned it: *"Almighty and Eternal Lord God, Who by Thy Sacred Word has created heaven, earth, and sea, blessed and glorified be Thy Name and praised be Thy Majesty, and grant that through Thy humble servant Thy Sacred Name may be known and preached in this other part of the world. Amen."*

Taking a southerly course down the coast, Ponce rounded the Florida Keys, which he named the Martyrs, because the high rocks looked at a distance like men who were suffering, and then he sailed up the west coast of the peninsula to what may have been the present site of Pensacola. Again he turned southward, on May 23, and anchored at or near Charlotte Bay. This bay was to bear his name for many years—Bahía Juan Ponce. Here he had a bloody encounter with Indians, and decided to return to Puerto Rico.

Ponce's voyage had not been a missionary adventure. Although a Catholic, he had not ennobled his enterprise with any purposes specifically religious. The first missionary chapter would come later. To Ponce's credit, it was he who would write it.

On September 27, 1514, Ponce was commissioned by the Spanish king, Ferdinand V, to secure possession of his new discovery. The commission empowered Ponce to settle "the island of Florida," and to take with him a number of priests. "Treat [the Indians] as best you can," the king admonished, "seeking in every possible way to convert them to our Holy Catholic Faith."

Seven years passed before Ponce could get his colonization and missionary enterprise underway. In the meantime two events occurred that are worth our notice. First, an accident took place at sea which may have brought the first priest to Florida's shores. His name was Father Alonzo González, and he accompanied an ill-fated voyage of Francisco Hernández de Córdova from Cuba to the Bahamas in 1517. Stray winds blew Córdova from his course to Yucatán, where 56 of his party of 110 were killed by Indians. It is not recorded if Father González was among those killed. If he was not,

2

presumably he was with Córdova when stray winds blew Córdova's fleet against the west coast of Florida during the return to Cuba. Second, another explorer, Alonzo Alvarez de Pineda, discovered in 1519 that Florida was not an island, as everyone thought who had heard Ponce's account of the 1513 voyage. Instead, Pineda learned, the new land was a peninsula, and he himself fixed the western juncture to the mainland at Mobile river and bay, which he named after the Holy Spirit—Río de Espíritu Santo.

In 1521 Ponce de León at last embarked from Puerto Rico in two ships with two hundred men and fifty horses, together with a variety of domestic animals and agricultural implements, gunpowder, crossbows, and other arms. Secular and regular priests accompanied the expedition to establish mission posts among the Indians. Their landing with Ponce in Florida is the first positively authenticated instance of the presence of Catholic priests on the mainland of the present United States.

Where precisely Ponce came ashore on the Florida coast is not known. Probably it was in the vicinity of Charlotte Harbor on the Gulf Coast. There he was immediately and furiously attacked by Indians. Many of his followers were killed, and Ponce himself was badly wounded by an arrow. He sadly re-embarked with his priests and people and returned to Cuba, where he died of his wound a few days afterwards. Noble in conception, the first missionary enterprise had been a conspicious failure before it could even take root.

Only five years later, misfortune struck another colonizing attempt farther north. Lucas Vásquez de Ayllón, a royal judge in Santo Domingo, sailed toward Florida with 600 men and women, including two priests and one lay brother of the Order of St. Dominic. The expedition followed the eastern seaboard of La Florida as far north as the Chesapeake Bay, where Ayllón's party disembarked on September 29, 1526, and began erecting houses and a modest chapel dedicated to St. Michael. Food supplies soon ran low, however, and widespread sickness followed the coming of winter cold. Ayllón died in the arms of one of the Dominican priests, and 150 famished and half-frozen survivors of his party decided to give it up and sail home to Santo Domingo. Thus, the second altar of Christian worship was abandoned like the first.

Pánfilo de Narváez was a tall, commanding man, fair-complexioned, red-bearded, and one-eyed (he had lost an eye trying to discipline Cortés, conqueror of Mexico). By all accounts he was a brave and resourceful soldier, and when in 1526 he returned to Spain after twenty-six years of royal service in the New World, King Charles I (as Charles V, Emperor of the Holy Roman Empire) awarded him settlement rights to all Florida.

On June 17, 1527, Narváez sailed from the port of San Lucar in Spain with six hundred colonists and soldiers. He set a course for the same Florida coastline where Ponce de León had twice been repulsed, the second time at the cost of his life. And like Ponce on his second voyage, he brought with him a company of priests to minister to the colonists and to evangelize the Indians: an unknown number of secular priests and five Franciscan friars. Of the secular priests only one is known to us by name—El Asturiano, "the Asturian." Superior of the Franciscan party was Father Juan Xuarez, named by Charles V as bishop-elect of Florida. Father Xuarez would never be consecrated, however. For all the talents of the leader, Narváez, the expedition was doomed to failure. Within seven years' time only four men of those who landed at Florida would still be alive.

One of the survivors was Alvar Núñez Cabeza de Vaca, treasurer and high sheriff, who wrote a long account of the expedition. From him we learn that enough misfortunes to discourage any but the most hardy of missionaries befell the voyagers at sea before they finally reached the shores of Florida. At last, with many thanksgivings, Narváez anchored in the vicinity of St. Clement's Point on the peninsula west of Tampa Bay. It was April 14, Holy Thursday of 1528.

Narváez and his missionaries were anxious to meet the Indians of the area before taking formal possession of the land. On landing the next day, therefore, they immediately set out toward an Indian village spotted from aboard ship. They found the village, but it was empty. The Indians had fled their huts and were hiding in the brush. The only cheering thing the Spaniards found was a gold ornament, which led them to think that more of the precious metal could be discovered farther inland.

4

The next day, Holy Saturday, Narváez solemnly took possession of Florida. To the unseen and unhearing Indians he delivered a formal declamation, which, because it indicates the missionary side of his enterprise, deserves to be quoted in part. He first explained how the descendants of Adam and Eve had spread abroad across the earth to form many nations, and how God had come to earth to save the nations "wheresoever they might live and be. Wherefore," he continued, ". . . I entreat and require you to understand this well which I have told you, taking the time for it that it just you should, to comprehend and reflect, and that you recognize the Church as Mistress and Superior of the Universe, and the Supreme Pontiff, called Pope . . . and that you consent and give opportunity that these Fathers and religious men may declare and preach these things to you."

Narváez and a large party of men then marched northward. Unfortunately, they lost contact with the fleet, which, despairing of their return, turned back toward Cuba. Cut off from all supplies, Narváez and his companions reached the country of the Apalache Indians near the present site of Tallahassee. There they discovered that they were unable to feed themselves off the land, and their plight was soon desperate. The men killed their horses for food and constructed five rough-hewn wooden boats, which they launched in the gulf, fifty men to a boat. Cabeza de Vaca relates the sad consequences: one after another, the boats foundered in the surf between Pensacola and Matagorda; most of the men drowned; eighty survivors were cast up on the Texas coast; gradually, the number dwindled through illness, exposure, and starvation.

After an incredible odyssey of seven years, during which they actually crossed the continent ocean to ocean, four lonely survivors of all that company of governor and officers, priests and friars, and mail-clad hidalgos finally reached Mexico and safety. Cabeza de Vaca was one of them. A Negro slave was another. There were two soldiers. The priests had all given their lives. Narváez, too, was dead.

Don Hernando de Soto, although only thirty-eight years of age, was a knight commander of the Order of Santiago. He was a veteran of the campaigns in central America, and had served under Francisco Pizarro in the conquest of the Incas. In 1538 he decided to "conquer, pacify, and populate" the peninsula of Florida and the lands extending westward to the Rio Grande. Almost alone among the Spanish commanders, he was undaunted by the failure of the earlier expeditions led by Ponce de León and Narváez. The desperate tale told by Cabeza de Vaca, companion of Narváez, only spurred him on to succeed where others had failed.

On April 6, 1538, De Soto sailed from the port of San Lucar in Spain with ten ships and a company of 620 men. His *cédula,* or charter, from King Charles I stipulated that he take "priests who shall be appointed by us for the instruction of the natives of that province in our holy Catholic Faith, to whom you are to give and pay the passage, stores, and the other necessary subsistence for them according to our condition." Twelve priests in all accompanied the expedition to Florida, of whom eight were secular and four were regular.

After stopping for nearly a year in Cuba on the way, De Soto's fleet reached Florida's west coast on May 25, 1539. The bay in which he laid anchor was the same Tampa Bay in which Narváez had disembarked. De Soto named the bay Espíritu Santo—Holy Spirit. On June 3, he landed and took formal possession of Florida with all the usual ceremonies.

There were no Indians in attendance. Those who lived in that region, on seeing the approach of De Soto's ships, had lit warning fires along the coast and fled into the brush. Two Indians, captured by a Spanish patrol several months earlier for service as interpreters, made their escape on the day of the landing. De Soto therefore sent out two reconnoitering parties to capture natives to supply the loss of the interpreters, and to make a general exploration of the surrounding country. One of the patrols was led by Baltazar de Gallegos, a relative of Cabeza de Vaca.

De Soto had learned on his arrival of a Christian who lived among the Indians in one of the nearby villages, and Gallegos was ordered to investigate thoroughly if such a person existed. According to reports, the Christian was one of the men who had accompanied the expedition of Narváez eleven years before. After a severe march of ten days, Gallegos and his patrol of eighty men returned. With them was an "Indian," his body painted in livid colors, carrying a bow and arrows. Gallegos reported to De Soto that he had found this "Indian" at a point some eight leagues (twenty miles) inland, and that when the "Indian" became frightened of the Spaniards, he had called out to the Holy Virgin to be spared. De Soto agreed with Gallegos: this was the Spanish Christian.

A report on the incident was written by Luis Hernández de Biedma, the king's representative on the expedition: "The Christian had lived twelve years among those Indians . . . and . . . even after he had been four days with us, he still could not put together a whole sentence in Spanish. . . . He was so little acquainted with the country that he knew nothing about it farther than twenty leagues. . . ." After a time the Christian was able to tell his story. His name was Juan Ortiz. He had been enticed ashore from one of Narváez' ships by a group of Indians, who then captured and enslaved him. The tribal chieftain set him to work guarding the Indian dead from wild beasts. On one occasion Ortiz killed a wolf that had carried off the body of a child. Despite this act, he was eventually condemned to die. Before the execution could take place, he escaped to a neighboring tribe where he found refuge, and it was here that De Soto's patrol found him.

"When we realized that no gold was to be found here, we left the Port of Bahía Honda in order to move inland with all the men who had come, except for twenty-six horsemen and sixty footmen, who remained to guard the port until the Governor [De Soto] should communicate with them or bid them to join him. . . ." So wrote the king's representative, Biedma. And so began, on July 15, 1539, an extraordinary exploration. De Soto, his priests and soldiers, and the repatriated "Indian" Juan Ortiz, left their west coast encampment and marched northward into the trackless continent. Only three years later De Soto would be standing as far away as the Mississippi River.

In the first months, July to October, De Soto explored the center of the peninsula, passing through the regions of present-day Dade City, Ocala, Lake City, and Live Oak. In October he reached the principal town of the Apalache Indians near the present city of

7

Tallahassee, and there he passed the winter. On March 3, 1540, he broke camp and marched northward into that part of La Florida known today as Georgia. During the course of the next two years his indomitable procession passed through the central and northern part of Georgia, circled through the westernmost portions of the Carolinas, and traversed parts of Alabama, Louisiana, and possibly Texas.

The adventure was not without its casualties. Sickness and hostile Indians decimated De Soto's company. Four of the secular priests died during the first year. And in a fierce battle with Mobilian Indians near the Alabama River on October 15, 1540, all the vestments, chalices, patens, altar furnishings, and wheat and wine needed for Mass were destroyed. A later chronicler of De Soto's adventures, Garcilaso de la Vega (the Inca), recorded the result:

"Thereafter, an altar was erected and decorated on Sundays and holy days of obligation. Standing at the altar, a priest, vested in a buckskin chasuble, said the Confiteor, the Introit of the Mass, and the Oration, Epistle, and the Gospel, and all the rest up to the end of the Mass without consecrating. The Spaniards call this the *Misa seca* [Dry Mass]; and the one who said the Mass, or another priest, read the Gospel and delivered a sermon on it. From this they derived consolation in the distress they felt at not being able to adore our Lord and Redeemer Jesus Christ under the sacramental species. This lasted for almost three years, until the time they left Florida for the land of the Christians [Mexico]."

Although it is recorded that De Soto was not above the use of deception in his dealings with the Indians, nor averse to reducing them to slavery when it served his purposes, to his credit it is also recorded that he sometimes assisted the priests in instructing Indian chiefs and tribesmen in the basic beliefs of Christianity. On one such occasion—by a strange coincidence the same day, March 26, 1541, when his one-time commander, Francisco Pizarro, was assassinated in his palace in Peru, and, calling out "Jesu!" drew a cross with his finger in his own blood on the floor—De Soto fashioned and raised a towering pine-tree Cross at the town of Casqui on the western bank of the Mississippi, and proclaimed to the Indians of the place: "This was He who had made the sky and

8

the earth and man in His own image. Upon the tree of the Cross He suffered to save the human race, and rose from the tomb on His third day . . . and, having ascended into heaven, was there to receive with open arms all who would be converted to Him."

At another west-bank Indian town named Tamaliseu, which De Soto reached three years after the start of his overland journey, the explorer fell gravely ill, and appointed a successor, Luis de Moscoso, to lead the remainder of his men to safety. On May 21, 1542, he "confessed his sins with sorrow and compunction for having offended God," and died. A brave soldier, a man of invincible spirit and high resolve, a rude but earnest missionary, De Soto wrote one of the great chapters in Florida's Catholic history, and passed from this life beloved by his men, of whom three hundred remained of the six hundred who had landed with him at Tampa Bay. A group of soldiers wrapped his corpse in a mantle and bore it by canoe to the middle of the Mississippi. There, with the deepest reverence, they consigned the remains of their commander to the bed of the great river that he discovered.

On September 10, 1543, after a perilous journey by foot and on rough-hewn brigantines, the survivors reached Mexico and safety. Two secular priests, Rodrigo de Gallegos and Francisco de Pozo, two Dominicans, Juan de Gallegos and Luis de Soto, and one Franciscan, Juan de Torres, remained of the original band of twelve priests. The rest had their graves in the wilderness behind. So, too, Juan Ortiz, the Spanish Christian who had lived the life of the Florida Indian for eleven years, rested forever in the strange land of his captors. The dense American brush closed up behind the invaders and breathed again its primeval air. With the end of the De Soto expedition, Spain's fourth great effort in La Florida, there were still no permanent settlements, and the mass of savages remained unconverted worshippers of sun and sky.

Luis Cáncer de Barbastro was a priest of the Dominican Order, a native of Saragossa, Spain. In 1547, when he conceived the idea of going to Florida, he was already a veteran New World missionary, and a proven success with the fierce savages of Guatemala, where he had spent the last four years. "Alférez de la Fé,"

Standard Bearer of the Faith, had become his title of honor. And Guatemala, which had been called by Spaniards the "War Province" because of the warlike character of its Indians, was known at the close of Father Cáncer's short apostolate as the "Province of True Peace."

Cáncer read the stories of earlier expeditions to the unconquered and unconverted land of Florida. He talked with survivors of those expeditions. And he began to wonder: why could he not win over the Indians of Florida by the same means he had used in Guatemala? It seemed to him that the earlier missionaries to that province had been hampered rather than helped by the soldiers and armaments that accompanied them. He determined to try, by peaceable means alone, to convert the ignorant and seemingly intractable savages. In 1547 he asked the highest Church and civil authorities in Spain for permission to form an expedition.

On December 28, 1547, a royal cédula addressed to Don Antonio de Mendoza, Viceroy of Mexico, commanded that official to provide Father Cáncer with passage to his destination and all necessary supplies, including "whatsoever was needful for celebrating Mass." Early in 1549, the missionary set out from Vera Cruz, Mexico, on an unarmed vessel named the *Santa María de la Encina*. Three other Dominican priests accompanied him: Fathers Gregorio de Beteta, Diego de Tolosa, and Juan García. All three were seasoned New World missionaries. Father Gregorio had labored for many years in Mexico, and apparently had been the first Dominican to think seriously about the conversion of the Florida Indians: once, with another Dominican, he had set out to walk from Miva, Mexico, to the part of La Florida that lay north of Mexico, but had been forced to turn back for want of supplies.

Cáncer was convinced that his work would be fruitful only if he could work among natives who had not earlier been antagonized by the use of armed force. He had therefore prevailed upon the Viceroy of Mexico to issue the strictest orders to the pilot, Juan de Arana, to avoid all ports where Spaniards had previously landed. Arana, however, paid little heed to his orders. When on May 29 the shout of "land ahoy!" sounded from the topmast, the priests did not know it, but Arana had brought them

10

to a point near Tampa Bay, almost exactly the same place where, not many years before, Narváez and De Soto had landed and spread the terror of their arms.

Father Cáncer and his companions leaned over the gunwales of their ship and searched the coastline for signs of Indians. Seeing none, Cáncer decided to go ashore in a small landing boat. With him went Father Diego, a Spanish lay brother named Fuentes, an Indian woman interpreter named Magdalena, and Arana the pilot. Father Diego was the first to step ashore, and, following Cáncer's instructions, he climbed a tree to survey the surrounding country. As he did so, fifteen to twenty Indians came out of the woods and approached the shoreline cautiously.

As soon as he saw the Indians, Cáncer gathered up his habit, sprang into the sea and ran ashore in water up to his cincture, "and Our Lord knows what haste I made," he wrote later, "lest they [the Indians] should slay the monk before hearing what we were about. Reaching the beach, I fell on my knees and prayed for grace and divine help. I walked up to the plain where I found them [the Indians] gathered, and before reaching them repeated my actions on the beach. And rising from my knees I began to draw out of my sleeves some articles of Flanders, which, though of small account and of little value to Christians, were much prized by them and highly appreciated."

Cáncer explained later: "I had read in the Doctors, particularly in St. Thomas, Victoria, and Gaetano, that it is approved of and commended . . . to take to unbelievers . . . little presents such as these." He went on to describe what happened: "When they [the Indians] approach me, and after I give away part of what I brought with me, I go to the friar [Father Diego] who was coming toward me, and embrace him with much joy. We both kneel down with the Spaniard [Fuentes] and the Indian woman [Magdalena], and drawing out my book we recite the litanies, commending ourselves to Our Lord and to His Saints. Some Indians kneeled, others squatted, which greatly pleased me, and as they rise I leave the litanies half said and sit down with them in a hut. And I shortly learned the location of the harbor we were searching for, which was about a day and a half distance from there by land."

Father Cáncer returned alone to the ship to obtain more presents. But on his return to shore, he could not find any of his three companions. They had disappeared! And a sailor who had helped row the priest ashore was afterwards lured into the bush by Indians and was spirited away. Cáncer spent the remainder of the day on shore trying to unravel the mystery. Finally, at sunset, with no further word of their whereabouts, the priest sadly returned to his ship. The next day Cáncer and Father Juan García went ashore again, to find that not only were their friends still missing, but the Indians of the area had disappeared as well.

Once again despairing of any word from his friends, Cáncer returned with Father Juan to the ship. The sailors weighed anchor, and set a northerly course for the harbor of which the natives had spoken. After eight days of sailing along the coast and several more days of negotiating the entrance, Father Cáncer's ship sailed into a bay where it seemed suitable to establish a permanent settlement and mission. On the feast of Corpus Christi, Cáncer and Juan García offered Mass on shore. The next day Cáncer with Father Gregorio searched diligently throughout the surrounding area for their lost companions, but with no success. Then, just as they were about to leave, they spotted Indians approaching, and heard one of them shout in broken Spanish: "Friends, friends! Good, good!"

The two priests cautiously approached the Indian emissaries and responded to their overture. Father Cáncer shouted, "We are good men!" and he indicated by signs that he wished the three Spaniards and Magdalena to be returned to him. The Indians agreed —but it was treachery. Father Diego and the lay brother Fuentes had been massacred, and the sailor had been made a slave. Cáncer learned this agonizing news only after his return to the ship. In the meantime he was deceived again, this time by Magdalena. The Indian girl appeared suddenly on the shore among a crowd of natives. She had shorn herself of her Christian clothing and had taken on the old habits of her Indian upbringing. Deceitfully, she told Cáncer that the remainder of her "lost" party was enjoying the hospitality of the nearby chieftain; that she had convinced the Indians that the friars were on a peaceful mission; and that there were some fifty or sixty Indians gathered together to hear what the missionaries had to say.

Father Cáncer returned to his ship, full of expectation for the morrow. On board, however, he met an incredible stranger—a white man—who carried a report that the priest's friends were dead. The man called himself Juan Muñoz, and said that he was one of De Soto's soldiers, captured here ten years before. While Father Cáncer was ashore, Muñoz had escaped from his Indian master and paddled out to the Spanish ship in a canoe. He reported that the Indians had slain Father Diego and the lay brother—he had seen the scalp of the priest himself—and that they held the sailor in bondage.

Now came more bad news. The ship began to leak, and it was far from shore; meat and fish were spoiling; water was running low; many of the crew were down with fever; Juan de Arana had become increasingly fractious, and Cáncer found it hard to keep him from withdrawing.

Cáncer spent the day of Monday, June 24, on board ship writing letters to his superiors, arranging the things he wanted to take ashore with him, and setting down his adventures to date in a journal. It is to this journal that we are indebted for much of our information about the expedition. On Tuesday he attempted to go ashore with a party of sailors, but the sea was too rough. Wednesday the waters were still choppy, but by hard rowing Cáncer and his party reached the shore. With him went Father Gregorio and the De Soto campaigner, Juan Muñoz.

Before actually stepping ashore, the priests were given pause by the sight of Indians in the trees and of a sizeable group of Indians on a nearby hillock brandishing bows and arrows, clubs, and darts. Juan Muñoz shouted out a warning to the Indians to stop the hostile demonstration. But Cáncer said: "Be quiet, brother; do not provoke them." Father Gregorio urged his superior: "For the love of God, wait a little, do not land!"

Father Cáncer, however, leaped from the boat into the water and waded onto the beach. He called to the sailors to bring him a small crucifix that he had forgotten, and then walked toward the Indians on the hillock. Before reaching them, he fell on his knees

13

for a moment in prayer. It was his last prayer. As he arose, several Indians rushed forward and pushed him down the hill. A crowd of savages gathered around him. One took away his hat. Another, with the vicious swipe of a club, dispatched the priest from this life.

Thus died a remarkable missionary, a messenger of peace, a noble, brave, and gifted man. Father Gregorio could not persuade the captain to remain any longer, and so the voyagers who remained sailed back to Mexico. The year was now 1549, and still neither Spain nor the Church had a foothold in the land of flowers.

Although it seemed foolishness to some, Spanish priests and sea captains continued to dream of a colony in Florida. True, every effort to build permanently had been repulsed by the Indians. And priests who had tried heaping charity on the heads of the recalcitrant savages had been cruelly slaughtered for their pains. Florida was too important, however, to write off. Not only did the state of the Indians demand continued missionary efforts, but also Florida still loomed large as ever on navigators' maps as the strategic key to the Gulf and Caribbean trade routes. Still another reason for conquering the elusive peninsula came from Spaniards in Cuba. So many native Cuban women had married Spanish soldiers, one of the bishops on the island reported, a Cuban male "is lucky if he can get a wife eighty years old." The suggestion was therefore made by some that Florida would be an excellent source of Indian wives.

Faced with a growing number of persistent and authoritative appeals to do something about Florida, the Spanish king, Philip II, decided to promote yet another voyage out of Mexico. To head the expedition the Viceroy of Mexico chose Don Tristán de Luna y Arellano, son of the governor of Yucatán. Five priests and one lay brother, all members of the Order of St. Dominic, were appointed to accompany the undertaking and to see that the colonists followed the viceroy's instructions not to antagonize the Indians but "to settle, and by good example, with good works and with presents, to bring them to a knowledge of Our Holy Faith and Catholic Truth." The viceroy wrote to Philip II to assure the sovereign that the Dominicans named to the enterprise were chosen "because of their tried lives, learning, and doctrine," and because they were "of an age to be able to work among the Indians and learn their languages." Their names were Pedro de Feria, the superior, who resigned the priorship of the prospering house of St. Dominic in Mexico to undertake the Florida mission; Domingo de la Anunciación, a scholar said to have mastered all the Mexican dialects; Domingo de Salazar, later Bishop of the Philippines; Juan Mazuelas and Diego de San Domingo, both veterans of the Mexican missions; and Bartolomé Matéos, the lay brother, who had served as an artillery officer with Gonzalo Pizarro in Peru.

Accounts differ regarding the size of De Luna's expedition that set sail from the port of Vera Cruz, Mexico, on June 11, 1559. One account lists eleven ships carrying 500 soldiers, 1,000 settlers, and 240 horses; another lists fifteen ships carrying 1,500 soldiers and settlers, including women and children. The chronicles agree, however, on the main events. Favored by winds and weather, the expedition reached Florida's Gulf Coast after one month of sailing. On the eve of the feast of the Assumption of the Blessed Virgin Mary, August 14, the party landed at Pensacola Bay. De Luna wrote to King Philip: "I set sail on June 11, and until the day of our Lady of August, when it pleased God that the entire fleet should enter the port of Ichuse. As we entered on the day I say, I named the bay in your honor as Bahía Filipina del Puerto de Santa María."

So pleased was De Luna with the land he saw that he sent a shipload of settlers immediately to Spain in order to persuade other Spanish settlers to join his colony. Most of the other settlers were divided into two groups. De Luna sent the first group to reconnoiter the countryside by land. The second went up a nearby river by small boats. Dominican priests accompanied both groups. De Luna instructed the reconnaissance parties to return to the harbor within three or four days, with the consequence that the men took with them only enough food to last that length of time. The reconnaissance lasted longer than expected and produced nothing of importance. By river and by land the Spaniards saw only marshes and barren land. Food gave out after several days, and many of the

15

men fell sick from eating roots and leaves that were not edible. The two parties made their way back toward shore—and toward the churning black clouds of a tropical storm.

A fierce storm, probably a hurricane, bore down on the harbor out of the sea. Towering waves snapped anchor cables and battered the planks of all but two of the Spanish ships into tortured debris that piled up on the beach. Driving waves struck the beach with such force that those on shore had to flee inland for their lives. Many died aboard ship and on shore, including the Dominican lay brother, Matéos. For the survivors almost nothing remained of their store of provisions—enough food for a year had sailed in those ships—nor of their pieces of gold and other articles of value that they intended to use in trading with the Indians.

It was, then, to scenes of utter destruction and desolation that the two reconnaissance parties returned. But De Luna gathered the survivors and urged them to continue the colony at all costs. He left a captain with fifty men to guard the port and the two remaining ships, and set out with the rest of the settlers in search of food. The story of the colony for the next year and a half was a story of successive expeditions for this purpose, and of intermittent periods of raw hunger, when priests and soldiers were reduced to eating their horses and chewing the leather of their harnesses.

Human relations suffered under these pressures. In 1561 bitter dissension broke out among De Luna, the master of the camp, and the captains of the destroyed ships. At issue was the question whether another reconnaissance force should be sent into the interior. Fathers Domingo de la Anunciación and Domingo de Salazar were troubled by the outburst of argument and anger, and they attempted to bring peace to the settlement by leading the. soldiers and settlers each day in recitation of a litany. It was the Easter season, and the two priests were afraid that many of the people, with anger and hatred in their hearts, would not be able to receive worthily the Sacrament of Penance and Holy Communion. Finally, Father Domingo de la Anunciación decided to risk a prophecy.

During the offering of Mass at the beachhead at Ichuse on

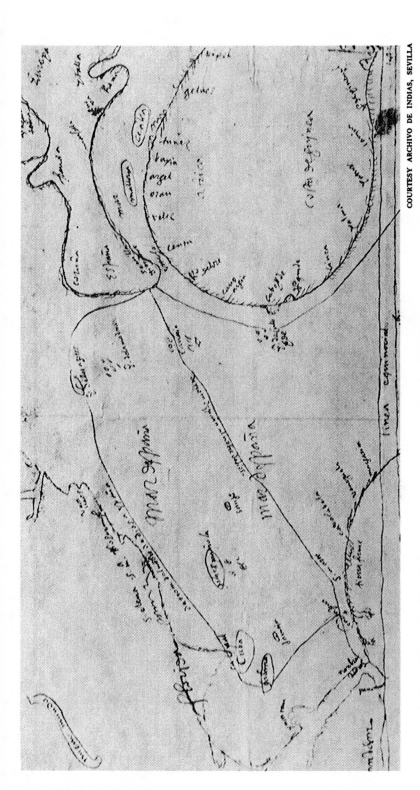

A 16th century Spanish map showing route of the treasure fleets from España (top right) to Nombre de Dios (Panamá), and the northern return route via Florida's east coast (left center). The New World—the North American mainland—bears the title "Nuevo Mundo."

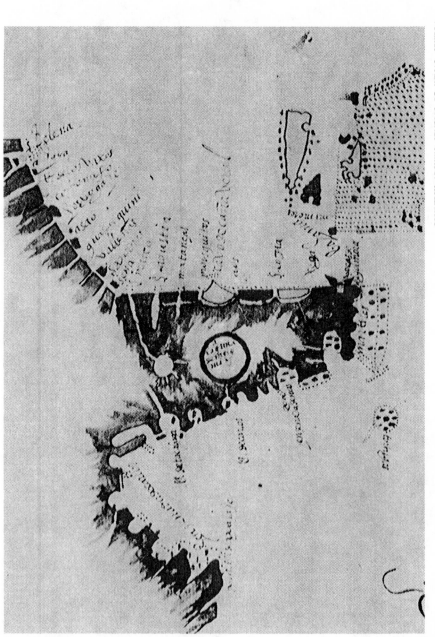

Late 16th century Spanish map showing shape of Florida as conceived by the navigators of that time. Circle in

Palm Sunday of 1561, he turned suddenly toward the people with the Sacred Host in his hands, and addressed De Luna. He questioned the governor about his faith. The governor stepped forward, knelt before the altar, and answered the priest's questions humbly. Father Domingo told the governor that if he would become reconciled with the captains and repent his sin in causing dissension and suffering among the people, before three days a ship would arrive in port with help to relieve the hunger of the colony. The governor was so struck by the confidence in the priest's voice, he turned to the congregation and announced his belief in the prophecy. While Father Domingo finished the Mass, the governor confessed aloud before all the people that he had been wrong. He asked the captains, the master of the camp, the soldiers, and the settlers to forgive him for the mischief he had done. A reconciliation among everyone present followed before the altar.

And lo, on the following day a great ship appeared on the horizon. It was from New Spain and it was laden with supplies for Tristán de Luna's men. It appeared that it was Father Domingo's prayer—and prophecy—which had been answered.

The vessel that entered the harbor of Ichuse was commanded by Angel de Villafañe, appointed by the viceroy to replace De Luna. With Villafañe was Father Gregorio de Beteta, who had accompanied the ill-fated expedition of Father Cáncer to Tampa Bay eleven years before. Villafañe and his men stayed only a short time in Florida. Then, leaving a garrison of fifty men at Ichuse, he left for Mexico by way of Havana carrying the remainder of De Luna's colony, now numbering fewer than three hundred persons. Father Domingo de la Anunciación remained with the soldiers in Florida for six or seven months until it was determined that the settlement was definitely not capable of surviving. The soldiers and Father Domingo returned to Mexico. And another attempt to settle and Christianize Florida reached an inglorious end.

In Spain consternation greeted the news of the failure of Tristán de Luna's colony. The Spanish Crown was displeased because, despite six well-planned attempts to do so, the banner of Castile and León had still not been permanently planted in the

17

elusive sands of Florida. Spanish military and naval leaders were frustrated and embarrassed by the failure of their arms to secure and hold a beachhead in this peninsula. That the arrows of primitive Indians had succeeded in driving off Spanish warriors on several notable occasions was humble pie that proud conquistadors were not prepared to eat. The gold that mail-clad hidalgos hunted in the El Dorado of dreams never seemed less real than it did among the bogs and swamps of Florida, and those Spaniards who disguised their greed for precious metal under the mantle of religion found that evil indeed was its own punishment.

No one was more disappointed, however, than the bishops and priests of Spain—mission-minded men who saw in Florida a field of souls ripe for the harvest. Every attempt to evangelize the Indians in this far-off country had proved to be as unstable and as impermanent as the waves that lapped the shores. Indeed, the historian of the abortive De Luna mission, Agustín Dávila y Padilla, recorded that the loss of life and expense incurred by that venture resulted in only one convert, an Indian woman of the Coosa nation baptized at the point of death. Despite the best efforts of the gallant, devoted, and self-sacrificing priests who endured indescribable privations in the American wild, and set up their crosses and preached their unfaltering faith as best they could during temporary halts along overland treks, the savages of Florida remained plunged in the crassest idolatry and ignorance. When would the priest have another chance?

Not for some time, decided Philip II. On September 23, 1561, the king expressed doubt that Florida was any longer worth the expense and effort of colonization. The king cited the opinion of Pedro Menéndez de Avilés, Spain's most experienced naval commander, who argued that Florida's shoreline was too low and sandy, her countryside too poor in resources, and her harbors too shallow to permit practicable settlement. Unless some crisis of state demanded it, there were to be no further attempts to colonize the peninsula. Such a crisis would arise, for example, if some new development endangered Spanish shipping in the Bahama Channel along Florida's east coast.

The Spanish treasure fleets sailed twice each year from Havana, where the gold-laden galleons and caravels joined together for mutual protection. The fleets passed northward through the Bahama Channel, or the Straits of Florida, until they reached the area of Bermuda, when they set course for the Azores. From the Azores to Seville the fleets were heavily guarded by men-of-war to prevent their capture by French pirates. The greatest danger on the voyage, however, came from navigating the Bahama Channel. This passage, discovered by Ponce de León on his first expedition, was only thirty-nine miles wide at its narrowest part; its waters were uncommonly rough; reefs at its entrance threatened the keels of heavily laden ships; and violent storms sometimes whipped the channel into cauldrons. Various wreckages along the coast attested the channel's terrors to Spanish navigators. What, then, if in addition to these natural hazards, French pirates should also infest this channel? And what if Menéndez de Avilés should change his mind?

II

For Altar and Throne

1565-1574

WHAT WAS ONLY A WORRY in the mind of the Spanish king in 1561 became a plain reality in the summer of 1564, when Huguenot adventurers under René de Goulaine de Laudonnière pre-empted the northeast coastline of peninsular Florida and began construction of a military fort. Called Fort Caroline, the French outpost was situated near the mouth of the River of May [St. Johns] where it commanded the northern discharge of the Bahama Channel, and enabled French warships to sally forth against the treasure fleets with dangerous ease. Laudonnière's force consisted of soldiers, sailors, and artisans. No clergy or farmers were included. The presence of this warlike band constituted a direct challenge to the claims of Spain in Florida, which had been recognized at least implicitly by France in the Treaty of Cateau-Cambrésis in 1559. Here, no doubt, was a crisis of state capable of changing the decision of a king and the mind of an admiral. And so it happened. When Philip II learned in the spring of 1565 that Jean Ribault, the great French sea captain, was assembling a fleet to reinforce Fort Caroline, he reacted angrily to what he considered a foreign encroachment upon the Spanish domain. A Spanish fleet, the king determined, must be dispatched at once to repel Ribault, destroy Fort Caroline, secure Florida again for Spain, and establish there, at long last, a permanent Catholic community. By coincidence, just the right man was seeking permission at that time to search for a son, lost somewhere on the Florida shoreline.

Pedro Menéndez de Avilés, Captain-General of the Indies Fleet, had served long and faithfully in the arduous campaigns of the Low Country and with the fleets that sailed regularly to and from New Spain. He knew the ports of the West Indies, the currents of the Caribbean, and the inviting shoreline of Florida. He also knew that Florida was populated by Indians whom no missionaries had yet been able to convert and hold, for lack of a permanent mission base. Menéndez heard the king's proposal. He thought of the possibility of finding his lost son, of Spain's economic dependency upon the treasure fleets, of the spiritual dangers to Florida's Indians that would come from "heretical" Frenchmen (most of the Fort Caroline colonists were Huguenots), and of the good that he himself could do as special viceroy of the Church in that as yet unconquered and savage province. He told the king that he would go, and accepted the office of Adelantado de la Florida. As Adelantado, he would be not only governor of the province, but direct representative of the sovereign himself.

The royal *asiento*, or contract, given Menéndez on March 20, 1565, plainly charged him with a missionary as well as a military responsibility: "As we have in mind the good of the salvation of those [Indian] souls," the king declared, "we have decided to give the order to send religious persons to instruct the said Indians, and those people who are Christians and our subjects, so that they may live among and talk to the natives that may inhabit those lands and provinces of Florida, and so that [the Indians] by association and conversation with them, might more easily be taught our Holy Catholic Faith and be led to good practices and customs and to perfect behavior."

On June 29, 1565, Captain General Menéndez sailed out of

21

the port of Cádiz with nineteen ships and 1,100 men, bound for Florida's east coast. Almost at once his fleet encountered severe storms which forced its return. Several days later, when the storms had abated, the Admiral set sail again, this time with an enlarged company of 1,504 soldiers, sailors, locksmiths, millers, silversmiths, tanners, sheepshearers, and farmers, some with their wives and children. An additional 1,000 soldiers and settlers were to follow later from Asturias and Vizcaya. Menéndez had had the good sense to recruit men skilled in tilling the soil, animal husbandry, and the hunting of game. It was for lack of these skills that earlier expeditions had shown such lamentable inability to live off the land.

Chief among the passengers were "four secular priests with faculties to hear confessions." In these four men lay the Church's hope of planting the Cross permanently in Florida's sands. We know three of their names: Francisco López de Mendoza Grajales, Rodrigo García de Trujillo, and Pedro de Rueda. As the Spanish vessels plowed westward through the Atlantic, Father López, who was fleet chaplain, made notes of the voyage. He recorded the fleet's arrival at the Canary Islands on Wednesday, July 5, where the ships took on wood and water. The following Sunday, he noted, the expedition raised sail again for the island of Dominica in the Caribbean.

Gonzalo Solís de Merás, a brother-in-law of Menéndez', also made notes of the voyage: "Having set sail from the Canaries, within a short time a fierce tempest arose, and the flagship with a patache broke away from the fleet, without being seen any more; and the next day a shallop turned back to land, for she was leaking badly and could not be helped." Only five vessels remained together. Father López was on one of them: "The five vessels which remained of our fleet had a prosperous voyage the rest of the way, thanks to Our Lord and His Blessed Mother. Up to Friday, the 20th, we had very fine weather, but at ten o'clock that day a violent wind arose, which by two in the afternoon had become the most frightful hurricane one could imagine. The sea, which rose to the very clouds, seemed about to swallow us up alive, and such was the fear and apprehension of the pilot and other sailors, that I pushed myself hard in exhorting my brethren and companions to repentance. I represented to them the Passion of Our Lord Jesus Christ, His Justice and His Mercy, and with so much success that I passed the night in confessing them."

The next day the storm roared even louder, and towering waves broke over the decks, forcing the captain of the ship on which López sailed to throw overboard the cooking apparatus, many barrels of water, seven millstones, the reserve rigging, and the ship's cable. The chaplain wrote: "The captain then resolved to throw all the chests of the men into the sea, but the distress of the soldiers was so great that I felt constrained to throw myself at his feet and beg him not to do it. I reminded him that we ought to trust to the great mercy of Our Lord, and, like a true Christian, he showed confidence in God, and spared the luggage. When Jesus Christ permitted the return of day, we looked at each other as at men raised from the dead, and though our suspense during Saturday was no less than that of the preceding night, light itself was a consolation to us. When night, however, found us again still in the same dangerous situation, we thought we must surely perish, and during the whole night I preached to the crew, and exhorted them to put their trust in God. Sunday morning came, and you can fancy how we rejoiced to see daylight once more, although the storm continued unabated all day, and until noon of the following Monday, when Our Lord deigned to have compassion and mercy on us, and calmed the fury of the winds and waves."

On August 5 the ship on which Father López sailed, with at least one other, made a landfall at the island of Dominica, where a small boat put ashore for wood and water. Three days later, the crews weighed anchor and set a compass heading for San Juan de Puerto Rico, which they reached on August 9. In the harbor they sighted three other ships of their scattered fleet, including the flagship *San Pelayo* of the Adelantado. "Loud cries of joy resounded on all sides," López wrote, "and we thanked the Lord that he had permitted us to find each other again, but it would be impossible for me to tell how it all happened."

The Spanish voyagers paused several days in Puerto Rico to replenish their store of provisions and to take on board horses and additional men that the king had agreed to furnish from the island garrison. Father López was asked to remain by Puerto Rican settlers. They offered him an attractive pastorate, but he refused, as he wrote later: "I wanted to see if by refusing a personal benefit for the love of Jesus, He would not grant me a greater, since it is my desire to serve Our Lord and His Blessed Mother."

Pedro Menéndez, meantime, had to face the problems created by his scattered fleet. The General was lacking over two-thirds of his expeditionary force, and he had no way of knowing when— or if—the remaining ships would arrive. He deliberated for a time whether he should await the balance of his fleet or press on toward Florida. Solís de Merás was with him when he made his decision, and he recorded it in these words: "Seeing that the people who were with him were persons of much reliance and bravery, despite the fact that many of the soldiers were not trained, he summoned all the captains to a council, and told them that he had not taken that expedition under his charge through vanity or personal interest, but for the honor of God, Who already appeared to be manifesting His mercies, since to show His hand visibly, He had permitted that the powerful fleet which sailed from [Spain] should arrive near Florida in an impaired condition in order that the success of whatever famous action could be achieved should be attributed to Him. Trusting in the Divine Will, he said, he held it proper that they should sail at once for Florida, without waiting for or seeking further aid."

With approval from all hands, Menéndez weighed anchor on August 15 and led his few ships to sea again, northward toward the Bahama Channel. On Monday, August 27, Father López noted, "while we were near the entrance to the Bahama Channel, God showed to us a miracle from heaven." He described it: "About nine o'clock in the evening, a comet appeared, which showed itself directly above us, a little eastward, giving so much light that it might have been taken for the sun. It went towards the west—that is, towards Florida, and its brightness lasted long enough to repeat two *Credos*."

The very next day the voyagers sighted land. It was Cape Canaveral (since 1963 Cape Kennedy), the thin finger of land that projected out from the center of Florida's east coast. It was "August 28, St. Augustine's Day," wrote Solís de Merás, "on which they sighted the land of Florida; all of them kneeling, saying the *Te Deum Laudamus*, they praised Our Lord, all the people repeating their prayers, entreating Our Lord to give them victory in all things." And Father López wrote: "Thanks to God and the prayers of the Blessed Virgin, we soon had the pleasure of seeing land, and found ourselves actually in Florida. . . ."

Pedro Menéndez himself recorded: "We discovered this land off Cape Canaveral, which is the latitude of 28 degrees, at the entrance of the Bahama Channel, and we sailed along the coast, seeking that harbor [of the River of May, site of Fort Caroline] as far as 29 degrees, for such was the report I had, that the Frenchmen were between 28 and 29 degrees. Not finding them, we went on as far as 29.5 degrees [slightly south of the site of the present Marineland]; and having seen fires on the shore on September 2, I ordered a captain ashore with twenty soldiers, to try to get an interpreter among the Indians, that they might give us knowledge of that harbor; and so the captain who went ashore joined them and talked to them, and they told him, by signs, that the harbor was farther on in a higher latitude toward the north."

Coasting along the shoreline farther north, the Adelantado came upon the harbor which the French called the River of Dolphins. The Indians called the site Seloy. It was, wrote Solís de Merás, "a good harbor, with a good beach, to which he [Menéndez] gave the name of St. Augustine," because that saint's feast was the day on which he had first sighted land.

The date was now September 4. Menéndez proceeded still farther up the coast and reached the mouth of the River of May early the next morning. There he sighted four French warships— reinforcements for Fort Caroline. Jean Ribault had won the race from Europe. Worried that the enemy force was strong enough to prevent the founding of a Spanish settlement, the Adelantado's council of captains urged him to return to the Caribbean to await the balance of his fleet. Menéndez, however, decided to engage the French ships at once. In making that decision, he set the seal of fate on 1565 as the year of his first settlement, for in the proposi-

25

tion of his captains he would not have returned to the harbor of St. Augustine until March of the following year.

A brief and inconsequential battle followed. Father López recorded that, "notwithstanding all the guns we fired at them, we did not sink one of their ships." The Spaniards, too, withdrew with no losses, and Menéndez, having satisfied for now his military honor, decided to retire. He put his flagship under full sail toward the newly named harbor of St. Augustine, and arrived there, just off the Indian village of Seloy, on September 6.

Father López described the sequence of events leading to the actual founding of the parish and garrison of St. Augustine: "Two companies of infantry now disembarked [on September 6], that of Captain Andrés Sóyez Patiño and that of Captain Juan de San Vincente, who is a very distinguished gentleman. They were well received by the Indians, who gave them a large house belonging to a chief, and situated near the shore of the river. Immediately, Captain Patiño and Captain San Vincente, both men of talent and energy, ordered an entrenchment to be built around this house, with a slope of earth and fascines, these being the only means of defense possible in that country, where stones are nowhere to be found. The energy and talents of those two brave captains, joined to the efforts of their brave soldiers, who had no tools with which to work the earth, accomplished the construction of this fortress of defense, and when the General disembarked, he was quite surprised with what had been done.

"On Saturday the 8th, the General landed with many banners spread, to the sound of trumpets and salutes of artillery. As I had gone ashore the evening before, I took a Cross and went to meet him, singing the hymn, *Te Deum Laudamus*. The General, followed by all who accompanied him, marched up to the Cross, knelt, and kissed it. A large number of Indians watched these proceedings and imitated all they saw done."

A solemn Mass was then offered in honor of the Nativity of the Blessed Virgin Mary, the feast day observed, then as now, on September 8. Solís de Merás records that after Mass, "the Adelantado had the Indians fed and dined himself." It was the first community act of religion and thanksgiving in the first permanent settlement in the land. It was also the beginning of the parish of St. Augustine and of the permanent service of the Catholic Church in what is now the United States.

The Spaniards christened their landing site Nombre de Dios—Name of God—by which name the site is still known today. Shortly after the landing, Menéndez and his priests erected there, among the redmen of Seloy, the first Christian mission to the North American Indian. Nombre de Dios became the baptismal name of a new nation. From that place, for 198 uninterrupted years, priests and laymen would carry Christianity and civilization into the wild interior: first diocesan, then Jesuit, and finally Franciscan missionaries would drop their lamps of faith and knowledge into the darkness as far as Virginia to the north, and Texas in the west, and write their names into one of the least known but most heroic chapters of American and Catholic history.

According to traditions maintained by the Spanish population of St. Augustine over the next two centuries, the landing site was situated on the mainland, on the north side of a creek called Macaris, known today as Hospital Creek, about a quarter of a mile north of the city gates of the eventual Ciudad de San Agustín that was marked out and erected by Menéndez' successors in the sixteenth and seventeenth centuries. Both the location of the landing site and the reverence with which it was regarded by the Spaniards of St. Augustine were indicated by cartographer Juan Joseph Elíxio de la Puente in a carefully drawn map of the city executed in 1769. The map's key points out the place and reads, in part: "Place called Nombre de Dios, which is the same where the first Mass was said on September 8, 1565, when the Spaniards under the command of the Adelantado Pedro Menéndez de Avilés set out to conquer these provinces; and afterwards, an Indian village was built there, with a chapel, in which was placed an image of María Santísima de la Leche."

Three days after the landing, Menéndez wrote home to Philip II: "As for myself, Your Majesty may be assured that if I had a million [ducats] more or less, I would spend it all upon this undertaking, because it is of such great service to God Our Lord, for the increase of our Holy Catholic Faith, and for the service of

27

Your Majesty. And therefore, I have offered to Our Lord all that He may give me in this world, all that I may acquire and possess, in order to plant the Gospel in this land for the enlightenment of its natives; and in like manner I pledge myself to Your Majesty."

Although it has startled many readers of Spanish Florida history to discover that men warred mercilessly against each other in the sixteenth century as they do unremittingly in our own, it is a fact that Menéndez accomplished with dispatch and thoroughness the military portion of his mission. Marching overland in mid-September, Menéndez and his five hundred fighting men captured Fort Caroline and slew the entire garrison, excepting women and children and youths not under arms. Father López observed that the Spaniards "found many packs of playing cards with the figure of the Host and Chalice on the backs, and many saints with crosses on their shoulders and other playing cards burlesquing things of the Church." Soon afterwards, catching Jean Ribault and two groups of shipwrecked soldiers at Matanzas Inlet south of St. Augustine, Menéndez exacted their unconditional surrender, and then coolly "gave them to the sword," sparing only the Catholics among them and youths not under arms, about seventeen in all. This act was committed with the same *sang-froid* of French cruiser captains off the coast of Holland; of Jacques Sorie, who had slaughtered the residents of Havana several years before; and of Dominique de Gourgues, who would wreak French revenge on the Spanish occupiers of Fort Caroline (renamed San Mateo) only three years later. The Adelantado returned then to St. Augustine, wrote Solís de Merás, where "some persons considered him cruel, and others, that he had acted as a very good captain should." Historians in that city are still judging him both ways.

Discharge of his mandate, military necessity, inability to feed the French captives from his meager stores—over a hundred Spaniards would die from starvation during the coming winter—these appear to have been reasons which led Menéndez to carry out his instructions so completely. Although France and Spain were not formally at war, police actions of this sort were common occurrences where national ambitions collided in foreign lands or on the seas. They were cruel times; one can imagine the fate of

Menéndez had he fallen into the hands of Sir Francis Drake! To Menéndez it seemed necessary in this instance to sacrifice mercy to justice, and if that marked him with "an indelible stain," as the Catholic historian John Gilmary Shea concluded in the last century, it was the sole stain on an otherwise admirable breastplate.

In October of the same year Menéndez petitioned the Society of Jesus (Jesuits) in Spain for additional missionaries to the Indians, who seemed everywhere friendly and receptive to the diocesan pioneers. He assured Father Diego de Avellañeda, provincial of the Jesuits in Andalusia, that while he waited on the Jesuits he would dispose the Indians by every kindness to receive their doctrine gladly. In voyages along the Florida peninsula and up the Atlantic coast in 1565 and the year following, Menéndez erected crosses at various points and left Spaniards of marked religious zeal to instruct the surrounding tribes in the elements of Christianity. Most of these lay missions were administered from military outposts, which by 1567 ran in a chain from the fort of San Felipe at Santa Elena (Parris Island, South Carolina) around to the Gulf Coast of the Florida peninsula.

All of this territory, and more, was referred to in official documents of the time as Las Provincias de la Florida. The various districts were usually designated by their Indian names: South Carolina was Orista, Georgia along the coast was Guale, and the vast interior was called Tama. The northeast corner of the Florida peninsula around St. Augustine was known as Timucua. South of Timucua, in the region of Cape Canaveral, was Ais. Bordering Ais to the northwest was Potano. The southeast Atlantic coast was called Tequesta. The southwest Gulf coast was known as Calusa, or Carlos. Within this stretch of shoreline Menéndez had three permanent settlements served by diocesan priests—St. Augustine, San Mateo (Fort Caroline), and Santa Elena—and a line of forts at Ais (St. Lucie), Tequesta (Biscayne Bay), Carlos (Charlotte Harbor), and Tocobaga (Tampa). Another settlement attempted on the Chesapeake had failed.

At St. Augustine Father López was *cura*, or pastor, named to that office by Menéndez with the concurrence of the Bishop of

Santiago de Cuba. In June, 1566, a relief expedition arrived in the harbor with five more diocesan priests, who were placed under Father López' direction. Writing to Spain in 1567, López styled himself "vicar of Florida," and complained of a slight illness. We catch his name in the records once more, in 1569, when he interceded for a group of mutineers at St. Augustine. After that the pioneer cleric disappears into the twilight of history; there is no known record of his death and burial.

The first authenticated missionary success with the North American Indians can be attributed to Father Sebastian Montero, one of the five diocesan priests who arrived at St. Augustine with the relief expedition of 1566. Father Montero, a native of Ecija, came as chaplain to the company of Captain Juan Pardo, and accompanied Pardo and three hundred men to their station at San Felipe, the fort of Santa Elena. In August, 1566, Pedro Menéndez ordered Pardo to make an overland reconnaissance of Orista in the direction of New Spain, or Mexico. The Adelantado directed him to visit the Indian *caciques*, or chieftains, to construct a chain of inland forts, and to "see that the Indians became Christians," as Solís de Merás recorded.

Pardo departed from Santa Elena on November 1 with 125 soldier-volunteers and his chaplain, Father Montero. In the course of their march westward, Pardo and his men explored the cypress lands that lie between the Broad and Edisto Rivers, visited a series of Indian towns that De Soto had passed through twenty-six years before, and halted, finally, at the snow-crowned barrier of the Chattooga Ridge in present-day Oconee County, South Carolina. Here was the important Indian village of Joara, or Juada, the "Xualla" of De Soto, at the gateway of the Appalachians. Pardo renamed the place Cuenca, after his native city in Spain, built a blockhouse where he stationed a sergeant with thirty men, and began to march back toward Santa Elena, following the course of several "copious streams." In the vicinity of what is now Anderson County, South Carolina, the Spaniards stumbled on the great town of Guatari, royal residence of two noble *cacicas*, or chieftainesses, of the Wateree tribe.

"Here I stayed fifteen or sixteen days, more or less," Pardo

wrote later, "where those chieftains asked me to give them someone to instruct them, and so I gave them the priest of my company
and four soldiers. . . ." Until very recently this was the last word
about Father Montero that history had; indeed, even his name was
lost to history and remained unknown for most of the next four
centuries. Now we know, from recently discovered documents,
that Sebastian Montero remained among the Guatari Indians for
six years, and that he enjoyed a considerable success with them. Witnesses reported later in Seville that the priest taught the Indians
four basic prayers (the Our Father, the Hail Mary, the Creed, and
the Hail Holy Queen) "and other Christian things that are necessary to them for their salvation." He taught them to worship regularly on Sundays and holy days, to abstain from meat on Fridays,
and to observe the Commandments. Of equal interest, Montero
taught them the Spanish language, including the skills of reading
and writing, with the result, as one Spanish soldier testified, "that
many of them understood much of it through his direction and instruction, especially the principal *caciques* with whom he worked
a good deal. . . ."

Captain Pardo returned to Guatari on another and longer expedition in 1567, and renamed the town Salamanca. During this
second march Pardo marked out a line of advance around the northern and western flanks of Santa Elena, and erected a string of garrisoned forts that stretched as far as the Chattahoochee River. Not
only did Spanish arms now prevail throughout this great Indian
region, but the Cross of Christianity as well, for Pardo commanded
the soldiers in his garrisons to "teach them [the Indians] and let
them know how they are to give service to God our Lord. . . ."
Unfortunately, and unaccountably, that interior chain of outposts
was abandoned in the following year. And Father Montero himself withdrew from Guatari in 1572 for reasons of failing health.
As subsequent events turned out, the priest from Ecija was the
last, as he had been the first, priest-missionary in the Orista back
country of La Florida. He seems to have left there no traces of
himself, nor of his labors. Still, it can be written now, belatedly,
that Father Montero at Guatari produced the first evangelical success to which the infant mission center could lay claim.

31

In September, 1566, the Jesuits finally came to Florida. Just shortly before, Menéndez had written a complaining letter to the Jesuit provincial of Andalusia, saying of the Indians, "I had told them that these religious [Jesuits] were coming on the next ships and would soon talk with them and instruct them on becoming Christians; and now, as no religious came, the natives think that I am a liar; and some of them have become angry and accuse me of deluding them; and the unfriendly chiefs laugh at them and at me."

It was in a Flemish pinnacle that the first Jesuit band arrived September 14, near the mouth of the St. Johns River: Father Pedro Martínez, superior, Father Juan Rogel, and Brother Francisco Villareal. Unexplainedly, their vessel had missed the harbor of St. Augustine, and Father Martínez with six Flemish seamen and two Spanish soldiers rowed ashore to ask directions. While they explored the coastline on foot, a storm at sea drove their ship away. The party on shore was left without food, and, getting into their skiff again, Martínez and his companions coasted along the beach to look for Indians. They found both Indians and food, and managed to stay alive until September 28. On that date, while begging fish at a village on San Juan Island, they were suddenly attacked by forty Indians and all but four cruelly killed. Father Martínez was strangled underwater and then clubbed. According to one of the survivors, the priest was not heard to utter a sound, but grasped the crucifix on his breast as he fell. His death was a martyrdom, and his name was afterwards invoked with awe among the members of his Order. But for the first Jesuit mission to La Florida, it was not an auspicious beginning.

Father Rogel and the lay brother had remained on board ship during Martínez' fateful venture on shore. Now the crew of their ship, desperately hungry and not knowing where they were, sailed south toward Havana, which they reached successfully, and where rescue ships sent by Menéndez discovered them. Early in 1567 the priest and lay brother were transported to Florida, Father Rogel to the military outpost near Charlotte Harbor where he began work among the surrounding Calusa tribes, and Brother Villareal to a point near the present city of Miami, where he undertook a difficult mission among the Tequesta Indians.

PEDRO MENÉNDEZ DE
AVILÉS, FOUNDER OF
FLORIDA (from a 16th
century painting)

Celebration of first Mass in St. Augustine, September 8, 1565, feast day of the Nativity of the Blessed Virgin Mary. The celebrant was Father Francisco López de Mendoza Grajales, first pastor of the pioneer settlement. Pedro Menéndez, founder of the settlement, is shown holding a banner (right). Engraving made from a painting commissioned in France by Bishop Augustin Verot in 1875.

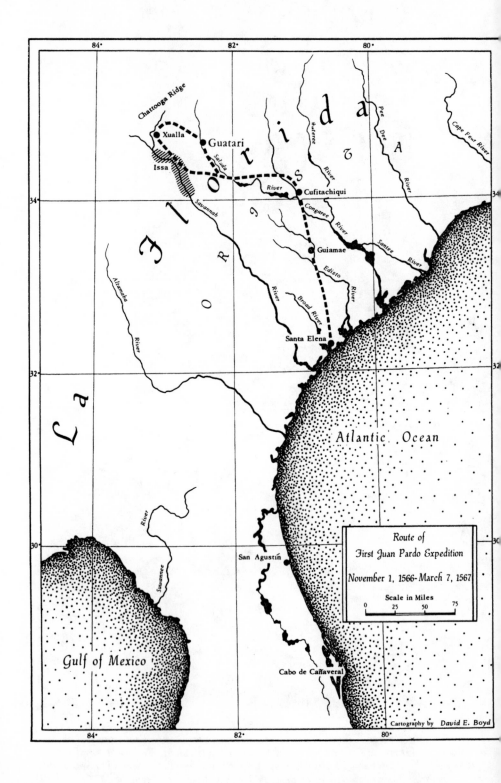

Route of
First Juan Pardo Expedition
November 1, 1566-March 7, 1567

Scale in Miles
0   25   50   75

Cartography by David E. Boyd

News of Father Martínez' martyrdom reached Spain and caused a large number of Jesuits to volunteer for the Florida missions. From these applicants, the Jesuit general selected a band of three priests, three lay brothers, and five novices. Father Bautista de Segura was appointed superior. Segura and his companions left for Florida in 1568. On their arrival, June 9, a plan for evangelizing Florida's Indians was carefully worked out. The missionaries distributed themselves along the eastern seaboard and resolved to stay at their posts until permanent missions were established and put into a flourishing state. By 1570, however, it was clear that this resolution was more difficult in realization than the Jesuits had expected. The Indians were not accepting Christianity with the quickness and fervor expected. A reorganization of the Jesuit effort resulted, and Father Rogel with one of the newcomers of 1568 was sent to search for better promise among the Indians farther north, on the Orista coastline, in what is now South Carolina. Rogel wrote back after eight months that he had managed to bring the Indians to belief in the Trinity and to a certain understanding of the Cross. However, when he began to preach to them about the evil character of the devil, they would have none of it. "When I began to treat of this, so great was the vexation and hatred which they directed at my words, they never again would come to listen to me; and they said to my people that they were very angry, and did not believe a thing I said, since I spoke ill of the devil."

Probably the main obstacle that faced the Jesuit missionaries was the migratory nature of these primitive peoples. The missionaries had difficulty keeping track of the various tribes, who moved constantly from place to place according to the seasons or hunting conditions—from pine woods to crop-raising fields, to acorn gathering sites. A good statement of the problem was sent by Father Rogel to Spain on December 9, 1570: "In order to obtain fruit in the blind and sad souls of these provinces, it is necessary first of all to order the Indians to come together, and live in towns and cultivate the earth, collecting sustenance for the entire year; and after they have thus become very settled, then to begin the preaching. Unless this is done, although the religious remain among them for fifty years, they will have no more fruit than we in our four years

33

among them, which is none at all, nor even a hope, nor the semblance of it."

In September, 1570, Father Segura traveled north with another priest, three novices, and three lay brothers to establish a mission at a site near the present city of Fredericksburg, Virginia. The adventure ended in tragedy. On February 4 and 9, 1571, only five months after the mission began, the missionaries were massacred by the Indians they had come to help. The martyrs' names were Fathers Segura and Luis de Quirós, and Brothers Gabriel de Solís, Juan Bautista Méndez, Pedro de Linares, Sancho Zeballos, Gabriel Gómez, and Cristóbal Redondo. The only survivor of the massacre to tell the tale was a little Indian boy named Alonso, who had accompanied the missionaries to Virginia from Santa Elena.

For the Jesuits this was the ultimate frustration. They had not a single successful mission to show for all their labor. In 1572 Jesuit authorities in Spain decided to abandon altogether the mission field of Florida. The few remaining missionaries were recalled to Mexico. Their order would not return again to Florida until 1743, when two Jesuit priest-explorers conducted a short-lived and unsuccessful mission in the Keys.

The Jesuit failure was a keen disappointment to Pedro Menéndez. The Adelantado had expected the Society of Jesus to succeed where, perhaps, another Order might have failed. Now this expectation had been dashed, and except for a small and tenacious band of diocesan priests, there was no missionary force in Florida to care for the unnumbered thousands of idolatrous Indians. The Jesuit withdrawal was all the more bitter for the fact that Menéndez himself had expended every effort, and every resource at his command, to fulfill the counsels made to him three years before in a personal brief from Pope (St.) Pius V: "You understand, we know well," the Pontiff had written him, "that those Indians should be ruled and governed with good judgment and prudence, that those who are still weak in the Faith, may be encouraged and fortified, and that the idolators may be converted and receive the faith of Christ, that the converts, who know the benefits of divine mercy, may praise God, and that those who are still unbelievers, guided by the example of those who have been rescued from their blindness, may follow them and be brought to a knowledge of the truth. But there is nothing more important for the conversion of these idolatrous Indians than to make every effort to keep them from being scandalized by the vices and bad habits of those who go to those lands from Europe. This is the keystone of the arch of this holy undertaking and in it is contained the very essence of your pious aim."

Now in 1572 Menéndez, too, went home, called there by Philip II to direct the organization of an "invincible armada" with which Spain hoped to clear the Flanders coast of pirates. He had crossed the ocean seven times in the interests of his colony. Now he crossed it for the last time, exhausted and impoverished—St. Augustine and Florida had cost him his health and his entire personal fortune. Apparently he counted it no special loss: a soldier in his command said of him, "He considered nothing but the service of God and of his Majesty, without looking to human interests." On September 8, 1574, while busy with his fleet at Santander in northern Spain, the Adelantado wrote to his nephew in Florida: "After the salvation of my soul, there is nothing I desire more than to be in Florida and there end my days saving souls. . . . This is my desire and it means all my happiness. May the Lord bring it about as He can, if He sees it necessary."

But nine days later the conqueror of Florida was dead.

The sunburnt, bearded body was removed from its steel corslets and dressed, according to his wish, in the simple habit of a Franciscan. Only the gentler side of his nature showed to those who viewed his remains. But the epitaph that was placed upon his grave at Avilés had the sound of trumpets. For to such a man, Spaniards insisted, the Nation owed a monument, History a book, and the Muses a poem:

> *Glory has grooved the furrows on thy brow,*
> *And seamed thy cheek, illustrious cavalier;*
> *The scars of wars and scorching suns appear*
> *On that bold front that none could force to bow.*
> —José-Maria de Heredia

III

Black Robes and Brown Robes

1574-1606

To the side of the black-cassocked diocesan priest there came to Florida in 1573 the first in a long and gallant line of Franciscan Fathers, or Friars Minor. Pedro Menéndez had arranged for the introduction of these Sons of St. Francis into the mission country soon after it was abandoned by the Jesuits, and the first band of the brown-robed friars reached La Florida at Santa Elena. In the beginning the Franciscans met the same obstacles in dealing with the Indians as had frustrated the Jesuit effort, and their labors seemed to have been confined to the garrison towns. In 1578 we find mention of a Fray Alonso Cavezas at St. Augustine and a Fray Francisco del Castillo at Santa Elena. During these first years the friars never numbered more than four or five.

Not until 1595 would the Order of Friars Minor launch a large-scale, concerted effort to win Florida's native population for the Church. How well they would then succeed is attested by the fact that only one hundred years after their coming they could account for over thirty thriving missions at which 26,000 Indians had been taught the catechism of Christianity and the rudiments of European arts and crafts. The hardships they met and overcame in working this triumph beggar the imagination, one reason why their story is still so little known. Another reason is that there is no consecutive chronicle kept by the Florida Franciscans themselves. The history of their labors must be pieced together from royal decrees, memorials, reports, letters, and fragments of a similar nature. But there is enough information of this kind to support the judgment that the Spanish mission system in Florida was one of the most heroic and successful humanitarian efforts for the amelioration and spiritual development of backward peoples that the American nation has experienced.

The Order of Friars Minor, founded by St. Francis of Assisi in 1209, was a mendicant order devoted to the ideal of "holy poverty." As such, its members were forbidden to possess private property, ride horseback (the mark of knighthood), wear other than the simple robe, cowl, and sandals of an Italian peasant, or have incomes beyond the alms that they daily begged. Yet in Florida where no gold or other riches had been discovered, and where the colonists themselves lived from hand to mouth, for a friar to live on alms alone was impossible. Recognizing this, King Philip II stipulated that each friar on the missions should receive from the local governor three reales a day for his maintenance, as well as his clothing, medicine, and the necessary furnishings and articles required for Mass. The friars, for their part, always referred to the royal honorarium as "the alms which your Majesty gives us." The Crown also provided for all the needs of the missions themselves, and for the transportation of the friars between Spain and Florida, and between St. Augustine and the individual missions along the coastline and in the interior.

The Crown, in fact, exercised direct jurisdiction over the entire mission process. By virtue of the *Patronato Real de Indias*, or Royal Patronage of the Indies, granted to the Spanish sovereigns in 1508 by Pope Julius II, the king was, for all intents and purposes, the vicar of the Pope in the ecclesiastical administration of the Indies, including La Florida. Missionaries to Florida were named by him, their stipends or "alms" were paid by him, their chapels, churches, and friaries were erected at his expense. The same royal jurisdiction applied to secular priests, and to their parishes. One cannot read the multitude of cédulas, asientos, and capitulations issued by the kings of Spain to the long succession of explorers and governors who came to Florida, and to the missionaries who accompanied them, without being struck by the prominence given to the command that they provide for the health, welfare, and conversion of the New World savages. No historian of note has questioned the sincerity of that command. Vast sums of the Crown's money were spent for this purpose, and there was no expectation of financial return. While the closeness of the Church-State alliance might not suit the taste of a later time, still it was probably the only really effective way to get the mission work done.

The first significant band of Franciscan missionaries arrived in St. Augustine on September 29, 1587. Numbering thirteen priests, the band was led by Fray Alonso Reinoso and included Fray Alonso Escobedo, a noted scholar, from whose metrical narrative *La Florida* we learn many of the facts about the group. Governor Pedro Menéndez Marqués, a nephew of the first governor, was so pleased by the missionaries' coming that he expressed himself in these moving lines:

> *Franciscan Fathers, so you have come*
> *From the distant parts of the East*
> *To settle this poor and barren nest*
> *Where the sun's fair face is hid.*
> *What humbly now I beg you all*
> *Is to teach these western tribes*
> *Who look upon Satan as a friend*
> *But their Maker, God, regard as foe.*

The missionaries were assigned to various nearby Indian towns. Fray Escobedo went to the pioneer mission, Nombre de Dios, where he soon had one hundred converts. The other priests, with the exception of Father Reinoso, went to missions under the names of San Sebastian, San Antonio, San Pedro, and San Juan del Puerto.

Father Reinoso returned to Spain to seek more priests. Curiously, few of these Franciscan arrivals stayed very long. In 1592 there were only three Franciscan priests and two lay brothers in the entire province. Perhaps because of the poverty of the land, Father Reinoso's recruits decided that the mission effort was doomed. It was true that the missions, like the garrison towns, were suffering at the time under severe financial strain. The new colony had not proved to be self-supporting; there were no prospects of mines; agriculture was poor; and aid from the mother country had been niggardly. Already Santa Elena had been abandoned, in 1586, because of economic difficulties and incessant Indian raids.

Then on September 23, 1595, a new band of Franciscans arrived who were destined to remain in Florida for many years. With this group, and with the new and efficient Franciscan superior in Florida, Fray Francisco Marrón, the friars' missionary program began in earnest. The missionaries were distributed along the coastline north of St. Augustine in Indian towns where already 1,500 Christians could be counted. There were five missions to the Timucuan Indians who inhabited the coastline between St. Augustine and what is now the Georgia border; in Georgian territory there were missions among the Guale Indians at what are now Cumberland Island, St. Simon Island, Jekyll Island, and St. Catherines Island. The friars who went out to the missions in 1595 were personally escorted by the governor, who knelt to kiss the hands of the missionaries before the assembled Indians, as a sign of the sacred authority granted to these bearers of the word of God.

A mission where there was a resident friar was called by the Franciscans a *doctrina;* a subsidiary mission station where the friar visited on Sundays and holy days was called a *visita*. A friar on the missions was called a *doctrinero*, i.e., one who taught Christian doctrine at the doctrina. The mission buildings themselves were of simple, even primitive, construction. Pine-tree trunks held up the roof and walls, and between these rough-hewn pillars small posts were interwoven with horizontal wattles, tied with leather thongs. Clay was then daubed on the latticework and, when dry, it was whitewashed on the interior. Palmetto thatching served as roofing, and wide eaves provided outside shade from the sun. Because of the scarcity of stone, and the unrelieved poverty of the colony, this wattle-and-daub type of construction would characterize the Florida mission compounds throughout their entire history.

A consoling sign of progress came two years later when twenty-two caciques came to St. Augustine to pledge their allegiance to the governor. Spain now had effective control over the coastline from Cape Canaveral in the south to Santa Elena Sound in the north, and over the seaboard tribes that inhabited those regions. Prospects for working amicably with the Indians looked bright. Missionaries could be sent safely, it seemed, to any point in that vast stretch of wilderness.

In the midst of this brightening picture there occurred a sudden and violent uprising by the Guale Indians in present-day Georgia. Called variously the Guale Revolt and the Juanillo Revolt, after the warrior Juanillo, son of the chief at Tolomato (on Pease Creek in McIntosh County, Georgia), it was an eruption of violence so serious that it threatened the continued presence of the Spaniards in Florida. It was a blow to the Franciscans particularly. For several of the friars the uprising brought martyrdom.

The trouble began when Fray Pedro de Corpa, the priest at Tolomato, reprimanded Juanillo for having other wives in addition to the one to whom he was lawfully married. Father Corpa told the warrior that there was a fundamental conflict between the savage and the Christian ways of life, and that if he desired to remain a Christian he would have to give up his polygamous habits. Juanillo resisted this instruction, however, and continued to possess his several wives, to the scandal of all the newly made Christians. Father Corpa, with the approval and aid of Father Blas Rodríguez at the nearby mission at Tupiqui, undertook a drastic measure to correct the wayward Indian. He deprived him of his right to succeed to the chiefship of Guale when his father should die, and transferred the right instead to another heir.

The results of this measure were not such as the two priests hoped for. On the morning of September 13, 1597, with two other Indians who were angered by the missionaries' attempt to enforce monogamy among the natives, Juanillo entered Father Corpa's dwelling while he was at prayer and fractured his head with a *macâna,* the Indian club. The priest's head was impaled on the point of a lance, and set up for the gaze of all at the *embarcadero,* or landing place. The remainder of the body was buried in the woods. The following day Juanillo persuaded the chiefs of seven other villages to join him in a murderous campaign against the Franciscans. On September 16 they accosted Father Rodríguez at Tupiqui, and told him that he, too, would have to die. The priest asked the insurgents for time enough to offer a last Mass, which he was allowed to do while his executioners sat waiting on the chapel floor. Following his Mass, Father Rodríguez distributed his few effects among the local Indians, admonished them to observe God's law, then knelt to receive the mortal blow. The Indians despoiled the priest's room of its sacred vessels and furnishings, and left his corpse a prey to bird and beast. Later a Christian Indian took the body to the woods and buried it. On St. Catherines, or Guale, Island, Father Miguel de Auñón and a lay brother, Antonio de Badajoz, patiently waited their own deaths. When scouts informed the missionaries that the rebel Indians were close by, Father Auñón celebrated Mass and gave Holy Communion to Brother Antonio. Then on September 19, they, too, fell under the macâna. Faithful Christian Indians buried their remains at the base of a towering wooden cross that Auñón had erected on the island. A military expedition sent afterwards by Governor Gonzalo Méndez de Canzo exhumed the friars' bodies and brought them back to St. Augustine where they were reinterred with great reverence. Another martyr was Fray Francisco de Verascola, the missionary at Santo Domingo de Asao. Known as the "Catabrian Giant" for his large physical proportions, Father Verascola was in St. Augustine to obtain supplies when the rebellion broke out. On the day he returned, two of the rebels took him in their arms as if to welcome him while the others killed him with an axe.

A living martyrdom was the fate of Fray Francisco de Avila at Ospo. He had already been apprised of the death of Father Corpa when rebel Indians appeared one night outside the hut that served for his friary. The Indians tried to entice the priest out of doors, saying that they had a communication from his superior. When Avila refused to answer, the Indians broke in. Avila hid behind a door, then, while the savages rummaged through his few possessions, fled outside to the cover of nearby rushes. The night was illuminated by a brilliant moon, however, and the priest was eventually sighted by the Indians, who wounded his shoulder, hand, and thigh with a volley of arrows. The priest was then forced to walk to the village of Tulafina, a good distance away, where he was tortured, and condemned to die. Finally, it was decided to spare his life in return for his services as a slave. The priest then entered upon a horrible captivity lasting nine months. In great pain from his wounds, he became the servant of everyone in the village, even of the children. He suffered from the cold and from constant hunger. All he had for food was what he could find himself among the wild produce of the Georgia coast. He had only scraps of cloth for clothes. The Indians attempted to make him enter a marriage contract and do other acts in violation of his vows or of his religion. Finally, in June, 1598, he was liberated by a Spanish military patrol, and taken to St. Augustine where food and medicines restored his health. Father Avila was the only survivor among the friars who knew anything about the causes behind the Guale revolt. When Governor Canzo therefore asked him to testify on the matter, Avila refused and invoked the immunity granted to clerics. He argued that he could offer no evidence without incriminating the Indians and thereby leading to their execution, and that Church law forbade him to do so. Canzo acknowledged his immunity and left him in peace. Years later, Father Avila went to Havana where, under Franciscan obedience, he wrote the account of his capture and captivity that we relate here.

The deaths of these Guale martyrs brought to seventeen the number of priests and lay brothers who had given their lives to the cause of their Faith in Florida. Now King Philip III, when he learned of the tragedy, seriously contemplated the abandonment of Florida. The loss of men and money that Spain had suffered over many years in her effort to colonize this province had become unbearable. The king demanded an investigation. He sent Fernando de Valdés, son of the governor of Cuba, to St. Augustine in order to determine how much if anything could be salvaged from the Guale Indian debacle. Valdés, to his surprise, found the Franciscans optimistic about the future of the missions and unanimous in their opposition to any plan for withdrawal. In formal depositions three of the friars described the success that the missions were enjoying among the more docile Timucuans.

Fray Pedro Bermejo, an eight-year veteran stationed at Nombre de Dios, reported that he had three Indian pueblos, or towns, with 200 Christian adults and children. The chapel at Nombre de Dios was a handsome stone structure complete with statues of the saints, and his Indians were by this time so well instructed they sang High Mass and Vespers on Sundays. Fray Francisco Pareja had 500 Christians in nine pueblos within his mission area at San Juan del Puerto near the mouth of the St. Johns River. And Fray Baltazar López had seven pueblos at San Pedro farther north, in which he numbered 384 baptized converts, and many others under instruction. López also noted that there were 1,200 Christian Indians in Guale who could easily be won back once the chiefs settled down. But Governor Canzo, all three priests agreed, would have to show a higher degree of cooperation with the missionaries than he had shown in the past, if the mission program was to succeed as it ought.

In 1603 Canzo made a personal visitation to the province of Guale to reassert Spain's dominion over it. He visited all the principal villages along the coast as far north as Santa Elena and succeeded in establishing peaceful relations with all the tribes. Later the same year Canzo's successor, Pedro de Ybarra, conducted another inspection of Guale, during which he founded new doctrinas at St. Simon Island, St. Catherines Island, and Sapelo Island. Ybarra promised to send more missionaries to the chiefs, who were asking for them again. By the end of 1603 the rebirth of the Guale missions was well under way.

The eventful course of the Franciscan mission system should not cause us to lose sight of the true pioneer clergy of Florida, the secular, or diocesan, priests. Although not primarily commissioned to work among the Indians, the diocesan priests did considerable work of this nature, and at Nombre de Dios they had been the sole missionaries to the Timucuans during the three years between the time of the Spanish landing in 1565 and the arrival of the Jesuits under Father Segura in 1568. The primary responsibility of the seculars was to care for the Spanish settlers. This was a full-time task, since the priests were never many in number, and the outposts erected by Menéndez along the Atlantic and Gulf seaboards were situated at great distances from each other, requiring the priests to undertake frequent and arduous journeys. The poverty experienced by these outposts often equaled the worst conditions found by the Jesuits and Franciscans among the natives. At St. Augustine and San Mateo over one hundred died the first winter; almost naked, the survivors suffered greatly from the cold. At the post of Santa Lucía farther south in the Ais country, conditions were so desperate in the winter of 1566 that the garrison was reduced to chewing shoes, leather belts, snakes, rats, and dwarf palmettos to stay alive. When Indians attacked the post in force, killing twenty-three of the soldiers in a fierce contest between arquebuses and arrows, Father López de Mendoza Grajales, who happened to be on the scene at the time, slipped out with a sub-lieutenant and several men and endeavored to reach Havana and help. None of the crew knew navigation, however, and the small boat in which they sailed was driven back to shore by foul weather. A relief ship finally arrived to bring food and replacements.

St. Augustine was more or less continually served by secular priests during the early years. Records are scant, but we know that in 1584 there were two seculars in the garrison town, and that they drew the same rations and pay as that of a common soldier. One of these priests was Rodrigo García de Trujillo, who had come over with Menéndez in 1565. He was pastor of St. Augustine in the summer of 1586 when the town was plundered and burned to the ground by the English corsair, Sir Francis Drake. Though absent at intervals, Father Trujillo apparently served twenty-eight years in the old settlement, until 1593 when broken in health, he had to retire. He was replaced for a brief time by Father Diego Escobar de Sambrana, whose name is the first to appear on the still extant parish registers. The first entry records the baptism of "María, legitimate daughter of S. Ximenes de la Queva and María Melendez, his wife" on June 25, 1594. In July of that year Father Sambrana left the parish, and was replaced by Father Marrón, superior of the Florida Franciscans. Marrón served in this capacity until 1597, when he was replaced by an Irish-born secular.

Father Ricardo Artur (Richard Arthur) was the first pastor at St. Augustine of whom we have any substantial record. He was also the first Irish priest to serve in what is now the United States. Although details of his early life are lacking, he probably had served as a layman with the Irish Brigade and Legion formed by Sir William Stanley to help the Dutch in their revolt against Spain in 1586. This so-called "Wild Geese" brigade later went over to the side of Spain. Father Artur arrived in St. Augustine by ship from Spain in June, 1597, in company with the newly appointed Governor Canzo.

Father Marrón turned over the parish to Artur, we read in the records, "while preaching one Sunday in the principal church in this city." Underlining the different responsibilities of the regular and secular clergy, the records add that Marrón could no longer serve as pastor "because he was a Franciscan friar." (Nine years later the Franciscans would not be so obliging.) On February 10, 1598, the Bishop of Santiago de Cuba, Don Antonio Díaz de Salcedo, confirmed Artur's appointment as pastor of St. Augustine and also made the Irishman his vicar and ecclesiastical judge for the entire province of Florida. All persons, Franciscan friars as well as lay colonists, were instructed to obey him in all ecclesiastical matters, and not to interfere with the performance of his office under pain of excommunication. The next year Artur was appointed *visitador* as well. By this office he was empowered to visit and inspect the friaries of the district. Relations, which had never been very warm between regulars and seculars in the Indies, no doubt cooled with this news that an Irish-born newcomer had been named to rule the veteran Spanish Franciscans.

There are no descriptions of the parish church at St. Augustine at this time. The first church had been destroyed in Drake's raid of 1586. In the rebuilding, wood would have been used since it was not until the next century that the colonists learned to use the coquina shellrock which abounded below the sands of nearby Anastasia Island. We know that on March 14, 1599, the Franciscan monastery burned down, as well as a number of houses, and that the friars had to move into a hospital completed by Governor Canzo the year before.

This hospital—dedicated under the title Nuestra Señora de la Soledad,—Our Lady of Solitude—is worthy of notice as the first hospital in what is now the United States. Except for the brief period of its occupancy by the burned-out friars (1599-1605), it would serve as a hospital for most of the next century and a half. When the friars moved into La Soledad, Governor Canzo erected another hospital at his own expense, and dedicated it under the name Santa Bárbara. By 1605 the friars had moved into new quarters and opened up a small seminary. Thus, St. Augustine gained the distinction of also having the first school in what is now the United States, antedating by more than a quarter-century the educational foundations in English and Dutch colonies to the north.

As a Crown colony, Florida was not subject in its civil and judicial administration to the *audiencia* (tribunal) of Santo Domingo, as other Spanish settlements in the general geographic area, but directly to the Spanish Crown. Ecclesiastically, too, Florida was in great part controlled by the Crown, by virtue of the patronato real. Certain jurisdiction, however, was exercised by the Bishop of Santiago de Cuba, whose see was situated at Havana, and in 1606 it fell upon that prelate, Juan de las Cabezas de Altamirano, to make an official visitation of his distant charge. Many in Florida, including the governor, felt that such a visitation was long overdue: none of the converted Indians or second-generation Spaniards had yet received the sacrament of Confirmation. Bishop Altamirano arrived at St. Augustine on March 15 on board a captured English pirate ship, and the colonists turned out in force to greet him, the first consecrated bishop to visit Florida. For the drab presidio town it was an event of the first magnitude, and the panoply and pomp must have startled the Spaniards as much as it did the Indians.

The week following the bishop's arrival was Holy Week. On Holy Thursday Altamirano consecrated the holy oils and chrism. On Holy Saturday he ordained more than 20 young men, some from Cuba, the rest from Florida families. (It is not recorded if these were major or minor orders.) On Easter Sunday he conferred confirmation on 350 adults and minors at St. Augustine's parish church. And on the Sunday following, he began his visitation of the missions, going first to nearby Nombre de Dios, where he confirmed 216 Indians and 20 Spaniards—soldiers, fishermen, hunters—who lived in that settlement. Then came the Guale missions in Georgian territory to the north, where he confirmed 1,652 Indians, and remonstrated against their near nudity; and the Timucuan missions, which by this date went westward to San Diego Salamototo on the St. Johns near Tocoi and as far as San Francisco de Potano near present-day Gainesville. Altogether, in territory now Floridian, the bishop confirmed 981 persons, Indian and Spanish.

On his return to St. Augustine, the bishop spent a good part of his time ironing out jurisdictional problems that had arisen in the relations of the friars with the governor. He concluded from his investigation that one reason for the strained relations was the youth and independent spirit of some of the friars. "The labors and hardships of the Fathers in their missions," the bishop wrote to Philip III, "are indeed very great; and it is much to their credit to have produced the fruits that I have seen in several of their charges here. Beyond a doubt, they eat their bread in sorrow in these places." However, he went on, "the religious best adapted to these provinces are those who have reached the age of forty, and are humble rather than learned—those who have been brought up on Spanish goodness and piety, trained in the austerities of their institutes, and have, to use the expression common in the Order, 'trampled worldly wealth under foot.' "

Altamirano also took note of the ambition of certain of the Franciscans to gain control of the parish church at St. Augustine and of the chaplaincy at the fort. The Franciscans based their petition on the fact that they had actually filled those posts when, from time to time, a secular priest was not available. The bishop's comments to the king on this matter are interesting because they point up the independence of the friar, who, unlike his diocesan counterpart, was exempt from direct obedience to the bishop: "I can only tell your Majesty that my predecessor, although he belonged to that [Franciscan] Order, did not wish a religious to be parish priest or chaplain here because of certain difficulties, not the least of which was that they [Franciscans] worked when they wished to work and took off when they did not. Neither the bishop nor the governor could call them to duty, for on such occasions they pleaded, as it suited them, their privilege of exemption. For my part, because of what I have seen, I declare that I would not venture to entrust this parish to them, unless your Majesty positively commands me to do so."

The parish remained in diocesan hands and the Franciscans concentrated again on the missions. Priest, friar, Indian, creole, soldier, and official took heart from the episcopal visitation. A vast and relatively disjointed stretch of primitive territory inhabited by aborigines had been consolidated under the touch of the highest authority the Church could offer. Bishop Altamirano went home to Cuba. And Florida readied itself for the Golden Age.

First page of the Parish Registers of St. Augustine. The earliest entry, dated June 25, 1594, and signed by the pastor, Father Diego de Sambrana, records the baptism of an infant named María. The Registers, the oldest written records of American origin in the United States, are preserved in the Mission of Nombre de Dios in St. Augustine.

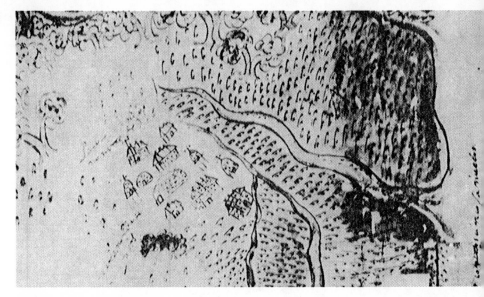

COURTESY ARCHIVO GENERAL DE INDIAS, SEVIL

(Upper) *Spanish map, dated 1595, gives the earliest known portrayal of the Mission of Nombre de Dios. Legend above the group of wooden buildings reads "Pueblo de Indios Nombre de Dios"—Indian village Nombre de Dios.*

(Right) *Chapel of the Mission of Nombre de Dios. Several earlier chapels stood on this site in Spanish times, but were destroyed by cannon fire or storms. Present reconstruction dates from 1915.*

(Left) *The statue of Nuestra Señora de Leche y buen parto (Our Nursing Mother Happy Delivery) is similar to that of Mar enshrined under the same title by 17th cer tury Spaniards at the Mission of Nombre Dios.*

IV

The Golden Age

of the Florida Missions

1606-1675

T HE STORY OF THE RAPID GROWTH of the missions that followed Bishop Altamirano's visit and reached its zenith
three-quarters through the seventeenth century is also the
story of a long succession of hardships, obstacles, and
worries. The hardships came from the nature of the work and from
the forbidding circumstances in which it was often carried on. The
obstacles were raised by Spaniards, usually governors or governors'
officials, who compromised the spiritual labor of the friars and ex-
ploited the converted Indians for purposes not religious; a particularly egregious example of this predatory policy would arise in the
1650's during the administration of Governor Diego de Rebolledo.
The worries were occasioned by the constant threat that Spain
would withdraw from Florida for economic reasons, leaving the
mass of Indians to their savagery. This threat came very close to
reality in 1607. The incident deserves the attention of our narrative,
for it discloses that the Golden Age almost did not happen.

By 1607 King Philip III had reached the conclusion that the
presidio of St. Augustine was serving the defense of the West In-

dies only indirectly, and at a disproportionate cost. He knew that no mines or other sources of wealth had been discovered in the area, and that the bar that blocked its shallow harbor allowed entrance only to the smallest ships; also that when the town was not being inundated by the sea it was, as one of the Franciscans put it, "impossible to walk a quarter of a league without coming in contact with swamps or sloughs . . . with the result that we are marooned"; that the land was poor for agriculture and out of the path of commerce; that without an annual subvention of food and other necessities from Mexico and the Caribbean, the colony could not survive; and that a determined foreign corsair, such as Drake in 1586, could easily overwhelm the present fort whenever he wished. With the support of his advisers, Philip recommended to Governor Ybarra that he abandon St. Augustine, except for a corporal's guard of 150 men, dismantle the mission system, and arrange to transport any baptized Indians who wished to leave for Española.

Ybarra vigorously objected to this plan, arguing that Spain's continued presence in strength on the peninsula was necessary to the maintenance of Spanish suzerainty over the continent. But it was probably the protest of two Florida Franciscans that carried the day: Fathers Francisco Pareja and Alonso de Peñaranda pointed to the long years that their Order had labored to Christianize the Indians, suffering all manner of torments and even martyrdom— was all this to be set aside lightly? The 6,000 Christian Indians would never consent to leave their native habitat, and to abandon them would be unthinkable. "Therefore," they declared, "directing our eyes toward God, Our Master, from Whom we hope to receive perfect protection, we beg your Majesty who is a most Christian king . . . that you protect the presidio and permit it to be strengthened. Besides, more religious should be sent to answer the needs of the field." To these arguments the king reluctantly consented. The Florida missions were saved.

In 1612 the Franciscan system in Florida and Cuba was raised to the dignity of a Province, under the title Santa Elena de la Florida (St. Helen of Florida). Eight friaries, or convents, were included in the new province, over which Fray Juan Bautista de Capilla was named superior. In the same year the additional Florida missionaries that the Franciscans had asked for arrived, twenty-three in number. The next year eight came, and in 1615 twelve more. By 1615 twenty convents in the principal villages of Guale and Timucua could be counted. By this date the missionaries had ventured into the heart of Timucua, and as far west as Apalache. Timucuan country occupied the northeast corner of the peninsula, from the Atlantic west to the province of Potano (near the Gainesville of today), thence northwest to the Aucilla River (dividing today's Taylor and Jefferson counties). In the northwest corner lay the populous province of Apalache, which occupied all the fertile, rolling land between the Aucilla and Ochlockonee Rivers, and had the heaviest concentration of Indian population around the present-day site of Tallahassee. Here the Franciscans were eventually to enjoy their greatest success. To the south, on the Gulf Coast from Tampa Bay to the Keys, were situated the Calusa Indians, and on the southeast coast lived several small, independent tribes who were connected by race and language, and sometimes by politics, with the Calusas. To neither of these southern groups were the Franciscans to make serious overtures, and neither figures prominently in our story. It was in Timucua and Apalache that the friars concentrated their effort.

One priest in particular deserves credit for opening up the northwestern reaches of Florida's interior. His name was Father Martín Prieto. In 1607 he made a number of exploratory trips into the lands of Timucua west of St. Augustine and succeeded in bringing back one of the *caciques* for Christian instruction. The following year, after the cacique had been baptized at St. Augustine along with fifty followers, Father Prieto and the cacique traveled through all the villages of Timucua, and then passed across the Aucilla River to establish relations with the Apalache Indians, who "went about," said the priest, "as naked as on the day they were born." Prieto wrote of the Apalaches: "Seventy caciques came together with all their people. . . . They had abundant food consisting of cakes made of maize, and flour of the same, and thus they awaited me. Having arrived at the Plaza of Juitachuco, I testify I saw more than 30,000 Indians and I am not surprised . . . that [being] the first time they ever saw a Spaniard in their land in these times." After

1608 the Franciscans kept in regular contact with these distant tribes. Not until 1612-15, however, when the Franciscan forces were augmented to a total of thirty-eight missionaries, were they in a position to spread out toward the new lands.

In 1614, at the beginning of the Franciscan push westward, Florida was visited by Fray Luís Jerónimo de Oré, O.F.M., a native of Peru, who had been appointed commissary-general of the Indies and assigned the task of recruiting missionaries for Florida. Oré was a distinguished scholar and linguist, and shortly before coming to Florida he had read Garcilaso de la Vega's *La Florida del Inca*, an account of the De Soto expedition written from interviews with the survivors. The commissary-general made an extensive investigation of the missions and of the methods that the friars were using to develop them. Satisfied that good progress was being made there, he returned to govern the Franciscan Province of Concepción in Spain. In 1616 he visited Florida again as visitor general to hold a provincial chapter and to make a new study of the doctrinas in the Indian territories.

Together with his secretary, Father Oré traversed the entire mission system by foot and by canoe. He covered the St. Johns River missions and the missions in Potano, as far west as the Suwannee River. From there he headed northeast to the Guale Indian missions on the Georgia coast. In each place he personally examined the Indians as to their knowledge of Christian doctrine and found them to compare favorably with the Spaniards. He also found that many of the natives had learned the art of writing. Oré later published his findings in a book, *Martyrs of Florida*, toward the end of which he singled out for special praise Fray Francisco Pareja, "one of the religious who has been most useful in the conversion of the Indians."

Father Pareja, a native of Auñon in Spain, had come to Florida with the first large contingent of Franciscans in 1595. What especially impressed the visitor general was the fact that Pareja had compiled a Timucuan dictionary and grammar and had composed in that language several books of a catechetical and devotional nature. These books, Father Oré found, were always in the Indians' hands. "With ease," Oré reported, "many Indian men and women have learned to read in less than two months, and they write letters to one another in their own language." Oré asked Pareja to give an account of the religious state of the Florida Indians at this stage in their development, and was so impressed by what he heard that he published the friar's account in his book. The account gives an illuminating picture of mission life.

To the question whether the converted Indians showed themselves to be true Christians, and not just savages over whom had been placed a thin veneer of the white man's religion, Father Pareja answered that many of the men and women were so fervent in their new beliefs, and so well instructed, that they catechized other Indians. The baptized Indians regularly assisted at Mass on Sundays and feast days, "in which they take part and sing." From the visitas, or mission stations, the outlying tribes came to the doctrinas to hear the *Salve Regina* sung on Saturdays, then stayed overnight for Mass the next morning. The Indians were also regular in the recitation of morning and evening prayers, and showed a consoling initiative in things spiritual. Whenever a missionary left the doctrina for an extended journey, it was not unusual for the men and women to approach him for confession first, saying, "perhaps I shall die before your reverence returns." In each of the principal towns there was a church and a community house, in which the Indians came together to teach one another singing and reading. They had extirpated all signs of their former superstitions and in all things, including morality, most of the Indians were living as true Christians ought. In fact, Father Pareja added, "Many persons are found, men and women, who confess and who receive [Holy Communion] with tears, and who show up advantageously with many Spaniards. And I shall make bold to say . . . that with regard to the mysteries of faith, many of them answer better than the Spaniards because the latter are careless in these matters."

As for the missionaries themselves, Father Pareja described to Oré the utter privation suffered by many of the friars in the field. Not only food and clothing, but sometimes even vestments for Mass were lacking to the priests. When the necessities for Mass were exhausted, the missionaries went without meals·in order to purchase them with the reales saved. Once Father Pareja and Father Pedro Ruíz at a nearby doctrina were reduced to fashioning a chalice from lead. The priest complained that funds and supplies that should have been provided to the missionaries were being held back by government officials at St. Augustine, "since it seems to them that the soldiers are the necessary ones [here], and that we are of no use. . . ."

"But," Father Pareja argued, with justification, "we are the ones who bear the burden and the heat; we are the ones who are conquering and subduing the land."

In 1633 the Indians of Apalache received their first full-time resident missionary. A doubtful Franciscan authority estimated at that time that there were some 34,000 Indians in that province alone, "of whom now over 5,000 are baptized." Both figures were probably exaggerations. In 1635, writing to the king, Fray Francisco Alonzo de Jesús, custodian of the Province of Santa Elena de la Florida, wrote that Florida was in dire need of priests for the newly opened mission in the northwest. Of twelve friars who had been sent out in 1630, he wrote, one died on the voyage from Spain, two others had to be left in Cuba to recuperate from illnesses contracted on the voyage, and five had died from the severe and continuous labors of their apostolate to the Indians in Florida. He went on to say: "The friars suffer greatly in this mission field. They must walk barefooted in this cold land when going about from mission to mission. The Indians are very widely scattered about in forty-four doctrinas. For this great number there are only thirty-five religious. Many times it is necessary for a missionary to walk eight or ten leagues to hear a confession. All of which sufferings are augmented by the fact that the missionaries get very little aid in the form of assistants who might lighten some of their burdens. Some of the priests, being so overburdened with work and seeing so many Indians without hope of converting them, become discouraged and return to Spain."

Those priests who remained, about forty-three in all, kept at the job of conversion, despite the seemingly hopeless odds. The more Indians they brought into the Faith the more time they had to give to ministering to the faithful, and the less time, correspondingly, they had to devote to new conversions. Yet all the while during the 1630's and 1640's, they were being importuned by new tribes and villages which sought their ministrations. Sometimes pagan Indians would come to the doctrina, watch with awe what was going on, and then disappear. After several weeks they would return and say to the missionary, "Father, we have a house for you and a church. Come and instruct us, for the Christians have already told us it is of great importance for us to go and see the *Utinama* [the All-Powerful One] who is in heaven above."

Convert-making was a slow and painstaking process. The records leave no doubt that the natives were not admitted to baptism until they had undergone a long and thorough preparation as *catecúmenos*, or initiates. There was never a note of hurry in this regard, nor was there coercion of any kind. Even after baptism, the convert, now called a *cristiano*, had to convince the missionary that he understood the basic theology behind Penance and the Eucharist before he could receive those sacraments. The cristianos were made to understand, furthermore, that they had taken on new obligations of faith and morality which must be rigorously observed, under a day-by-day Christian discipline. The only veneer to be found in this conservative missionary program was the quasi-Spanish culture that sometimes characterized villages where the cristianos were also *muy españolados*—very Hispanisized. There the Indians had Christian names prefixed by *don*, and recited the prayers of Catholic Europe.

Although the number of missions and Indian converts increased with each passing decade, no similar progress marked the material lot of the missionaries and Indians. We learn some of the practical problems of the priests' life in the field during the 1640's from a "memorial" by the Franciscan provincial, Fray Francisco Pérez. Writing at St. Augustine in July, 1648, Father Pérez said that there were then forty-three Franciscans at work in Florida. They lived, he said, among much material poverty and spiritual frustration. Maize, or Indian corn, was the only crop harvested in the entire province, and often the land was too sterile even for maize. The poor soil conditions were largely the result of poor farming, and the missionaries expended a great deal of their time in trying to get the Indians to cultivate the fields properly. Not only had the Indians proved to be discouragingly lazy, but most of them, from poverty, lacked hoes and axes and other basic farming tools. Some of the Indians went about completely naked for lack of clothes.

Commodities that New Spain was charged with sending to Florida each year had not arrived intact for ten years. This assistance, which originated at Mexico City and was called the *situado*, was largely eaten up by the expenses of first procuring it and then shipping it to St. Augustine. In transport it was subject to shipwreck, piracy, and the dishonesty of officials. With the situado arriving in depleted shape or not at all, the Indians were so hard pressed by hunger they often disappeared into the woods to hunt for acorns, palm berries, water grapes, and wild roots in order to keep their bodies and souls together. When this happened, the missionaries would have to follow them into the wilds and minister the sacraments to them under jungle conditions. In his account Father Pérez could only hint at the hardships suffered by these selfless men of God—the constant hunger, the long and exhausting treks overland, the ceaseless torments from mosquitoes, and the risk to life that came from frequent wars between the tribes. It was a truly apostolic life, he wrote, completely devoid of all ambition for human glory.

Adding to the missionaries' ordinary problems, some of the Apalache Indians revolted against Spanish rule in 1647. At issue was the exploitation of the Indians for personal services by a military garrison stationed in the province. Although the missionaries opposed the military in this matter, three of their number were killed in the outbreak. Royal Treasurer Francisco Menéndez Marqués, with a small force, easily quelled the uprising, executed twelve of the rebels, and sentenced twenty-six others to forced labor on the fortifications at St. Augustine. The severity of the sentences was a setback for the Franciscans, who argued, unsuccessfully, that their program in Apalache was seriously compromised as a consequence. It was bad enough to have provoked an uprising, they said, but the punishments meted out only increased the Indians' grievance. The disenchantment of the Indians with the white man's justice continued to grow as civil officials began to inflict new indignities on the natives. In 1648 the Franciscans, taking the Indians' part, protested to King Philip IV that the governor, the royal officials, and the soldiers were exploiting the Indians and their impoverished condition by forcing them to cultivate their private gardens. Even the married men, the friars said, were being taken out of the doctrinas and worked so hard for such long periods that many of them were dying. Some were being kept under conditions of forced labor, away from their wives and children, for as long as a year. As a result of this plea by the priests, a royal order was issued from Spain directing the governor and the officers of the presidio at St. Augustine to give scrupulous obedience to ordinances given earlier on just treatment of the natives. And so the problem was solved, for a time. It would crop up again eight years later.

In 1655 the Franciscans claimed 26,000 Christianized Indians in thirty-eight doctrinas. Seventy friars, the highest number ever, were in the field. The Florida missions were riding the crest of the Golden Age. Then in 1656 Indians in both Timucua and Apalache raised a serious rebellion, and the mission program faltered. Governor Diego de Rebolledo feigned surprise, but the Franciscans had known for some years that a crisis of this kind was coming. When the governor attempted to cast blame for the incident on the friars, arguing that they must have mistreated the Indians, the friars threw the charge back in Rebolledo's face. The sole blame, they said, rested with him: The immediate cause of the uprising, as attested by the Indians themselves, was the governor's program of forced labor, under which Indians had been conscripted to carry corn and other supplies from the interior to the coastal presidio of St. Augustine.

Father Juan Gómez de Engraba, who had been in Florida forty-six years, testified that the Indians were loaded down like mules or horses, and required to walk as much as one hundred leagues under the burden. Many of the Indians suspected that Rebolledo planned to kill them when they reached St. Augustine. They remembered that under Rebolledo's predecessor, Pedro Benedit Horruytiner, of two hundred Indians who walked to St. Augustine, only ten returned to their homes. The rest had died of hunger on the way. Rebolledo dispatched soldiers under Sergeant Major Adrian de Canizares to put down the revolt. This the governor's men did, but with such extreme cruelty that six priests who were in Apalache at the time left the province in disgust, and took ship at the Bay of Apalache for Havana. Tragically, they were all drowned when a violent storm swallowed up their vessel during the crossing.

Although they felt an understandable resentment toward the Spanish civil authorities who had enslaved them, the Indian rebels of 1656 did not carry the same feeling toward their Franciscan Fathers. They realized that these men of God, Spaniards though they were, had pleaded their case to the king and had stood up boldly to the local governor in defense of Indian rights. Relations between the Indians and the priests were even enhanced during this unhappy period by the fact that the Franciscans continued their ministrations, without rebuke to the Indians, and without any care for what the government at St. Augustine might think about their civil obedience. During the height of the hostilities, for example, one of the friars went by night to the mission Santa Elena de Machaba in Timucua, where the rebels were gathered, so that they should not be without the sacraments.

In the end the Franciscan position was vindicated. Governor Rebolledo was formally condemned by the Council of the Indies. Relying on such reports as those of Father Gómez, the Council decided that an example had to be made of Rebolledo before Florida was lost to the Crown and all the good work of Christian conversion brought to naught. In 1657 it was decided to send orders for the immediate arrest of the governor and for his detention in one of the *castillos* of Havana until he could be transported to Spain for trial. Ironically, Rebolledo died before these orders could be carried out.

The Franciscans were now enabled to get on with the work of "reducing" the Indians to Christianity, as they described the process of conversion. One of their first acts after Rebolledo's death was to press for the return of all displaced Indians to their proper homes. Among the displaced were many Indians of the

province of Timucua whose pueblos had been moved by Rebolledo from their original sites to new sites along the principal road
that led from St. Augustine to Apalache. Although the late governor's action had seemed wise in theory, experience showed that
the change of sites had brought more bad results than good. Most
of the transplanted Indians, once taken out of their natural environment, fled into the woods to live with their infidel cousins,
where they might easily die in apostasy. The Franciscans urged
that these Indians be allowed to return to their homes, as subsequently was done.

Relations between the Franciscans and civil authorities continued strained during the next two decades. A particular nettle in
the side of the friars was the military garrison that St. Augustine insisted on stationing in the center of the Apalache mission country.
The soldiers and their arms were there not for any altruistic reasons,
but to guard the fertile Apalache lands that were then being
farmed for corn and developed for cattle raising. The friars argued
that their presence was unnecessary, as there was nothing in Apalache that an enemy might want. Besides, the presence of the military offended the spirit of peace that the friars were trying to in-
culcate in their charges. Finally, and this was their principal objection, the soldiers gave bad example by their disrespectful language
and conduct toward the friars. The soldiers went about saying
that the friars were good for nothing but to say Mass, one Franciscan complained to St. Augustine, "When the Indians see that
the soldiers show no consideration to the friars, they themselves
lose respect for us. The religious then speak to deaf ears when they
talk about sufferings and hard labor; the Indians flee off to the
woods to return to their pagan ways."

In St. Augustine the secular clergy maintained their pastoral
influence over the capital, and by mid-century showed appreciable
progress in their organization of the town's Catholic life. In 1646
there were three priests in the town, a pastor, assistant pastor, and
a chaplain to the three hundred soldiers of the garrison. The regular force of seculars never seems to have gone beyond four, although there is mention of five clerics in the town during 1655.

Before 1666 the duties of sacristan were performed by a soldier; after that date a priest-sacristan was stationed in the principal church. The regulations governing the diocesan clergy in the Indies specified that the secular priests were to be supported by tithes on all produce of the land. However, since there was little in the way of Florida produce, the priests' rations depended largely on annual subventions from Mexico. Their salaries, which ranged from 200 to 283 ducats each, were paid by the Crown from Church tithes collected in Cuba. The same regulations stated that the regulars were not permitted to interfere where seculars were already established—in St. Augustine there seems to have been little, if any, cooperation between the two. The seculars were obliged to teach the Spanish language to the Indians and to give them doctrinal instructions in that language. At a later date, however, jurisdiction over the Indians within St. Augustine passed to the Franciscans. The parish priests had work enough to keep them busy in the presidio: three hundred soldiers with their dependents, a few farmers and tradespeople, the civil list, and resident Indians; the royal hospital of La Soledad, another hospital for the treatment of the poor, confraternities of the Blessed Sacrament and of the Holy Souls, and hermitages of San Patricio (St. Patrick) and Santa Bárbara.

The parish continued to share the dreadful poverty of the town. In 1606 the Bishop of Santiago de Cuba had found a wooden church in fair condition, but so poor it could not boast a single candle; in 1623 the building was described as old and crumbling, and still without adornment; in 1635 and 1645 petitions to Church authorities outside Florida for assistance in repairing the wretched condition of the church went unheeded. In 1668 the church was sacked during a nighttime raid by English pirates under Robert Searles, a sacrilege which caused the pastor, Francisco Sotolongo, to protest to the Crown over what he considered the military incompetence of the governor. The parish was so poverty-stricken by 1673 that during a portion of that year the sacristan-priest complained that Mass could not be celebrated for lack of hosts and wine. The enduring destitution of St. Augustine and Florida was one reason, along with the scant population of the province, why

Florida was never erected to the dignity of a diocese during Spanish times, although the possibility had been raised by the Council of the Indies in 1655, and would be put forward again in the century that followed. In the meantime, St. Augustine and Florida were sorely in need of an episcopal visitation.

On August 14, 1674, the Bishop of Santiago de Cuba, Gabriel Díaz Vara Calderón, wrote to Queen Mariana of Spain to acknowledge two royal cédulas of the previous year. In them Queen Mariana, a member of the House of Austria and a religious person much interested in the spread of Christianity in the New World, had directed Bishop Calderón to make an episcopal visitation of the provinces of Florida. Calderón had held the Cuban see since 1671, and within his jurisdiction was the nearby mainland of La Florida. In the beginning he had attempted to govern the province through the pastor at St. Augustine, Father Sotolongo. This nettled the Franciscans, however, who did not like being subject to a secular priest, and now, after the insistent letters of the queen, there was nothing for it but to go to Florida himself. Calderón told the queen that he would leave for Florida at once to administer Confirmation, correct faults and abuses, investigate the work of Indian conversions, and lend encouragement to efforts of the friars to extend the mission network into the country of Apalachicola, which bordered Apalache to the west. He added that he would take with him "chalices and all the necessary vestments of the Divine Cult."

Bishop Calderón arrived in St. Augustine on August. 23, 1674. The next day he ordained seven young priests, sons of the best families in St. Augustine—the first positively authenticated instance of ordinations to the priesthood to take place within what is now the United States. Shortly afterwards he left on his visitation to the missions. Where he went and what he saw during the next ten months was recorded in a remarkable letter written to Queen Mariana on his return to Cuba in 1675. The letter reported, as Calderón wrote in the opening sentence, "what has been discovered, up to today, concerning the entire district of Florida, both along the seacoast and inland." He went on to give a reasonably accurate description for his day of the entire southeastern United States, including a list of the principal Indian tribes; a brief geographical description of the entire coastline from Charleston around the Florida peninsula to the Apalachicola River; a description of the customs of the Christian Indians; and, most valuable of all, a list of all the missions of Timucua, Apalache, Apalachicola, and Guale, with measurements of the distances that lay between them. The Calderón report is an illuminating picture of the missions and probably the most valuable single document that remains to us from the Golden Age.

The bishop began with a description of St. Augustine, which seemed to him almost uninhabitable, owing to the poverty, hunger, and unhealthy, even hazardous, conditions that prevailed. The parish and its various works were adequately served, and the bishop produced no complaint about them. Then, he wrote, "Going out of the city, at half a league to the north there is a small village of scarcely more than thirty Indian inhabitants, called Nombre de Dios, the mission of which is served from the convent. Following the road from east to west, within an extent of ninety-eight leagues [a league was roughly two and a half miles] there are twenty-four settlements and missions of Christian Indians, eleven belonging to the province of Timucua and thirteen to that of Apalache." The bishop then enumerated the missions situated along the mission trail that began at Nombre de Dios and traversed the peninsula as far as present-day Tallahassee, giving the distances in leagues between them. His is the best list that remains to us, and it enables geographers and archaeologists to determine with reasonable accuracy the general areas in which the Franciscan settlements stood.

Setting out across the interior, Calderón arrrived after traveling ten leagues at the mission and village of San Diego de Salamototo, on the St. Johns River near present-day Tocoi. The bishop noted that the mission was at a spot where the St. Johns was "almost a league and a half in width" and "very turbulent." From that point it was twenty "uninhabited leagues" to the principal mission of Timucua, Santa Fé de Toloca, which stood about eight miles north of the present Gainesville. Nearby was the deserted mission and village of San Francisco de Potano.

Then followed, in order along the trail westward, the missions of Santa Catalina (near the Santa Fe River in Columbia County); Santa Cruz de Ajohica (near the junction of the Santa Fe and Suwannee Rivers); Santa Cruz de Tarihica, two leagues farther along the road; San Juan Guacara (on the Suwannee, near where Luraville now is); San Pedro de Potohiriba (on Sampala Lake in Madison County); Santa Elena de Machaba (near today's Madison); San Mateo (in Madison County); and San Miguel de Asyle (near the Aucilla River in Madison County). The Aucilla River formed the northern boundary of the province of Timucua. Now the bishop crossed into the country of the Apalache.

There he found the missions of San Lorenzo de Hibitachuco, La Concepción de Ayubale, San Francisco de Oconi, San Juan de Aspalaga, and San Joseph de Ocuya (all in Jefferson County); and the following missions in the area that is now Leon County: San Pedro de Patali, San Antonio de Bacuqua, San Damian de Cupahica, "also called Escambi," San Luis de Talimali, "which is the largest of all," La Purificación de Tama, "called Yamases," San Martín de Tomoli, Santa Cruz de Capoli, "called also Chuntafu," and Assumpción del Puerto. Of these Apalache missions, Calderón writes, two, La Purificación and Assumpción, he himself founded as missions, on January 27 and February 2, 1675, respectively, "gathering in Assumpción the three heathen nations, Chines, Pacaras, and Amacanos, who are gradually being instructed and baptized." The bishop's account also reveals that, "In the mission of San Luis, which is the principal one of the province, resides a military officer in a country house defended by pieces of ordnance and a garrison of infantry." (The presence of this garrison in the heart of the missions was resented by the Franciscans, who had often petitioned for its removal. Several times earlier the soldiers had been withdrawn, only to be sent back again each time.)

Going still farther to the west, Calderón entered the province of Apalachicola, where he dedicated a church in an Indian village renamed La Encarnación a la Santa Cruz de Sábacola, "wherein have gathered the great *cacique* of that province, with his vassals from Sábacola el Grande which I have converted to our holy Faith. . . ." To the north two missions, San Nicolás and San

Carlos, were inhabited by Indians of the Chacatos nation, "which fourteen years ago requested baptism and did not have their desire fulfilled until June 21 of last year, 1674." After mentioning some of the other great tribes who lived beyond the reach of the missions, Calderón then listed the Franciscan undertakings in Guale, north of St. Augustine.

In that province, the better part of which lay along the eastern shore of present-day Georgia, the bishop found the following missions: La Natividad de Nuestra Señora de Tolomato, two leagues north of St. Augustine; San Juan del Puerto (on Fort George Island at the mouth of the St. Johns River); Santa María (on Amelia Island); San Felipe (on Cumberland Island); Santa Buenaventura de Guadalquini (on Jekyll Island); Santo Domingo de Asahó (on St. Simon Island); San José de Zapala (on Sapelo Island); and Santa Catalina (on St. Catherines Island). "All are settlements of Christian [Indians]," the bishop wrote, "and in the last named Your Majesty has an officer with a good garrison of infantry." He noted that twenty-four leagues to the north of Santa Catalina was Port St. George (Charleston, South Carolina), "now an English settlement."

In the great hinterland that lay between Port St. George and the Spanish mission centers in Apalache, Calderón heard, "there dwells, in encampments, without fixed dwellings, the numerous nation of the Chichimecos, heathen, so savage and cruel that their only concern is to assault villages, Christian and heathen, taking lives and sparing neither sex, age, nor state of life, roasting and eating the victims." Whether this actually was the accustomed behavior of the tribes in the interior, such at least was the opinion held of them by the Indians along the coast. As for the Florida peninsula south of St. Augustine, Calderón noted that there were as yet no missions at all among the tribes of the Calusa nation.

Next to his enumeration of the Spanish mission sites, the most interesting feature of Calderón's report was his description of the Christian Indians themselves: "In the four provinces of Guale, Timucua, Apalache, and Apalachocoli [sic] there are 13,152 Christian Indians to whom I administered the holy sacrament of Confirmation. They are fleshy, and rarely is there a small one, but

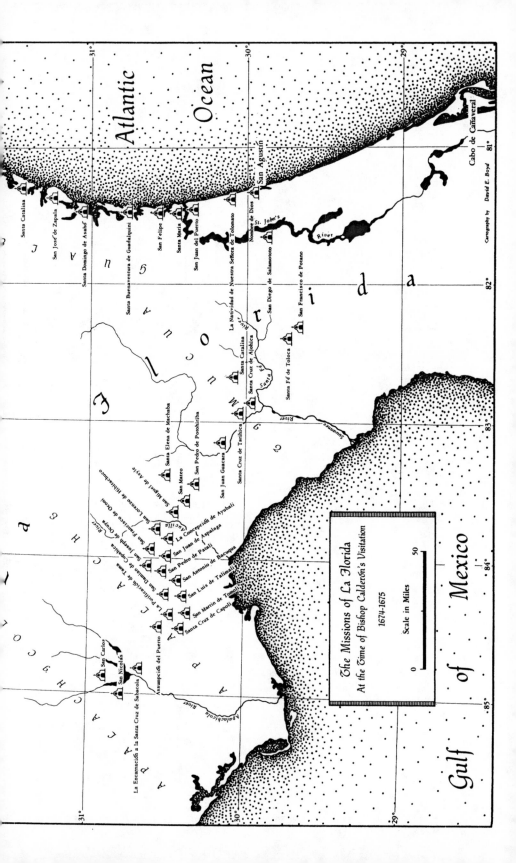

The Missions of La Florida
At the Time of Bishop Calderón's Visitation

1674-1675

Scale in Miles

0   50

Cartography by   David E. Boyd

Atlantic

Ocean

Gulf   of   Mexico

Cabo de Cañaveral

San Agustín

Nombre de Dios
La Natividad de Nuestra Señora de Tolomato
San Juan del Puerto
Santa María
San Felipe
Santa Buenaventura de Guadalquini
Santa Domingo de Asaho
San José de Zapala
Santa Catalina

St. John's
River

San Diego de Salamototo
San Francisco de Potano
Santa Catalina de Ajohica
Santa Fé de Toloca
Santa Cruz de Tarihica
Santa Cruz de Ajohica
Santa Fé River
Suwannee River

Santa Elena de Machaba
San Pedro de Potohiriba
San Mateo
San Juan Guacara
San Miguel de Asyle
San Lorenzo de Hibiniachuco
Arcilla
La Concepción de Ayubali
San Francisco de Oconi
San Juan de Aspalaga
San Joseph de Ocuya
San Pedro de Patali
San Damian de Cupahica
La Purificación de Tama
San Antonio de Bacuqua
San Luis de Talimali
San Martin de Tomoli
Santa Cruz de Capoli

Apalache

Assumpción del Puerto
La Encarnación a la Santa Cruz de Sabacola
San Carlos
San Nicolás

Apalachicola River
Chattahoochee River

ARTE
Y pronunciacion en
LENGVA TIMVQVANA, Y
Caſtellana.
¶ COMPVESTO Y DE NVE.
uo ſacado à luz, por el Padre Fray Franciſco
Pareja, Diffinidor, y Padre perpetuo de la Pro
uincia de Santa Elena de la Florida, Religioſo
de la Orden de nueſtro Seraphico Padre S.
Franciſco : y natural de la Villa de Au-
ñon, del Arçobiſpado de Toledo.

Impreſſo Con licencia en Mexico.
En la Emprenta de Ioan Ruyz. Año 1614

COURTESY SMITHSONIAN INSTITUTION

*Title page of dictionary in the Indian lan-
guage of Timucua, written by Franciscan
Father Francisco Pareja in 1614.*

(Above) *First page of letter written in
1675 to Queen Mariana of Spain by
Gabriel Díaz Vara Calderón, Bishop of
Santiago de Cuba, describing the city of
St. Augustine, headquarters of the mis-
sion chains.*

(Right) *Artist's reconstruction of wattle
and daub technique used in the Spanish
missions. Upright poles have horizontal
wattles lashed in place, with the frame-
work covered with clay (daub).*

(from *Here They Once Stood*, University of
Florida Press)

they are weak and phlegmatic as regards work, though clever and quick to learn any art they see done, and great carpenters as is evidenced in the construction of their wooden churches which are large and painstakingly wrought." The Indians' weapons were the bow and arrow and the hatchet called macâna. The men went half-naked, with the skin of some animal worn from the waist down; sometimes they wore a coat of serge without a lining, or a blanket. Most of the women wore "a sort of tunic" made from *guano*, the so-called Spanish moss. "Four thousand and eighty-one women," Calderón wrote, "whom I found in the villages naked from the waist up and from the knees down, I caused to be clothed in this moss like the others."

The ordinary diet of the Indians consisted of "corn with ashes" —lye hominy—pumpkins, beans, and such game and fish as they could catch. The usual beverage was water, and they never touched wine or rum. "Their greatest luxury is [a drink] called *cazina*, which they make from a reed that grows on the seacoast, which they cook and drink hot. It becomes very bitter and is worse than beer although it does not intoxicate them and is beneficial." The Indians slept on the ground in warm weather. In winter they slept inside their houses on frames of reed bars covered by bearskins. Fires set in the center of the houses made blankets unnecessary. The Indian house was called a *bujio*. "It is a hut made in round form, of straw, without a window and with a door a yard high and half a yard wide. On one side is a granary supported by twelve beams, which they call a *garita*, where they store the wheat, corn and other things they harvest." In the center of each village was a great bujio, or council house, constructed of wood and covered with straw. It was round and had a "very large" opening at the top. Most council houses, the bishop reported, could accommodate "from 2,000 to 3,000 persons." The interior sides were furnished with niches, which served as seats for the chiefs and as lodgings for warriors and transients. Dances and festivals were held in them around a fire that blazed in the center, beneath the roof opening, and the missionary priest was always present to prevent indecent conduct.

A fascinating account of the Indians' practice of Christianity closed the bishop's report: "As to their religion, they are not idolators, and they embrace with devotion the mysteries of our holy Faith. They attend Mass with regularity at eleven o'clock on the Holy Days they observe, namely, Sunday, and the feasts of Christmas, the Circumcision, Epiphany, the Purification of Our Lady, and the feast days of Saint Peter, Saint Paul, and All Saints' Day, and before entering the church each one brings to the house of the priest a log of wood as a contribution. They do not talk in the church, and the women are separated from the men, the women on the Epistle side [of the altar], the men on the Gospel side.

"They are very devoted to the Virgin, and on Saturdays they attend [church] when her Mass is sung. On Sundays they attend the Rosary and the *Salve* in the afternoon. They celebrate with rejoicing and devotion the Birth of Our Lord, all attending the midnight Mass with offerings of loaves, eggs, and other food. They subject themselves to extraordinary penances during Holy Week, and during the twenty-four hours of Holy Thursday and Friday . . . they attend standing, praying the rosary in complete silence —twenty-four men, twenty-four women, and twenty-four children—with hourly changes. The children, both male and female, go to church on workdays, [and] to a religious school where they are taught by a teacher whom they call the *Athequi* [interpreter] of the church—[a person] whom the priests have for this service; as they also have someone deputized to report to them on all parishioners who live in evil."

Thus ended the bishop's letter to Queen Mariana. His visitation had lasted ten months. He had inspected every mission in the far-flung province, confirmed 13,152 Spaniards and Indians, corrected abuses and suppressed irregularities, begun or restored six doctrinas, and expended the equivalent of eleven thousand dollars for the amelioration of the living conditions of the Indians. He returned to Cuba in late June, 1675, and died there a year later, some say from the hardships endured on his visitation.

The year 1675 marked the finest hour of the missionary movement in Florida—the highest point, as events would determine, to which the aspirations of the Franciscans led. Greater numbers of missionaries had labored in the missions before that date, but never before had their results been so consoling and impressive. Given the trying circumstances under which they labored, it was an amazing accomplishment. In building the mission network described by Calderón, they had had to win over the friendship and confidence of savage tribes, withstand a sometimes hostile or indifferent civil government, and survive the torments, physical and psychological, that came from living among aborigines in the woods and thickets and maize patches of a primeval land. The rude wattle-and-daub buildings of their mission compounds were a far cry from the baroque monasteries of old Spain. Yet from living stones they had built a story that will linger long after the monasteries may have passed. It is a story that loses none of its luster from the fact that it came to an unbelievably tragic end.

V

Decline and Ruin

1675-1763

ONE YEAR AFTER Bishop Altamirano's episcopal visitation of Florida in 1606, English settlers began a foundation on the James River in Virginia. By the time of the second visitation, Bishop Calderón's in 1674, Englishmen were settled as far south as Charleston. During the last quarter of the seventeenth century, the dimensions of La Florida would contract still farther, and English hegemony over the Atlantic coast would reach as far as the present border between Florida and Georgia. Lands associated for nearly a century and a half with the Spanish missions suddenly found themselves overrun by Indians under the captaincy of English Carolinians. Drawn on by a profitable trade in skins, the English moved out from Charleston into the Yamassee and Creek country of central and western Georgia, where, with their cheaper and more abundant supply of manufactured goods (and firearms, which Spaniards had never provided the Indians), they easily won the trade and friendship of the interior tribes. With the tribes in tow, they then moved east to the coast and south toward the Gulf. Within a few years the Guale country was lost to Spain and all its missions destroyed; the bright prospects that Bishop Calderón had seen for the conversion of the Apalachicola Indians vanished under the persuasion of the Carolina traders; and although it would have seemed incredible in 1675, the prosperous missions of Timucua and Apalache lay in ruins, and awash in the blood of slaughter. What made the tragedy all the worse was that the fervor and disinterestedness of many of the missionaries fell apart before the missions did.

The number of missionaries in Florida increased following Bishop Calderón's visitation: from forty in 1676 to fifty-two in 1680. On the surface everything seemed to be going well. A synod of the Diocese of Santiago de Cuba was held in 1684 that served to strengthen discipline among both Spanish and Indian Christians. A special section was devoted to Florida, which ended with an admonition to the missionaries to "watch with all attention and vigilance for the relief and good treatment of the Indians," and "not to consent that any person, ecclesiastical or lay, should maltreat them in word or deed. . . ." One of the strictures written into the section on Florida declared that, "The Indians shall not play ball"—a regulation that would be curious to us today did it not refer to a "game" that was more mayhem than sport. In response to a formal challenge issued by one village to another, forty or fifty Indians on a side would wrestle over a deerskin ball with the aim of kicking it into the hollowed top of a goal post. Whichever side performed this feat eleven times won the match. The scrimmaging was so rough, as one of the missionaries described the affair, that "when the pile is broken up four or five are stretched lifeless, others have their eyes gouged out, and many arms and legs and ribs are broken. Buckets of water are poured on the survivors, while substitutes replace the disabled, and the game starts all over in the hot sun; and so it goes on till sunset." It is little wonder that the Church banned the game of "ball."

In 1679 the pastor at St. Augustine, Sebastian Pérez de la Cerda, informed the governor that he and a group of secular priests stationed in Cuba desired to go as missionaries to the Calusa Indians who inhabited the lower Gulf side of the Florida peninsula. (The year before, a Franciscan mission to the Calusa country had come to a speedy and comical conclusion. The friars entered one of the villages at night in solemn procession, hoping, no doubt, to conquer "Jericho" with one elegant display. But the Indians fled into the woods, terrified. When the friars repeated the performance the next evening, the Indians came at them with their hatchets. The noisy visitors were stripped of their brown robes, but they got out with their lives.) A royal cédula for the secular mission was issued in October, 1680. It directed the governor of Cuba to appropriate three hundred gold ducats for each priest's transportation expenses. The first secular in Cuba to offer himself for the work was Doctor Don Juan de Cisneros, senior canon of the Cathedral Church of Santiago de Cuba, a man of letters and of high virtuous repute. Seven other seculars stepped forward to join him. The necessary funds, however, were not forthcoming as ordered, and the project languished. It was revived in 1687, but there is no record that any seculars came to the Calusas as a result.

In 1688 Florida was visited by a young secular, Father Juan Ferro Machado, emissary of the Bishop of Cuba. Machado's visit proved a great success, especially in correcting some abuses that had crept into Florida's ecclesiastical life. He seems not to have gotten along very well with the Franciscans, however, who disputed his right to inspect them, and one of their number, Fray Francisco Ayeta, wrote a polemic charging that Florida was not even a part of the Cuban diocese. For his part, Machado criticized the friars for not having unified all the Indian tribes under one language, as had been done in Peru—despite the fact that conditions in Florida and Peru were not at all comparable. Finally, Machado recommended that Florida be erected into a separate diocese. The proposal for a separate diocese had been made before, by two of Florida's governors, Rebolledo in 1655 and Juan Marqués Cabrera in 1683. Only two of the twenty-three bishops of Cuba since the foundation of St. Augustine had visited the peninsula, pleading the great distance or the danger from pirates (which was very real). The feeling in Havana was that Florida ought to be cut off from the cares—and the funds—of Cuba, and be allowed to shift for itself ecclesiastically. It was never to be. But from this date forward the idea became increasingly popular.

In 1693 an expedition led by Don Andrés de Pez landed at Pensacola Bay, site of the ill-fated Tristán de Luna colony of 1559-1561. With Pez was Father Carlos de Sigüenza y Góngora, a well-known professor of mathematics in the University of Mexico. The priest chanted the *Te Deum* and then surveyed the shore for a suitable site for a settlement. When he was satisfied that he had chosen a good location, the Spaniards marched to it in procession, chanting the Litany of Loretto. A cross was set up, and Father Sigüenza offered Mass. It was St. Mark's Day, April 25. Thus began again the story of Pensacola, although a permanent settlement was not established until five years later. As the second large Spanish settlement in Florida, it would one day rival St. Augustine as headquarters of the province. As early, in fact, as 1693, before a single building had been built, Andrés de Pez was proposing that St. Augustine be partly abandoned in favor of the new site, a proposal that was hotly contested by the Franciscans. We know that there were two Augustinian Fathers and several Franciscans in Pensacola when a French expedition visited the site in 1699. But a search by one historian through Spanish documents relating to Pensacola's early history failed to turn up any evidence of missionary activity among the Indians during these first years.

The frequency of English incursions into Guale country increased during the 1670's and reached the northernmost mission stations by 1680. In that year a band of Creek Indians allied with the English struck the mission station of Santiago de Ocone on Jekyll Island. A few of the Christian Indians were killed, but the remainder, under a Spanish lieutenant, successfully withstood the attack. Shortly afterwards, an attacking force of three hundred Indians under English leadership laid siege to the doctrina of Santa Catalina on St. Catherines Island. Although heavily outnumbered, Captain Francisco Fuentes with five Spanish and sixteen Indian musketeers managed to drive off the attackers.

Governor Cabrera now ordered a general retreat from the exposed missions of northern Guale, and endeavored to persuade the converted Indians of those parts to relocate on the islands of Santa María, San Juan, and Santa Cruz farther south. The Indians, how-

71

ever, refused to go. Many revolted and fled into the woods, or, responding to blandishments of the English, joined the warring tribes of the interior. The friars heaped kindnesses on the caciques who remained, in an effort to counteract the influence of the Carolinians. But it was in vain. The populations of the northernmost islands, aroused to action by the cacique of the Yamassees, revolted and passed over to the English in a wholesale exodus during 1684.

Armed by their new friends, these same Indians unexpectedly crossed into the Spanish territory of Timucua the next year and laid waste the mission of Santa Catalina near the Santa Fe River. They burned the pueblo and murdered many of its Christain inhabitants, captured others to sell as slaves, and carried off the vestments and sacred vessels. About this same time a series of pirate raids on the missions south of Zapala, on Zapala itself, and on the station on Jekyll Island added to the debacle. The Spaniards might have held out against one enemy alone; but the combination of heathen and apostate Indians, aggrandizing Carolinians, and covetous buccaneers was more than their 290 Spanish soldiers could handle. The defense perimeter began to shrink, and with it, the dimensions of La Florida.

In 1686 the few remaining Guale mission Indians who had not gone over to the English were removed to Santa María, San Juan, and Santa Cruz (apparently a newly established mission). The Zapala garrison retreated southward with the frontier to Santa María. The northern missions were now completely abandoned, and the Spanish-English border stood at the St. Marys River. When the English Quaker Jonathan Dickinson was shipwrecked below St. Augustine in 1697, he recorded that the missions among the Timucuans at this date were still active. At Santa Cruz, three leagues north of St. Augustine, Dickinson and his companions found that the Christian Indians were a civilized and industrious group who were well-schooled, modest, reverent, and as diligent in their devotions as were any of the Spaniards. Above Santa María on Amelia Island, however, he reported that no missions any longer remained. What the English destroyed they did not replace.

Why had the Indians so quickly repudiated their allegiance to

Spain and to the Church? Surely, the firearms and other inducements with which they were plied by English adventurers formed the major and immediate reason. Yet the English had also been able to play upon certain injustices, real or fancied, that hot debates between the priests and Spanish civil officials had called to their attention. After the attack in 1680 on Santa Catalina in Guale, for example, the defending officer, Captain Fuentes, informed the governor that many of the Indians were repudiating their allegiance to Spain because of maltreatment that they had received in the doctrinas. Fuentes reported that, against all existing rules, some of the friars were demanding stipends from the Indians, were forcing them to perform personal and menial services with no recompense, and were exacting heavy penalties for disobedience to their orders. Similar charges against the "arbitrary and overbearing" attitude of the friars occurred periodically in official reports during the next two decades, particularly in the papers of Governor Cabrera, who confessed to being a bigot where Franciscans were concerned. Some of the charges had the ring of exaggeration about them, as though the civil officials were anxious to offer the friars as scapegoats for the loss of Guale, and to screen their own indisputable harshness toward the Indian during these years. One such report in 1691 maintained that "three hundred Indians in the mission of Nuestra Señora de la Candelaria de la Tama had taken refuge in the woods to avoid the whip of Fray Domingo Sanctos." Whatever the truth of charges such as these, and Governor Cabrera was not disposed to question them, they made their way to Spain in 1697, where the Council of the Indies issued instructions for the friars to treat the natives well in both word and act, and to see that "suavity and sweetness" guided their mutual relations. The episode was an unfortunate one, not only because it contributed to the loss of the Guale missions, but also because it formed the only stain on the otherwise glorious habit of the Florida Franciscans.

Within the Franciscan house itself, a certain amount of apathy could be discerned during these years, as the century drew to a close. There seemed to be something lacking in the Franciscan spirit—something vital that had marked these men before in heroic measure, and now was conspicuously absent. The missions atrophied. For many months certain villages went without Mass. The friars settled down to routine, or else allowed themselves to be worried sick where the English would strike next. Fray Blas Martínez de Robles, with thirty-seven years' service in five missions, lamented that, except for the robes, the Franciscan Order had ceased to exist in Florida. But it had not. Only a few years later, Franciscans would be defending the Faith with their lives.

The terrible climax to this story of decline and ruin began in 1702 with the outbreak of the War of Spanish Succession (Queen Anne's War in America), in which Spain was allied with France against England. Governor James Moore of Carolina seized on the war as an opportunity to attack St. Augustine itself. With a force of one thousand men, half English, half Indian, Moore descended on the city by both land and sea. The marauders forced the missions back from the St. Marys to San Juan, sent the Christian Indians scattering in fright, took three Franciscans captive, and put to the torch three churches and convents on the island of San Marcos. On October 22 the overland and naval forces joined in a futile siege of the Spaniard's new fort at St. Augustine, Castillo de San Marcos, whose broad shellrock battlements had been completed in 1696. The entire population of 1,500 soldiers and civilians spent over fifty days inside the fort while Moore's men, without bombs, could do little more than fume outside. Frustrated, the English raised the siege and prepared to retire to Carolina. Before withdrawing, however, they wreaked vengeance on the old Catholic city, burning down its parish church, the hermitage of Nuestra Señora de la Leche, and the convent and chapel of the Franciscans. The friars' library had already been burned on the first day of invasion. Of that incident a Protestant clergyman of the time said: "To show what friends some of them [Moore's men] are to learning and books, when they were at Saint Augustine, they burned a library of books worth about £600, wherein were a collection of the Greek and Latin Fathers, and the Holy Bible itself did not escape, because it was in Latin." As they retired, the English attacked the mission stations of San José and San Francisco, killed many of the mission Indians, and took five hundred others away as captives. Meanwhile, in the heart of Timucua another English-led raiding party had devastated the church and pueblo of Santa Fé. The land of the missions was dissolving into a land of terror. Apalache would be next.

Discredited by the St. Augustine fiasco, Moore soon resigned as governor of Carolina. In 1703, however, with eyes lusting for the wealth of Apalache, the Carolina assembly commissioned Moore to drive the Spaniards out of that frontier province, and gave him authority to enlist fifty whites and over one thousand Creek Indians. Crossing the Ocmulgee River, Moore's warriors surprised the mission village of La Concepción de Ayubale on the morning of January 25, 1704, and quickly penetrated as far as the council house before the friar, Fray Angel de Miranda, could gather enough Indians with muskets to stay the attack. Father Miranda stationed his men in the church and held out for nine hours. Then, his ammunition exhausted, he was compelled to surrender.

Word of the attack reached the nearby presidio of San Luis Patali, and Captain Alonso Dias Mexía, with thirty Spaniards, two friars, and four hundred Indians, rushed to give assistance. Twice they drove Moore back, but in the evening they, too, ran out of ammunition and had to surrender. Moore was immensely satisfied with himself for having "regained the reputation we seem to have lost." He then proceeded to enhance that reputation. At Ayubale, and the next day at Patali, his men slew the three priests, and committed acts of gratuitous barbarity on the Christian Indians. Fray Juan de Parga Araujo was beheaded, and his body butchered. Fray Manuel de Mendoza's body was later found in a charred state, his hands and a half-melted crucifix sunk into his flesh. Father Miranda's remains were never found. To a Spanish rescue party that reached the two towns several days later, the scene was one of indescribable horror: scalped and mutilated bodies of men, women, and children lay about the ground, or hung from stakes. The few survivors who came out of the blood-bath to tell the tale had consoling stories of heroism. The governor passed them on to the king: "During this cruel and barbarous martyrdom which the poor Apalache Indians experienced, there were some of them who encouraged the others, declaring that through martyrdom they would appear before God; and to the pagans they said, 'Make more fire so that our hearts may be allowed to suffer for our souls. We go to enjoy God as Christians.' "

By the time James Moore withdrew from this second invasion of the peninsula, eight out of the fourteen doctrinas in Apalache had been laid waste. It was a paralyzing blow. Timucua had learned the Englishman's touch in 1702; now it, too, experienced complete disaster, as raiders carried on the killing and wanton destruction during 1706 and 1707. By 1708 the Florida missions were no more. In that year the government at St. Augustine estimated that ten to twelve thousand mission Indians had been carried off to Carolina as slaves. The few remaining Christian Indians in Florida, perhaps three hundred men, women, and children, had removed to St. Augustine where they huddled for safety beneath the cannon of the Castillo. Even there, the governor told the king, "some are carried off and killed each day while on excursions they make to procure wood and palm [hearts] for their subsistence."

For James Moore, who was concerned about "reputation," his acts in Apalache won him a secure place in history. But the advent of the Englishman into Florida never received quite the same publicity as the advent of Menéndez, and for reasons best known to academic historians, no "black legend" ever grew up around him.

St. Augustine was without a parish church for the first time in its history. The crude wooden structure burned by Moore's men was no great artistic or economic loss, but its destruction left the 1,500 Catholics of the city no place in which to worship. Father Martín de Alacano, from the nearby mission of Nombre de Dios, recorded that the English destroyed everything in town "with the exception of the hospital and twenty houses." It was the chapel of this hospital, Nuestra Señora de la Soledad, that the priests took over for daily and Sunday Mass, keeping in use the hospital wards, which remained either in the same building or in an adjacent one. When the Council of the Indies learned that the parish church had been destroyed, it recommended to the king that 20,000 pesos be appropriated to build a new one. Nothing ever came of this proposal, however, and the inadequate facilities at La Soledad had to serve until 1763. Funds actually were sent to rebuild the Franciscan Convent of the Immaculate Conception; but somehow they dissolved as they passed through the hands of civil functionaries. Until 1755 the Franciscans managed in a rude co-quina rock chapel and frail wooden huts for living quarters.

Remains of the destroyed hermitage of Nuestra Señora de la Leche stood at the mission of Nombre de Dios, a "cannon shot from the *castillo*." It was patiently rebuilt from coquina rock, the shell conglomerate that was now being used extensively by the Spanish engineers. The reconstructed chapel ran north and south, 33 by 15 feet, and easily accommodated the estimated forty Christian Indians who could still be found at the pioneer mission. Most of the Indians at Nombre de Dios by the 1720's were Yamassees, Carolina Indians who had once been allies of the English, but now were settled peaceably among the Spaniards. Some of the Yamassees went north on occasion to raid outposts of their former friends. In March of 1728 they were attacked themselves by a combined English-Indian force under Colonel John Palmer, a member of the Commons House of Assembly in South Carolina. Palmer attacked the Yamassees head-on at their strongest point, which was Nombre de Dios. He killed thirty, wounded and captured many more. When the survivors retired to the Castillo, Palmer burned the her-mitage chapel on March 20 and carried off the few statues and al-tar furnishings that adorned the little building. Among the statues was a figure of the Blessed Virgin nursing the infant Jesus, Nuestra Señora de la Leche y buen parto—Our Nursing Mother of Happy Delivery—under which title the Spaniards of Florida had venerated Mary since early in the seventeenth century. The special devo-tion had originated in Madrid in 1598, when a reported miracle persuaded King Philip III to erect a shrine under that title in the Church of San Luis in Madrid. (The original statue and shrine were destroyed by Communist elements of the Loyalist army on May 13, 1937, during the Spanish Civil War.) In the mop-up after this latest English raid, Florida Governor Antonio de Benavides decided to break up the remaining stones of the mission, lest they be used in the future as shelter for an attacking enemy. A new chapel and hermitage were therefore built inside the outer defense line, or hornwork, that crossed the south line of the original mission property. And a new image of the Mother and Child was ordered from Spain.

Violence also erupted around the infant church at Pensacola. In May, 1719, the Spanish fort and settlement were invested by French warships, and being too weak to withstand a siege, had to surrender. The two priests of the settlement, both Franciscans, were given safe escort to Havana. Spanish arms later recovered the fort, only to lose it a second time to Frenchmen under the Count de Champmeslin. When the French decided that they could not hold the site, they destroyed the fort and the town by fire. The church went up in flames with the rest. When in 1720 the site was restored to Spain by treaty, a new fort and church were built on the western extremity of Santa Rosa Island. Some years later the settlement was moved to its permanent location where a third church was erected.

The most significant religious event to occur in Florida during these years after the destruction of the mission chain was the arrival in 1709 of Florida's first resident bishop. Although the bishops of Cuba had pressed since 1690 for the erection of an independent bishopric in Florida, the Council of the Indies determined that the peninsula could best be governed ecclesiastically by an auxiliary bishop of Cuba who should have permanent residence in St. Augustine. Under this arrangement Florida would not itself be a diocese, and the auxiliary bishop would not exercise ordinary jurisdiction over the province; both province and bishop would remain directly subordinate to the See of Santiago de Cuba. King Philip V acted favorably on this arrangement and proposed it to Pope Clement XI who gave approval in May of 1703. Named to the new post was Dionisio Resino, the oldest priest in Cuba.

Several years' delay ensued before the new bishop could be consecrated, as the bishop of Cuba, the governor of Florida, and the king argued the question who should support the auxiliary bishopric financially. An equitable solution was reached, finally, in 1708, and Resino was consecrated early the next year in Yucatán. He arrived to a warm welcome at St. Augustine on June 23, 1709, after a narrow escape from eleven English warships. Unfortunately, all the buildings of the parish were in ashes, except for the chapel of La Soledad; no episcopal residence could be provided; and, with the loss of the missions, the Franciscans had almost no Indians to present for confirmation. Disheartened, Resino sailed back to Cuba only three weeks after his arrival. Two years later he died.

The question whether Florida should be raised to an independent diocese was debated again in Cuba and Spain. The arguments continued until 1723, when the see in Cuba finally agreed to underwrite another auxiliary bishopric. Nothing was done about it, however, until 1731 when Francisco de San Buenaventura y Tejada, professor of theology and guardian of a Franciscan convent in Seville, was appointed to the post. Buenaventura sailed from Spain the next year, was consecrated at Vera Cruz, and arrived at St. Augustine in July, 1735. He was shocked to find the capital in a state of spiritual decadence: families were racked by scandals, drunken Indians roamed the streets, English traders preached heretical doctrines on street corners, and the parochial church at La Soledad was an unkempt disgrace—"when it rains it is the same as being outside."

The bishop put a new roof on the church, reinforced the planking it had for walls, and built a stone sacristy alongside. He gave new encouragement to the pastor and three assistants of the parish; gathered the children of the town in the church three days a week to teach them their catechism; struck out at immoral behavior, private and public, and prohibited gambling in the local taverns; opened a classical school for young boys—the only school in Florida since the English invasion; promoted religious processions through the streets of the town; and, by April, 1736, conferred the sacrament of Confirmation on 630 Spaniards and 143 slave and free Negroes. In 1740, when St. Augustine was invested for thirty-seven days by a powerful English land and sea force under General James Oglethorpe, the bishop roused the zeal of the population with pious exhortations, and with each round of the English cannonading led the people in choruses of *Ave Maria!* (Under this title he composed a description of the siege, which was printed at Seville in 1740.)

Buenaventura was presented for the See of Yucatán in 1745 and left St. Augustine the same year. By the date of his departure he had sparked a moral regeneration in the rude frontier town, which now was once again remarked for its stable moral life and its civilized amenities. Unfortunately his successor was not equal to the same task. Father Pedro Ponce y Carrasco, of Cuba, was named auxiliary in 1745 but did not arrive in Florida until nine years later. Although a man of high intellectual and moral repute, the new prelate lacked the vitality required for the Florida post, and he sailed home to Cuba only ten months after his arrival.

The last bishop to rule in Florida before 1763 was the Bishop of Santiago de Cuba himself, Pedro Agustín Morell, a native of Vera Cruz. He came to St. Augustine not by design but by an accident of war. In 1762 Havana was seized by British forces under the Earl of Albemarle. Bishop Morell was forcibly ejected from his cathedral—carried out in his episcopal chair—and placed on a British man-of-war which took him as a prisoner to the English settlement at Charleston, South Carolina. Morell thus became the first bishop to enter the limits of the thirteen original English colonies. After two weeks of detention, he was allowed to go to St. Augustine, which he reached in early December, 1762. He took the opportunity of his involuntary presence in Florida to make an official visitation. Between December 29 and April 11 of the following year the bishop inspected the parish of St. Augustine and the few remaining towns of Christian Indians in the province, confirming altogether 639 persons. In the spring the clergy of Cuba were able to send a ship to convey their bishop back home.

What of the Franciscans during these years? Their headquarters convent in St. Augustine had been burned in 1702 and their chain of missions had been wiped out during the years from 1702 to 1708. Except for the few remaining Christian Indians around St. Augustine, there had been almost complete loss through enslavement or apostasy of the thousands of aborigines that their Order had labored so long to Christianize and civilize. Understandably, Franciscan morale was at a low point. In 1715, however, there came a breakthrough that gave high promise that the friars

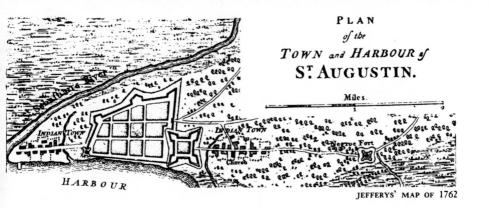

PLAN
of the
TOWN *and* HARBOUR *of*
ST. AUGUSTIN.

Miles.

HARBOUR

JEFFERYS' MAP OF 1762

(Left) *Francisco de San Buenaventura y Tejada, Auxiliary Bishop of Santiago de Cuba, resident in Florida.*

(Lower left) *Luis Ignacio Peñalver y Cárdenas, Bishop of Louisiana and the Floridas.*

(Lower right) *Hat and staff typical of those used by Franciscan missionaries in Florida during the early 18th century. Hook at end of staff was used for carrying bundles.*

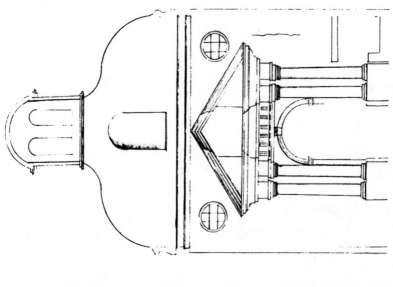

Relics from the Spanish missions of Florida. (1) Sherds of a Spanish olive jar, incised with letters believed to be the name of Father Domingo Criado, San Francisco de Ocomi. (2) Fragmentary rosary found in Apalachee. (3) Corpus from crucifix, somewhat misshapen by fire, San Francisco de Ocomi.

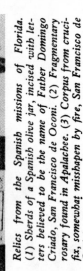

First plan of the façade for the parish church of St. Augustine, drawn by Spanish Royal Engineer Mariano de la Rocque. When completed in 1797, however, the actual façade was somewhat different, particularly in the belfry.

might get their circle of missions under way again: in that year caciques representing perhaps 50,000 Indians from 161 villages—Yamassees, Lower Creeks, Apalaches—came to St. Augustine to ask friendship and protection. Their alliance with England had collapsed. The Franciscans sent an urgent request to Spain for more hands to help reap this sudden and unexpected harvest. Unfortunately the Crown was three years late in acting on the request, and by the end of 1719 only nine new friars had arrived in the province. Ten more came in 1722, but the number was still grossly insufficient. And of these nineteen recruits, all but two became discouraged by the hardships of Florida mission life, and left for Cuba. By 1724 there was a Franciscan in only 11 of the 161 receptive Indian villages. Financial support also failed to materialize, and the new missions foundered.

The most serious reason behind the failure of the mission revival was a bitter struggle for control of the Order that broke out in the 1720's between the Creoles, colonial-born, colonial-trained Franciscans, and the newly arrived recruits, or peninsulars, from Spain. The Creoles had been left in control of the Order in Florida after the disasters of 1702-1704, and when all but two of the new arrivals from Spain retired to Cuba during the 1720's, the Creoles remained even more firmly entrenched by default. Then in 1732 nine new friars arrived from Spain and the factional dispute broke out anew. The Creoles treated the peninsulars in a fashion that can only be called cavalier: they gave them no briefing or training; assigned them to hostile villages; shifted them about at frequent intervals, with the result that they had no chance to learn the individual languages; and restricted their participation in chapter and conventual administration. Not inaccurately, the peninsulars charged the Creoles with abusing their new-found authority and with acting in a manner that was detrimental to the success of the missions. The climax came in 1735. In that year the peninsulars held their own separate chapter election, and the rift became definite and open. For several years the unsavory and acrimonious division continued. Newly arrived Florida Governor Manuel de Montiano described the condition of the Order in 1738 as a "deep abyss of enmity and disunion." In seeking a solution to the im-

passe, the Bishop of Santiago de Cuba and the Franciscan commissary-general of New Spain sided with the Creoles. King Philip V,
however, took the part of the peninsulars, and forcefully declared
in their favor in 1737 and again in 1739.

That settled the factional struggle, but nothing seemed to help
the missions themselves, which continued to decline in numbers and
influence. With no military protection and no supporting funds,
with no means of protecting their Indian charges against the inducements of English traders, with little or no assistance from civil officials at St. Augustine, it is no wonder that the missionaries had to
abandon one after another their mission villages. In 1738 twenty-
five priests were serving in Florida; by 1759 only ten remained.
During these years the Franciscans also lost their jurisdiction over
the Indians of St. Augustine. In 1746 the Crown awarded ecclesiastical jurisdiction over *all* Christians residing in St. Augustine—
Spaniards, Creoles, Indians, *mestizos* (persons of mixed Indian and
Spanish blood), mulattoes, and Negroes—to the pastor and assistant
pastors of the parish church. The prestige of the seculars went
up, and that of the Franciscans correspondingly went down. The
only substantial accomplishment of the friars during these waning
years of the first Spanish period in Florida was the construction,
finally, of a new monastery. Begun in 1724, and occupied by the
friars for the first time in 1737, it was a handsome coquina rock
structure, 168 feet long, 18 feet wide, and 18 feet high, that stood
at the south end of the town overlooking the Matanzas River.
Twenty-five cells were provided, more than enough for the number of friars who remained in the city.

By mid-century it was obvious that the Church's effort to re-
cover its fortunes after the devastating raids of 1702-1704 had
failed. Although enough recovery had been made to assure the
continued routine presence of Catholicity in Florida, there was
nothing during these years to resemble the missionary expansion of
the previous century. Catholic life in the province was, at best,
static. Only two parishes and a handful of missions could be shown
as the result of two centuries of Spanish labors. Economically the
province had not fared much better, and in 1763 the Spanish
Crown decided finally to rid itself of the destitute colony. The

occasion was the conclusion of the Seven Years', or in America the French and Indian, War, during which English forces captured the prize port of Havana. England agreed to return Havana on the condition that Spain cede to her either Puerto Rico or Florida. In the First Treaty of Paris signed in 1763, Florida was chosen by King Charles III to be the more easily expendable property, and in the spring of that year the transfer of sovereignty was formally made. On July 20 a regiment of redcoats paraded through the plaza of St. Augustine under the shocked gaze of 3,096 Spanish soldiers and civilians. The ancient presidio surrendered on paper what she had never yielded on the field. The first Spanish period of Florida came to an end. And one year later no more than eight Catholics, all laymen, could be found anywhere on the peninsula.

VI

Second Spring

1768-1790

I N THE TERMS OF HER OCCUPATION of Florida, England pledged
generous religious guarantees to the Catholic Spaniards who remained: "His Britannic Majesty agrees on his part to allow the
inhabitants of the country above ceded, the liberty of the
Catholic religion and that in consequence his Britannic Majesty will
give the most exact and effectual orders that his new Roman Catholic subjects may profess the worship of their religion according to
the rites of the Roman Church, so far as the laws of Great Britain
permit." However consoling this pledge may have been, it was not
enough to persuade the disheartened Spanish population to remain
after word was received that Charles III was offering new homes in
Cuba and Mexico to all his former subjects in St. Augustine and
Pensacola who wished to leave. A wholesale exodus from both
towns followed.

So many Catholic families sold their holdings (often at great
sacrifice) and took ship for Cuba, it became clear to the priests at
St. Augustine that the parish there would soon have to follow the
parishioners. The Franciscan friars, too, made ready to leave. To

guard against seizure of the Church properties by the British government, the pastor and the Franciscan superior arranged for Juan Joseph Elixio de la Puente, royal auditor of the colony, to sell the properties at nominal sums to John Gordon, a wealthy English Catholic from Carolina. The episcopal residence (southeast corner of King and St. George Streets) was sold for $1,000.00, the Franciscan Convent of the Immaculate Conception for $1,500.00, and the hermitage of Nuestra Señora de la Leche for $300.00. To Jesse Fish, an agent of Gordon, the pastor conveyed the property and unfinished walls of a new parish church. Unfortunately, the device failed of its purpose. British authorities refused to recognize the transactions. Taking a strict interpretation of the patronato real, England decided that the properties in question were originally owned, not by the Church, but by the Spanish Crown, and hence had already been conveyed to British ownership by treaty.

The new occupiers of St. Augustine therefore disposed of the Church properties as they saw fit: the episcopal residence was given to the Church of England for the use of Reverend John Forbes, M.A., the Anglican rector, and later, in 1772-75, it was reconstructed as a state house; the Franciscan monastery was made over into a barracks for the troops; the hermitage of La Leche was converted into a hospital; and the site of the parish church was taken over as an extension of the parade ground. The British also requisitioned the hospital-parish church of La Soledad, which they renamed St. Peter's and used for an Anglican church; in 1773 they added a wooden spire, clock, and bells to the old building. Thus, the system of royal patronage and the fact that no Catholic priests had come with the English to assume control over the ecclesiastical properties resulted in their complete loss to the Church.

The interior furnishings of the Church buildings, meanwhile, had been successfully removed. A schooner, *Nuestra Señora de la Luz*, arrived at Havana in February, 1764, bearing all the altars, images, vestments, canopies, candlesticks, bells, and other objects that had decorated the parochial buildings and the Franciscan convent. Also on board were fifteen folio volumes of parish registers (notations of baptisms, marriages, funerals, etc.) that formed a continuous record of the pioneer Catholic community from 1594

85

to the day of embarkation. The registers were placed in the archives of the Bishop of Santiago de Cuba, where they would remain for the next 143 years. By March 14 of the same year the last of the Spaniards themselves arrived in Havana—3,104 people on eight transports. The abandonment of Catholic St. Augustine was complete.

Although the English occupation of Florida was to last for twenty years, Catholicity was reborn in the province only five years after its sudden disappearance. The rebirth was worked by a remarkable priest at the head of an equally remarkable people. The story begins at the port of Mahón on the isle of Minorca, east of Spain in the Mediterranean. There, in the year 1767, a Scottish physician turned colonizer, Andrew Turnbull, began collecting colonists for a projected silk-worm, indigo, and cotton plantation on Florida's east coast. Although Mahón was at first only a collection point for the Greeks and Italians that Turnbull preferred, it eventually became the principal source for his company. By April, 1768, Minorcans formed the overwhelming majority of the 1,403 who had signed on as indentured servants.

Turnbull, whose wife was a Catholic, took care to enlist two priests for the colony. As pastor he was fortunate to secure Father Pedro Camps, a thirty-eight-year-old secular priest of Minorca who held a doctorate in theology from the University of Mallorca, and whose zeal and skill at preaching were widely respected on the island. Father Bartolomé Casanovas, an Augustinian, signed on as assistant pastor. Although neither priest was able to secure permission from his immediate ecclesiastical superior to join the expedition, owing to a rupture in communications, the Holy See at Rome gave its own consent, and directed Father Camps to consult with the bishop who ruled Florida on his arrival in America.

That arrival was never experienced by many in Turnbull's company. Some 148 colonists died on the eighty-day voyage from Gibraltar. One vessel, carrying 500 Negro slaves, was shipwrecked with the loss of all on board. Still, 1,255 men and women did arrive safely at St. Augustine—to that date the largest colony of Europeans to come to Florida at one time. Turnbull led the colonists south to his development site, opposite Mosquito Inlet, which he had named New Smyrna, after Smyrna, the birthplace of his wife. There he put them to work clearing the land under English overseers. At first the colony went well. Then, after a time, it became apparent that the tragedies at sea during the transatlantic crossing were only portents of more evils to come. Food supplies ran low; the colonists lacked clothes; living accommodations were primitive; soon men, women, and children were dying, sometimes as many as 15 in a single day. In August, 1768, 300 of the Italians rioted, and two of the ringleaders were executed in the punishments that followed. Loss of life to disease and malnutrition continued: deaths during the colony's first year amounted to 300 men and women and 150 children. Sickness and death, protests and punishments with but brief periods of relief—this was the story of the colony from its founding to its final collapse in 1777.

Father Camps and his assistant were hard pressed to keep up the Christian courage of their people. Although some 50 Italians, Corsicans, and Greeks attended the rude hut called St. Peter's Church, the great majority of parishioners were Minorcan, perhaps 175 families in all. Father Camps took every occasion to remind them of the strength that they ought to draw from their faith and from fervent reception of the sacraments. He taught the children regularly, promoted religious processions, and preached every Sunday of the year. In 1774 he lost the assistance of Father Casanovas, who was deported to Europe by Dr. Turnbull for alleged insubordination to colony officials. Camps made repeated attempts to communicate with Minorca and Havana to secure another priest for his maltreated people, but English authorities blocked all such appeals. The pastor labored on alone.

Father Camps had been told by the Holy See in 1768 to make contact with the bishop exercising ordinary jurisdiction over Florida. This was the Bishop of Santiago de Cuba, Santiago José Echevarría y Elguezúa. Making contact turned out to be more difficult than anticipated. Finally, in October, 1769, Camps persuaded two visiting Cuban fishermen to carry a message to Bishop Echevarría, in which he asked for Holy Oils and other necessities. Since Echevarría knew of no Catholic colony in Florida, he treated the message with suspicion. Sent off to Spain, the message went the rounds of innumerable councils and agencies and had to go as far as Rome before confirmation of the authenticity of the message could be given to King Charles III, and the Holy Oils dispatched as requested. The process had taken two years. In the meantime, Camps' temporary faculties, or powers of jurisdiction, had expired. Through another party of Cuban fishermen, the priest successfully got another message to Havana, and thence to Rome. In 1773 he learned from Echevarría that Rome had renewed his faculties for another twenty years.

In March, 1777, the Minorcans' cup of sorrow was running over. The ultimate frustration had been to learn that perhaps Turnbull would not grant them land of their own at the expiration of their indentures as had been agreed. Now two different groups of colonists made their way to St. Augustine, where they demanded justice from the English governor. Twelve of the emissaries were asked to state their grievances in writing and under oath. Responding to what he called "the shocking and unjustifiable actions . . . the distress, tyranny, and cruelty," Governor Patrick Tonyn issued orders releasing from their contracts all who had been maltreated and all who had signed when under legal age. The orders meant the virtual dissolution of the unhappy Turnbull experiment. As a consequence, attorneys for the colony released the Minorcans en masse, gave them each four quarts of corn and four days to get out. Under the leadership of the head carpenter, Francisco Pellicer (who had earlier risked death as one of the emissaries to St. Augustine), the half-starved refugees set out on foot for St. Augustine. Women, children, and old people marched in the center of the procession; the men, armed with stakes, took up the flanks. Three days later this half-starved but disciplined band reached St. Augustine and safety. Only six hundred—less than half—of the original group of colonists remained.

Some of the emancipated laborers, too weakened by sickness to travel, had had to remain behind. With them stayed Father Camps. The priest gave what aid he could to the sick, and confessed and anointed the dying. Turnbull's men frustrated Father Camps at every turn, possibly out of pique at the failure of the plantation. They denied him use of the sacred vessels in the church, and later held him a virtual prisoner when the sick colonists were taken to St. Augustine by ship. The date of his eventual release is not known, but he was in St. Augustine by November, when he entered his name in a new parish register: "On the 9th day of November, 1777, the church of San Pedro was translated from the settlement of Mosquito to the city of St. Augustine, with the same colony of Mahonese Minorcans which was established in the said settlement, and the same Parish Priest and Missionary Apostolic, Dr. Dn. Pedro Camps. [Signed] Dr. Pedro Camps, Parish Priest." The shepherd and his wronged flock had found a home.

One year before the flight to St. Augustine, Father Camps had sent a message to Bishop Echevarría via Cuban fishermen to ask to be relieved of his post as pastor of the Minorcans. Broken in health from his arduous service at New Smyrna, he thought that he ought to be replaced by a younger man. A replacement was also needed for Father Casanovas, he reminded the prelate. Camps' letter was forwarded to Spain, but nothing resulted from it until December 16, 1778, when Camps and his parishioners were no longer in New Smyrna. On that date the king commissioned two secular priest-volunteers for service in the English province. Interestingly, they were Irishmen: Fathers Thomas Hassett and Michael O'Reilly, both natives of Longford, Ireland. Hassett was twenty-seven years of age, O'Reilly was twenty-six. The two priests had just completed studies at the Irish College at Salamanca—El Real Colegio de Nobleses Irlandeses—founded in 1593 by Philip II as a place where Irish seminarians could be trained at royal expense for service in Ireland. It occurred now to the Spanish court that English-speaking priests could serve to equal advantage in the Anglicized province of Florida.

By April, 1779, the two Irish priests were in Havana and ready to take ship for St. Augustine. Unfortunately, by this time the English colonies in America were in revolt against their mother country, and Spain had openly sided with the patriots. Florida was blockaded by English men-of-war, and transportation to that colony from a Spanish port was impossible. While Father Camps continued his lonely and dangerous labors at St. Augustine, unaware that help was only a few hundred miles away, the two Irish priests could do nothing but turn their hands to other work. O'Reilly became chaplain to the Spanish troops in Cuba and at New Providence in the Bahamas, a post in which he won high official praise for his zeal and efficiency. Hassett ended up in patriot-held Philadelphia. When the Holy Oil stocks had run low in that city in 1779, the Catholic population appealed to Spain for new supplies. In the correspondence that followed, it was decided by the king that Father Hassett should be sent to Philadelphia to open a school for children. Accordingly, the priest left Cuba for Pennsylvania, arriving in May, 1782. By June of the year following, Hassett could report to Cuba that he had two schools in operation, "among the best on the continent," he averred. Neither O'Reilly nor Hassett was to remain in exile from his original appointment for very long, however. Spanish arms were in process of winning more battles in North America than they had won in several centuries, and within a few months of Hassett's 1783 report, all Florida was once again in Spanish possession. The second Spanish period was about to begin.

When England acquired the Florida peninsula from Spain by treaty in 1763, she also acquired eastern Louisiana from France. English suzerainty extended, therefore, from the peninsula westward in a thin line as far as the Mississippi. By royal proclamation in 1763 this entire territory, henceforth called the Floridas, was divided into two royal colonies: East Florida, which went west as far as the Chattahoochee River, and West Florida, which extended along the Gulf to the Mississippi. The northern frontier for both colonies was set at the thirty-first parallel, although later there were changes in this boundary. St. Augustine was capital of East Florida, and Pensacola, then only a crude camp of huts and military barracks, served as capital for the western colony. During the course of the American Revolution, Spain threw in her lot with the Americans and launched a surprise attack on British West Florida in 1779. The Spanish forces captured Mobile in 1780, and Pensacola a year later. By the end of 1781 they had effective control over the entire province. The remainder of the Floridas fell to Spain by treaty: East Florida was ceded back to the original possessors in the peace treaty of 1783 that concluded the war between England and the nascent United States.

Direct episcopal jurisdiction was first restored in West Florida. Even prior to the capture of Pensacola, Bishop Echevarría, of Santiago de Cuba, appointed a Capuchin priest from Louisiana, Father Cyril de Barcelona, to serve as *vicario*, or vicar forane, over West Florida. After Pensacola fell, Father Cyril sent a resident priest, Father Pedro Vélez, to serve the Spanish garrison at that site. Cyril himself was elevated to the episcopacy soon after. In 1784 he was named auxiliary-bishop of Santiago de Cuba, with jurisdiction over West Florida and Louisiana. In East Florida, meanwhile, Bishop Echevarría decided to establish Father Hassett as pastor of the Minorcan colony to succeed Father Camps, and to appoint a Spanish priest as pastor of the non-Minorcans. Through a mistake in the transmission of these decisions to the new Spanish governor of Florida, Vicente Manuel de Zéspedes y Velasco, Hassett was named pastor of both groups, as well as vicario of East Florida. Father O'Reilly was named assistant pastor, with the right of succession. Another priest, Francisco Traconis, was appointed chaplain of the hospital. When apprised of the mistake made in the documents sent to Zéspedes, Bishop Echevarría attempted to reinstate the plan for separate parishes. Zéspedes would have none of it, however, and insisted that Hassett serve both the Spaniards and the Minorcans as one group.

Hassett himself left Philadelphia by ship on June 10, 1784, unaware of the controversy, which ultimately was settled in Zéspedes' favor. His voyage nearly ended in tragedy. The Spanish frigate *Santa Ana* on which he sailed ran into a violent storm and was shipwrecked on the reef of Aroquito Key. To civil officials in Cuba the priest later wrote: "In this shipwreck your petitioner underwent the greatest sufferings and misfortunes that can be imagined, and in addition, lost everything he possessed, including his books, personal papers, and the king's orders. . . . Thanking God for having saved his life, and climbing up on the reef badly injured, and in the same clothes in which he had been aroused in

91

fright from his bed, he spent a week there in recovering from shock and his wounds before he was able to proceed." Hassett was picked up and taken to Havana. There is no date for his eventual arrival at St. Augustine. However, it was probably not much before October 8, 1784, when the first entry in his name appears in the new parish registers.

Fathers O'Reilly and Traconis had already preceded Hassett to the East Florida capital, arriving on June 26. And prior to that date, on June 12, the Spaniards had taken formal possession of the colony, with salutes of artillery, and Benediction of the Blessed Sacrament given by the ailing Father Camps. By the time Hassett arrived, the old seacoast presidio had taken on much of its original Spanish character again, although there were fewer residents than before, and many of the buildings had been substantially altered along English lines. Father Hassett was shocked at the state of Catholicity in the town. A chapel fitted out by Father Camps on the ground floor of a residence near the city gates had served the Minorcans since 1777, and was still the sole place of Catholic worship at the change of flags. The new pastor thought it "wretched" and "lacking in all things appropriate for the celebration of the divine liturgy."

Although the former hospital-church of La Soledad was still standing, it had been gutted by the departing English, and the royal engineer, Mariano de la Rocque, described it at this time as a "useless pile of masonry." The Franciscan monastery was no longer good for anything but barracks, to which purpose the British had converted it. The old bishop's house, however, had been improved under British rule, and Father Hassett decided to open his parish church in the upper story of that 50-by-90-foot masonry building. He granted that it was not the most suitable place for worship —one had to mount a steep stairway, the quarters were cramped, and raucous laughter came from a nearby guardhouse—but it would have to do until the king appropriated sufficient funds to build a new church. As for altar furnishings, they had all been removed to Cuba in 1764, and "the things found here in the hands of the priest of the Minorcans are so few and in such poor condition that they are practically useless, almost as bad as having nothing. . . ." Hassett's remarks suggest the penury suffered for seven lonely years by Father Camps and his gallant flock.

Only a few of East Florida's former Spanish residents, uprooted in 1763, returned to the colony from Cuba. At the same time over 16,000 British subjects left. In 1787 only 900 white persons and 490 Negro slaves could be counted in the entire province. In West Florida the capital town of Pensacola was left with 265 inhabitants. Minorcans formed the bulk of the civilian population in St. Augustine—perhaps 469 persons, including the few Italians and Greeks who had escaped with them from New Smyrna. Father Hassett was disappointed to find that he was making no headway with the Minorcans, owing to his ignorance of their dialect, a variant of Catalan. The disappointment of Father Camps was even keener, since he had hoped to retire. Now the old priest realized that he had to stay on, rather than leave his people without the services of a priest knowing their native language. Hassett reluctantly agreed to this arrangement, which amounted to the creation of a parish within the parish. Apparently Hassett did not go to the trouble of seeking approval of the arrangement from higher authorities, for trouble it would have been: the slow-moving processes of government, ecclesiastical and lay, that resulted from the application of the patronato real were notorious at this time for holding up plans and projects far past the time of their practical use.

One Hassett-sponsored program for the Minorcans was a conspicuous success, a school opened for their children in September, 1787. It was apparently the first free school in what is now the United States, and its twenty-six rules remained in force for thirty-five years. Father Traconis, in addition to his duties as chaplain, took on the task of instructing the first grades. A layman, José Antonio Iguíñiz, was examined and found qualified to teach the higher grades. Instruction was given in reading, writing, arithmetic, and geography. The rules under which the school was conducted are still striking for their high standards, respect for discipline, and practical good sense. A brief sampling follows:

"No one shall be qualified to teach except upon examination and approval of the ecclesiastical and civil superiors of the province. . . . Throughout the year the schools shall be opened at seven o'clock in the morning and at two in the afternoon. At no time shall the pupils be dismissed in the morning before twelve o'clock, nor in the afternoon in winter before sunset. . . . As each pupil enters school in the morning and in the afternoon, he shall greet with proper courtesy first his teacher and then his fellow pupils. He shall then hang up his hat in the [proper] place and seat himself in all modesty. After blessing himself in the name of the Blessed Trinity, he shall take up the book or paper with which his study is to begin. . . . The teachers shall not permit children in the school with contagious diseases, such as the itch. . . . The schoolrooms shall be swept at least once a week by the pupils themselves. . . . The length of a pupil's absence [from the room] shall be measured by the movement of a pendulum hung from the ceiling of the classroom, which pendulum the pupil himself will put in motion at the time of his going out, the teacher taking note whether the pendulum is still in motion when [the student has] returned. . . .

"The schools shall be divided according to the capacity and advancement of the pupils, by numbers and separate seats into distinct classes, and to the first or most capable of each class shall be given some title, reserving for the first of the highest class the title of Emperor of the whole school, and these titles shall prevail until others more striking can be found. . . . The teacher shall never allow his pupils to pass on to new matter until the old is thoroughly learned. . . . The teachers shall endeavor to obtain the most instructive books to be read by their pupils. They shall not permit any other language than Spanish to be spoken in the school. . . . The pupils shall ask with most profound humility that the blessings of their parents accompany them on their way to and from school, and whenever they meet any of their elders in the street, they should salute them with proper courtesy. . . ."

With the return of Florida to Spain, the Franciscan friars of the province of Santa Elena in Cuba sought royal permission to reoccupy their convent at St. Augustine and to restore their system of Indian missions. Governor Zéspedes argued against their petition, saying that the convent had been completely remodeled to serve as a barracks, and that the situation of the Indians at the moment was too unstable to give any hope that they could be made to settle down in Franciscan doctrinas. Two Franciscans eventually did come to St. Augustine in 1789 when Hassett requested help for Father Camps, whose state of health had become alarming. Neither of the friars knew the Minorcan language, however, and their presence in the town proved to be ineffectual. They were recalled a year later. Missionary thoughts also occupied the minds of the governor and of the secular priests during these years, but not with respect to Indians. Hundreds of Anglo-American frontiersmen lived in the northern reaches of East Florida, and according to all reports they were well disposed toward the Catholic Church. Instead of obliging them to become Catholics, as Spanish law at first required of all English residents, Charles III had ruled that special parishes should be erected for them, and that Irish priests who spoke their language should be sent to them, not to exert undue pressure, but to win them over by gentle preaching.

In 1787 Zéspedes and Father O'Reilly made a lengthy tour of the north country to discover how many Irish priests might be needed for work among the Anglo-Americans in East Florida. Their findings were that three new parishes would be sufficient, one on the North River just above St. Augustine, another on the St. Johns River, and a third on Amelia Island near the Georgia border. Zéspedes reported: "I tested the principles of all the British inhabitants that I met during my journey and found most of them disposed to receive instructions in the Catholic religion, and all of them disposed to let their children be brought up in it." A similar encouraging report was sent to Spain by authorities in West Florida, where three parishes for Anglo-Americans were also proposed. By August, 1787, West Florida's request for priests was answered: four Irish seculars, trained in Spain, arrived at New Orleans ready for work. East Florida's petition somehow got caught in the paper mill of Spanish officialdom, and was not acted on until 1791. By that date the chances for making converts among the border people would not be nearly so good. It was another case of lost opportunity resulting from the complicated machinery of the patronato real.

Heretofore the two colonies of East and West Florida had been included within the jurisdiction of the Bishop of Santiago de Cuba. On September 10, 1787, the Holy See at Rome divided the diocese to form the new diocese of San Cristóbal, with its see at Havana. The mainland provinces of Louisiana and the Floridas were placed under the jurisdiction of San Cristóbal, to which a Cuban priest, José de Trespalacios y Verdeja, was appointed as first bishop. The organization of the Church in the Floridas at this time can be seen more clearly in the accompanying table.

DIOCESE OF SAN CRISTOBAL DE HAVANA
Bishop José de Trespalacios y Verdeja

CUBAN PROVINCES
under Bishop Trespalacios

JOINT PROVINCE OF
LOUISIANA-WEST FLORIDA
Cyril de Barcelona, auxiliary bishop, and vicario of the joint province, resident in New Orleans

PROVINCE OF EAST FLORIDA
Father Thomas Hassett, vicario of the province and pastor of St. Augustine

Although Bishop Cyril was directly responsible for confirmations and other episcopal functions in East Florida, it was not until 1788 that he inspected the peninsular church. He arrived by ship at St. Augustine on July 18 of that year, accompanied by a priest-secretary and two pages, and took up residence in a rented house. The official visitation began on September 14, when the people of the parish were formally assembled and Bishop Cyril read to them the Edicto de Pecados Publicos—the Edict of Public Sins. This document, a part of the rubrics of a visitation, was a solemn appeal to the faithful to inform the bishop of any abuses that had arisen in the district, whether through the fault of the priests or of the parishioners. All delinquencies were to be reported in detail: did the pastor offer Mass regularly and with edification? was he remiss in the administration of the sacraments or in the other duties of his pastorate? was he tardy in opening the church doors, or in ringing the bells that announced services? did he dance or play musical instruments at weddings, or engage in private business enterprises? The parishioners were expected to report to the bishop all cases where couples lived in concubinage or caused homes to be broken, or gave bad example to their children. Doctors were to be accused if they failed to inform their seriously sick patients of the gravity of their condition so that they might receive Extreme Unction.

The searching inquisitiveness of the Edicto, with its temptations for the gossipy, was probably a surprise to the few English-speaking members of the parish. To the Spaniards it was a more familiar experience. Still, if the notarized acts of the visitation are an indication, comparatively few people took this opportunity to divulge the misdemeanors of their neighbors. The reports on Fathers Hassett and O'Reilly were uniformly good, although two of the parishioners, Don Bernardo de Madrid and Miguel Iznardy (interestingly, the captain of the frigate on which Father Hassett had been shipwrecked in 1784), criticized their failure to preach in the Spanish style, and said the people preferred to hear Fathers Camps and Traconis. Father Camps was especially singled out for praise by the people of the parish. Bishop Cyril himself was impressed by the four priests of the town, and by their general administration of the parish. He cautioned Hassett, however, that he would have to show greater care in the keeping of the parish registers. The bishop directed that henceforth all baptismal, confirmation, and other entries in the registers should be written in Spanish instead of Latin, and he left model formulas to be followed for each category of entries. Cyril was also critical of the fact that almost none of the 651 Negro slaves in East Florida had been baptized. He reminded the Fathers that the diocesan statutes required slaveholders to see that their slaves were instructed in Christian doctrine and prepared for baptism within six months after their purchase. Cyril decreed that slaveholders who failed to do so would incur excommunication from the Church. Father Hassett was told to have the church bell rung at a certain time on Sundays to summon the slaves to regular instruction classes.

Bishop Cyril remained at St. Augustine through the winter. His census of the East Florida population shows that there were altogether 1,078 white men, women, and children in the province. Of this number, 296 were former British subjects. By 1789 only 98 of the English residents had been converted to the Catholic religion. Thereafter the conversion rate would be about 20 a year, never as numerous as King Charles III had expected. One reason, Cyril saw, why the English residents did not come over to the traditional faith of the Spaniards was the failure of the Crown to provide priests and supplies for the three Anglo-American parishes that had been projected for the northern districts. The bishop appealed to the king for this assistance, but, again, nothing was done about it.

Cyril left St. Augustine in June, 1789, and two years later, in February, 1791, he began a similar visitation of the parish at Pensacola. There 572 souls could be counted, 292 of them white. Of the Negroes 114 were Catholic, 161 Protestant. The capital of West Florida was still only a small frontier settlement, mostly in ruinous condition, except for a few elegant houses, one tavern, and the store of Panton, Leslie and Company, which was selling, one traveler complained, at 500 per cent profit. The state of religion in the town was apparently no better. French-speaking parishioners had not confessed their sins for as long as five years, since the sole priest in the town, Father Esteban Valorio, did not know the language. The year before Bishop Cyril's arrival, only seven Catholics received Holy Communion during the Easter season, which was one of the grave precepts of the Church. Cyril saw to it personally that 70 more parishioners satisfied this obligation during the period of his visitation. Except for his failure to learn French, Cyril found no cause for criticizing Father Valorio, who seemed to be laboring with commendable zeal in adverse circumstances. Cyril's visitation gave much-needed encouragement to the pastor and his struggling flock. Unhappily for Cyril, he came under criticism himself two years later, and was removed from his post to Spain by order of King Charles IV. There, in a Capuchin monastery, he died in 1809.

Such was the situation of the Church in the territory now

known as the state of Florida as the last decade of the eighteenth century opened. Two parishes were solidly established, at St. Augustine and Pensacola. Catholic life was a predominant feature of the two towns, and as a result of Bishop Cyril's visits, it was more active than it had been at any time since the Spanish restoration. Still, the condition of the Church was overly dependent on factors other than religious zeal, particularly on economic and political influences. As a quasi State body, administered under the terms of the patronato real, the Church felt keenly the ebb and flow of Florida's secular fortunes. When the State was strong, which was rarely, the Church reaped the benefits; when the State was weak, the Church's influence also waned. When, in 1788, government employees at St. Augustine had to go without salaries for six months, the decay in the local economy precipitated a similar decadence in the moral state of the town's population. The Church could have spoken to the situation with a purer and thus more effective voice had it not been identified so closely with the State whose obligations were in arrears. In Pensacola the depressing poverty of the town had been reflected in the poverty of the Church, both materially and spiritually, at the time of Bishop Cyril's visit. Now, as the *fin de siècle* approached, Father Hassett at St. Augustine complained frequently in his correspondence about "this miserable colony" or "this dying colony," in which religion continued to suffer from economic misery, from a political administration that was routine if it was not stagnant, and from the maladjusted conditions of everyday life. Civil officials, for their part, were stating at the same time that the peninsula offered Spain no special advantage in the propagation of religion, and that the Church was being supported purely by subsidy in an area from which, in fact, military prudence suggested withdrawal. As for immigration, there had been no great influx of Americans to give growth in the form of new towns and settlements. And trade was effectively stifled by the monopolistic system of commerce enjoined by the Spanish colonial system. A dearth of money, want of trade, and a lack of inhabitants—the Church lived amidst these debilitating influences as the century neared its close. The Second Spring had been consoling, but it was not promising.

VII

The Spanish Twilight

1790-1821

O N MAY 19, 1790, Father Camps died. Twenty-two years the valiant old shepherd had cared for the spiritual needs of his Minorcan countrymen in the distant land of East Florida. Although for the last eight years he had desired to retire as a canon in the Cathedral of Mallorca, he refused to leave while there was no other priest who spoke the language to replace him. His death was a sad loss to St. Augustine, where not only the Minorcan but the entire Spanish population mourned him. Newly arrived Governor Juan Nepomuceno Quesada now put in a request to Spain for a successor, and in 1792 he arrived—Narciso Font, a Minorcan-speaking Franciscan from Villa de Agramunt. Not the most talented of preachers, Father Font's pulpit defects were sharply noted by his Minorcan charges, who, still grieving their beloved Father Camps, probably would not have been impressed by any successor, however eloquent. Father Font's stay was of short duration, however, for he died on January 13, 1793. Although another request went out for a Minorcan-speaking priest, and some labor was expended on the project in Spain, none ever came, and the Minorcans gradually merged their "parish" with the territorial Parish of St. Augustine.

In 1791 St. Augustine also lost Father Traconis, chaplain at the hospital and *maestro* in the local school, who finally secured what he had long desired, a benefice in his Cuban homeland. Father O'Reilly was pressed into service as teacher. Although O'Reilly spoke four languages and could count other scholarly attainments as well, he found difficulty in adding school work onto his normal parochial schedule, and his health broke down in consequence. In searching for another replacement, Father Hassett devised a compromise whereby the teaching post (which paid very little in salary) was linked with that of apothecary in the royal hospital. Under this arrangement a qualified layman, Rafael Saavedra de Espinosa, was induced to accept the post. The teaching staff was now entirely lay.

Despairing of the early arrival of Irish priests who had been promised by Spain to staff parishes for the Anglo-Americans, Father Hassett decided in 1790 to visit the northern regions of Florida and do what missionary work he could alone. In mid-April he set out in a launch accompanied by four soldiers, and during the next five weeks he traversed the St. Johns, St. Marys, and Nassau Rivers, traveling altogether about 600 miles. In the scattered settlements he found many men and women who had never seen a priest, nor even a Protestant minister, in their entire lives. Mostly newcomers from Georgia and the Carolinas, their state of spiritual abandonment was distressing to the priest, and his pastoral sympathy went out to them. From family to family Hassett trudged, instructing children and adults in the elements of Christian doctrine. To every family he gave catechisms in the English language that had been printed in New York at the Spanish king's expense. The instructions were received so eagerly and rapidly that Hassett was able to baptize 78 children and 51 Negro slaves before his departure.

When he returned to St. Augustine on May 31, Hassett reported the gratifying results to Bishop Trespalacios. This report, plus another to the newly arrived Governor Quesada, finally stung authorities in Spain to act on the long-ignored request for Irish priests. On May 21, 1791, a royal order cleared the way for three Irish clerics to depart as soon as possible, and in December of that year the clerics were aboard ship sailing for St. Augustine. Their names were Michael Crosby, Michael Wallis, and Constantine Mc-Caffrey. Father Crosby was a secular priest, twenty-seven years old, a native of Wexford. He had studied three years of philosophy and two years of theology at the Dominican College of Seville, and although he lacked the final two years of preparation in theology, the Archbishop of Seville consented to his early ordination because of the urgency of Florida's request. Father Wallis was a Dominican, of the Dominican House of St. Paul in Seville. He, too, lacked the final two years of theology, as also did the third priest in the party, Father McCaffrey, a Carmelite, twenty-seven years old, a native of Mullingar, Ireland. The priests arrived at St. Augustine in December, 1791, and pending their assignment to the projected northern parishes, they were stationed at St. Augustine to assist Father Hassett. As events turned out, the three priests never reached their intended assignments.

Father Wallis showed a disturbing emotional instability almost from the start, and he finally suffered a complete mental collapse on October 1, 1794, after which Father Hassett sent him to Havana for treatment. Father McCaffrey developed sickness two years later, and in August, 1796, had to leave for Havana. The lone secular, Father Crosby, stayed on at St. Augustine, although he, too, fell sick with stomach troubles and at one point, in 1812, asked to be relieved. As a consequence the northern parishes never got beyond the planning stage, and, to the great regret of Fathers Hassett and O'Reilly, thousands of English frontiersmen continued to live out their days without baptism and the consolations of religion. Again the cumbersome operation of the patronato real, the sickly conditions at St. Augustine, and the impoverished state of the province as a whole had resulted in lost opportunity, if not tragic omission. The formation of an active English Catholic colony in Florida to rival those in Maryland and New York, which seemed so possible to Father Hassett in 1790, never materialized. And Catholic life in Florida continued to contract around the twin parishes of St. Augustine and Pensacola.

The priests were not the only Irishmen in St. Augustine during these years. The Irish-born Hibernia Regiment had been stationed in the presidio for several years prior to 1788, and the region had become used to such names as Lieutenant Colonel Guillermo O'Kelly, commandant of the garrison, and his adjutant, Captain Eduardo Nugent. Among the civilian population there were a number of persons of Irish descent: Edward Ashton, Groves Doran, George Fleming, John Hudson, and Honoria Clark. Carlos Howard, secretary of the government, was probably Irish. The most celebrated Irishman of the second Spanish period, however, was Lieutenant Juan O'Donovan, who had successfully executed a clandestine marriage with Dominga de Zéspedes, daughter of the first Spanish governor of the second period. One night in the spring of 1785 Father O'Reilly had been summoned to the home of the chief engineer, Mariano de la Rocque, ostensibly on a sick call. When he entered the home, there stood O'Donovan and the governor's daughter, side by side, holding hands. Before the startled priest realized what was going on, the two lovers exchanged marriage vows, thus fulfilling, so they thought, the canonical requirements for a valid marriage—the exchange of vows before a priest and witnesses. The infuriated Zéspedes produced the couple later before Father Hassett, who, as ecclesiastical judge for the province, determined that, since there was some doubt about the union, the marriage should be validated. Following the validation ceremony, O'Donovan was sent a prisoner to Havana for a term lasting until March, 1787, when he returned to St. Augustine to take up residence with his bride for the first time.

If the O'Donovans lived happily ever after, the same cannot be said for Fathers Hassett and O'Reilly, who continued to be bedeviled by matrimonial problems. In Spanish law there was no provision for marriages between non-Catholics, whether before a Protestant minister or a civil official. Yet among the non-Catholic Anglo-Americans residing in Florida there were numerous instances of couples going across the Georgia border to be married by Protestant clergymen. Other couples simply called in the neighbors for witnesses, exchanged vows, and recorded the ceremony in a book. Both procedures violated the letter of Spanish civil and religious law, which recognized only marriages performed before a priest. The matter engaged the attention of Father Hassett because of the possibility that Catholics might attempt marriage under the same circumstances. Hassett was also worried how he should treat Anglo-American couples who desired to become Catholics: need their marriages be validated? Again, Hassett was at a loss to know what he should do when non-Catholics, wishing to marry non-Catholics, came to him for the ceremony—which, after all, was the law.

After a great deal of debate on the problem in Spain, a decision was handed down in November, 1792, by Bishop Agustín Rubín de Cevallos, of Jaen, the competent juridical authority. Bishop Cevallos ruled that Protestant and non-Christian couples could be married by the parish priest, acting solely as the official witness of God and of the State to the expression of conjugal consent, but not within the church building, nor with the use of any sacramental formula, nuptial blessing, or ecclesiastical vestment. Indeed, the bishop went on, all such couples were obligated to be married in this manner; and all previously contracted unions, clandestine or otherwise, were to be rectified in line with the new regulations. This last provision, not surprisingly, turned out to be difficult of execution, and was never rigidly enforced. As late as 1802, when Father O'Reilly cited a non-Catholic couple to appear before his ecclesiastical tribunal on the charge that they had attempted marriage in Georgia before a Protestant minister, the governor, Enrique White, persuaded the priest to drop the matter, on the argument that the decree of 1792 had never been officially promulgated in the northern districts where the couple resided. The more lenient practice of the American church to the north also contributed to the tempering of Spanish zeal on this point: in the United States, the Church readily recognized as valid and binding all marriages between Protestant or non-Christian partners performed before ministers or civil officials, provided the couples were free to marry and there were no other invalidating impediments.

The one truly great accomplishment of the Church during the second Spanish period was the construction, at long last, of a new parish church for St. Augustine. Not since Moore burned the *iglesia mayor* in 1702 had the members of the parish possessed a church to call their own. Even the old parish church of the 1600's was little more than four walls and a roof, and its dilapidated condition had been condemned in both ecclesiastical and civil reports long before Moore got hold of it. Still, it was better than hospital chapels and upper storys of bishops' houses. And it was better than the church building begun sometime before 1737, which never progressed beyond the weathered foundation that still stood in the plaza, across the street from the governor's house. Understandably, ever since the restoration of Spanish rule, St. Augustine's consuming religious desire was to build a new, decent, commodious, and if possible, ornate parish church. Tentative efforts in that direction began in 1784, when Father Hassett wrote to the captain-general of Cuba, Bernardo de Gálvez: "It becomes necessary . . . that Your Honor take steps toward building an appropriate temple at the most fitting location, of the necessary extension, capacity, cleanliness, and proportions, which are completely lacking at present." Governor Zéspedes seconded the recommendation, but two full years elapsed before the community learned that King Charles III had acted on it.

By a royal decree of December 8, 1786, the king ordered a new house of worship to be built, the cost to be defrayed by applying to it the value (3,537 pesos, 1.5 reales) of the plate and vestments removed from St. Augustine to Havana in 1764, plus the rentals of eleven houses in Cuba that were owned by the "Church of Florida" (thanks to a gift from one of St. Augustine's early parish priests). This sum, the Minister of the Indies wrote to Bishop Echevarría of Santiago de Cuba, "his Majesty holds and considers sufficient for a decent and appropriate church for that settlement." Zéspedes agreed that this financial arrangement was adequate, since future rentals of the Cuban properties would swell the building fund. Several months later, however, he was disappointed to learn from Bishop Echevarría that the same royal order authorizing construction of the church also authorized an increase in salary for Fathers Hassett and O'Reilly, the increase to be paid from the future rentals of the Cuban properties! If only that year's rentals

were available to the construction, Zéspedes had to write Echevarría, then a new church was out of the question. The valuation of
the pre-1763 church furnishings was plainly inadequate "to construct from the foundations a parish church with suitable bell
tower, especially in a presidio where the poverty of the parishioners does not permit effective giving of alms for the advancement
of such a holy and indispensable work. . . ." Resignedly, however, Zéspedes commissioned preliminary drawings and used the
limited funds given him to gather materials for building.

During the episcopal visitation of Bishop Cyril de Barcelona in
1788, the preliminary plans were subjected to close criticism, as
bishop, governor, and pastor tried to devise means to reduce the
cost of the building. The first set of plans, drawn up by the royal
engineer, Mariano de la Rocque, were rejected by Cyril as too expensive. Rocque estimated that 11,358 pesos would be needed to
build a church large enough for the five hundred faithful of the
parish. "It should be built," he added, on the supposition that the
city's growth would carry it toward the south, between María
Sánchez Creek and Matanzas Bay, "in the same place that it was
formerly," i.e., on the site of the old hospital-church of La Soledad.
Bishop Cyril thought that the cost could be reduced substantially
by the use of salvaged stone from La Soledad and from the ruins of
the hermitage of Nuestra Señora de la Leche north of the city. He
came up with the figure of 8,400 pesos, 3.25 reales. Zéspedes disagreed with both estimates. He did not think that such a church
as St. Augustine wanted and needed could be built for so little.
And if it turned out that the costs were higher, as he predicted,
he disagreed with Bishop Cyril that the difference could be met
by alms contributed locally: "Informed as I am of the misery of
these inhabitants," he wrote to Bishop Echevarría in Cuba, "I assure your Illustrious Lordship that, good as their intentions may be,
they are, and they will be, helpless as long as His Majesty does not
deign to arrange some class of commerce for the development of
the province. . . ."

The king approved Rocque's basic design in March, 1790, but
Spanish officials continued to debate the cost estimate, with the
result that two years passed before Rocque could proceed to work-

ing drawings and specifications. The engineer-architect made out a list of tools and equipment needed for the work—rollers, picks, shovels, barrows, carts, axes, hammers, and so on. Twenty laborers were employed. A general construction contract was awarded to former frigate captain Miguel Iznardy, and a sub-contract for lumber was given to Tomás Travers Proctor, whose admixture of English blood was obvious in his name. Father Hassett drew up a list of furnishings and ornaments needed for the new church, and submitted it to new Governor Quesada, who ordered the goods from Barcelona, through a merchant in Havana. As the plans took shape, parishioners offered what they could toward the cost of construction: lumber, lime, or free skilled labor; many offered maize or hens (which were appraised by the padres at six reales each).

Early in 1793 the government decided on the site for the new church, the Juana Perpall South Lot 142 in Block 18, which was bounded on the west by St. George Street, south by the plaza, east by the property of one P. Cecifacio, and north by the Treasury. This lot had passed through many hands since it was granted to John Dennett in 1766 by the English government. One of its owners had been the Reverend John Forbes, of the Church of England. On the lot in 1793 stood a two-story coquina house and an orange grove. The Spanish Crown purchased the lot from its owner on April 12, 1793, at a cost of 697 pesos and 6 reales. Later the same year—the exact date is not recorded—the cornerstone of the new church was laid and construction began. It was none too soon for Father Hassett and his parishioners. The bishop's house in which Mass was then being celebrated was in a state of near collapse. In September, 1793, Governor Quesada wrote to the governor of Cuba: "I ordered, in the first part of April this year, the start of construction of the new church, [which is all] the more urgent as the high house which is now serving provisionally as such, is entirely useless, fallen to the ground in various parts, full of posts to support the walls, and the use of certain parts of the building has been stopped in order to prevent, in the event of collapse, the fatal injury of the faithful who may be in it, as has already happened last year."

Before the foundations were laid, officials in Spain came up with several changes in the plan of the church, the most radical being enlargement of the building from 36 x 108 to 41 x 124 feet. In the final plan, Bishop Cyril's suggestion for the use of salvaged stone was followed, although both the quantity and the quality of the stone proved to be disappointing. Into the new building went coquina rock from the ruin of the hermitage of Nuestra Señora de la Leche, and from another unspecified ruin, which could have been either La Soledad or the chapel at the cemetery of Tolomato (which had been pulled apart for firewood during the English occupation). It is possible that the design of the façade of the new church closely resembled the façade of La Leche, and that changes introduced into the original plan were made to take better advantage of the salvaged stone. John Bartram, a traveler from the English colonies, described La Leche as it was in 1765: "Ye indian or milk church half a mile out of town is ye compleates[t] piece of architecter about ye town[.] at ye gable end[,] according to ye spanish tast[,] ye collums is fluted[,] hath ye capital & base & frize near ye derick order to ye square[,] above which is a prodigious sight of carved stone according to thair fancy. . . ." The majority of the coquina rock used in the construction came from the "king's quarry," three and a half miles away on Anastasia Island.

Although Father Hassett had been the first after restoration of Spanish rule to urge construction of the church, and although he was consulted frequently on the rubrical details of the building, the actual construction was not placed at any time under his direction. Here, as in so many other public functions of the Church in East Florida, one finds the ubiquitous hand of the patronato real. The choice of the site, the amount to be spent, the means of financing, the selection of the contractor, the custody of the parishioners' contributions to the building fund—all this came under the direct supervision of Governor Quesada, as agent of the king. While the arrangement was understandable in light of the king's substantial monetary interest in the program, it produced the usual series of long delays and transatlantic debates, with the result that a building which should have taken no more than one year to erect took four. And as erstwhile Governor Zéspedes had predicted, its final cost of 16,000 pesos was considerably above the first estimates. In August, 1797, Enrique White, the third Governor of East Florida to become involved in the building of the church, announced the completion of the work. Father Hassett by this date was far away: in 1795 he had been promoted to the office of vicar general of the newly erected Diocese of Louisiana. On December 8, the Feast of the Immaculate Conception, Father Michael O'Reilly, new pastor, and vicario of East Florida, formally opened the great quadrangular church. The proud parishioners accompanied their pastor in public procession as he carried the Blessed Sacrament from the old bishop's house on one side of the plaza to the new Church of St. Augustine on the other.

The completed edifice gave a beautiful aspect to the center of the ancient city. The walls of the façade (which still stands) swept upward in graceful ogee curves to a belfry surmounted by a cross, a design that was typical of many churches built in the Americas by the Spaniards in the eighteenth century. The façade itself was plain, with a finish of lime stucco. The lines were broken only by simple moldings, recesses, and cornices, and by four small windows placed in pairs to either side of the entrance. In the belfry were four bell niches, one above and three below. The westernmost niche held the oldest bell, on which was engraved: "Sancte Joseph, Ora Pro Nobis, 1682." Behind the belfry was a wooden balcony where the sacristans (or small boys, as usually was the case) rang the bells by pulling ropes attached to the clappers. The entrance area of the façade was neoclassic in design. To either side of the round-arched doorway stood Doric columns supporting an entablature, its frieze simply ornamented by three-channeled triglyphs, alternating with plain metopes. The projecting cornice of the entablature had several bands of molding, as did the pediment above. Above the pediment, breaking the plain expanse of the façade, was a niche in which was placed a statue of the parish patron, St. Augustine of Hippo.

The interior possessed the same simple dignity as the exterior. Small windows were placed sixteen feet above ground in the two-foot-thick walls. At the north end was the sanctuary with a wooden altar and steps ascending on both sides. On the east wall was an altar dedicated to St. Joseph and on the west another altar dedicated to the Blessed Virgin Mary. Above the entrance was a double gallery, an upper gallery for the choir and a lower one for the Negroes. The baptistry was in a recess near the entrance; here was preserved a crucifix salvaged from the ruin of La Leche after Palmer's raid in 1728. Two paintings decorated the interior side walls. One depicted the death of a sinner with demons awaiting the demise of their hapless victim, the other showed the death of a good man, his bed surrounded by hosts of angels.

It was, withal, the most splendid church in the Floridas.

Father Hassett, as seen above, was transferred from St. Augustine to New Orleans in 1795. The transfer occurred as part of a reorganization of the Church in Louisiana and the two Floridas. On April 25, 1795, the vicar general of Havana, Father Luis Ignacio Peñalver y Cárdenas, was consecrated bishop of a newly erected Diocese of Louisiana, in which both East and West Florida were placed. The area under the new bishop's jurisdiction stretched as far north and east as the confines of the diocese of Baltimore, and south and west to the boundaries of the Mexican dioceses of Linares and Durango. This part of the American mainland was now made independent of ecclesiastical authorities in Cuba for the first time. The see of the new diocese was fixed at New Orleans, and Bishop Peñalver arrived to take possession of it on July 24. To assist him in the administration of his vast diocese, Father Hassett was brought over from St. Augustine as canon and vicar-general.

Five months after his arrival, Bishop Peñalver issued an "Instruction for the Government of the Parishes of the Diocese of Louisiana," which was in greater part simply a restatement of the obligations of pastors toward their people. Two of the sixty-three paragraphs deserve notice. Particular stress was laid on the zeal that pastors should have for preaching the word of God, and they were told further to warn the Catholic people in their sermons against the atheism, deism, materialism, and other such errors that were being propagated in the neighboring United States, particularly by Protestants and bold spirits (*espíritus fuertes*). In another paragraph Peñalver ordered an annual census to be taken in each parish, in which was to be specified, among other things, how many Negroes, free and slave, Catholic and non-Catholic, were living within the parochial confines. His instruction on this point was motivated by a royal cédula of 1788 that commanded bishops and priests to give close attention to the spiritual needs of the Negroes. The cédula also codified all the slave laws that had been passed during the preceding years of Spanish colonialism. It is interesting that the provisions of this code were much milder than those of codes enforced in the English colonies. Slaves were taught to obey their masters, but they enjoyed a legal right to protest against harsh treatment. Masters were not allowed to make them work on Sundays and Holy Days. Slaveowners convicted of undue severity were fined. Slave marriages were encouraged and protected. If one partner in a marriage was sold to a different owner, the other had to be sold to the same owner. Slaves were to be properly fed and clothed, and given Christian instruction necessary to fit them for worthy reception of the Church's sacraments.

In East Florida no important events occurred during Bishop Peñalver's reign, and little progress was noted. The Church's influence, like the State's, was on the decline. Father O'Reilly, the new vicario, carried on the routine work of the parish, which now numbered about 2,000 souls. He got a helping hand in the person of Father Juan Cardoso in July, 1795. A Franciscan, Father Cardoso was assigned as chaplain of the hospital, a post that had been vacant since the departure of Father Traconis in 1791. Only three priests served in East Florida for the remainder of the decade—the third was Father Crosby. In 1802 Bishop Peñalver succeeded in having a young man ordained in Cuba for the lone East Florida parish, Juan Nepomuceno Gómez. On his arrival the young Father Gómez took on the work of maestro to eighty children in Father Hassett's still functioning school. East Florida continued to be plagued, however, by the familiar problems of too few priests, too little money, and too rigid adherence to time-consuming formalities. Bishop Peñalver never visited the province.

The state of the Church in West Florida offered no better picture, and for all the same reasons. Although the population of Pensacola had increased to 1,796 by the turn of the century, only one priest was in the town, Father James Coleman, from the Irish College of Nobles at Salamanca. The circumstances of his work were distressing, particularly the reluctance of his people to provide a decent place for Mass. Even Bishop Peñalver, when he visited the parish in 1798, was unable to persuade the people to make the necessary sacrifices for a new church. Meanwhile the temporary church fell slowly into ruin—walls buckled, windows broke, doors warped, and the floor fell through. As regards the moral condition of the town, there is no direct record, but if one may judge from the carelessness shown to the church building, it was, in all probability, not exemplary.

Although Bishop Peñalver exhibited courage and persistence in the administration of his vast diocese, eventually he felt himself crushed by the spreading weight of his problems, and after four years he asked in 1799 to be relieved. King Charles IV and the Holy See finally granted his request and in 1801 promoted him to Archbishop of Guatemala. In the meantime Father Francisco Porro y Reinado, a Spanish priest living in Rome, was selected to replace Peñalver. Bishop Porro was consecrated in November, 1801, but before he left for his diocese he learned of the possible retrocession of Louisiana to France, and delayed his journey. The news of the retrocession was confirmed later with the release of details of the secret treaty of San Ildefonso, and Porro was transferred by royal order to the See of Tarazona in Spain. It was unfortunate for his original diocese that he never arrived to take up jurisdiction, however briefly, because the arrangements made by Bishop Peñalver for temporary rule in the diocese resulted in juridical disorder.

Peñalver had left Father Hassett in command when he took ship for Havana in November, 1801, to accept the bulls appointing him to Guatemala. Father Patrick Walsh of New Orleans was named assistant administrator. Peñalver had authority to name an administrator only for the interim between his departure and his canonical possession of Guatemala; after that date the metropolitan, or archbishop, of the ecclesiastical province that comprised Louisiana and the Floridas would have to confirm Hassett in his office or else appoint a new administrator to serve until a new bishop arrived. Although this must have been known to Peñalver as the correct canonical procedure, his commission to Hassett inadvertently appointed him administrator not simply for the period that Peñalver remained Bishop of Louisiana, but until another bishop took possession of the see. When Bishop Porro's appointment to Louisiana was revoked, and he was assigned instead to Tarazona, no replacement was named for Louisiana, which now was a French possession. Responsibility for naming an administrator therefore devolved upon the metropolitan, or archbishop. But who was the metropolitan? At the time of its erection the Diocese of Louisiana was in the Archdiocese of Santo Domingo. In 1801, however, that archiepiscopal see was divided to form two new metropolitan sees, Caracas (Venezuela) and Santiago de Cuba, and for one reason or another Louisiana and the Floridas were included within neither one. Father Hassett was left with no alternative. After several abortive attempts to obtain a clear ruling on the duration of his powers, and with little confidence that he had canonical grounds for retaining the jurisdiction, Hassett nonetheless continued in his office of vicar-general and ruled Louisiana and the Floridas until his death on April 24, 1804.

Father Walsh now assumed jurisdiction over the diocese in virtue of the appointment given him by Peñalver in 1801. One year later, however, the validity of his powers was challenged by the Capuchin pastor of New Orleans, Father Antonio Sedella, and, more significantly, by the Bishop of Havana, Juan José Díaz de Espada y Landa. The New Orleans challenge erupted into schism, as Father Sedella and many of his parishioners openly defied Father Walsh's authority and withdrew their cathedral church from his control. Walsh appealed to the Sacred Congregation of Propaganda Fide in Rome to appoint someone with undisputed jurisdiction to take his place and restore order. Rome's reply was to tell Walsh that any jurisdiction he claimed had ceased, and that the Diocese of Louisiana had been given temporarily to the care of Bishop John Carroll of Baltimore. Unfortunately, through one of the inadvertencies that seemed to characterize this case, Bishop Carroll himself was advised that only the province of Louisiana (by this time a United States possession) came under his rule; nothing was said to him about that part of the Diocese of Louisiana that was under Spanish rule. Thus, East and West Florida continued to languish without firm episcopal control.

Bishop Espada's interest in the matter was aroused by a request from the captain general of Cuba to appoint chaplains for the Spanish soldiers in the Floridas. Doubtful about his competency to act in the Floridas, Espada asked the dean and chapter of the cathedral of Havana for their opinion of his canonical position. The chapter replied that, as the suffragan bishop nearest to Florida, he was empowered to exercise ecclesiastical jurisdiction in the area, *sede vacante*, the See of New Orleans being vacant. In a second opinion offered one month later, the chapter concluded that, in point of fact, the Diocese of Louisiana no longer existed, and that Espada had no choice but to act. Espada did so, and on September 13, 1806, he sent formal notice to all the faithful in both Floridas that he had dispatched the necessary canonical titles to Father O'Reilly at St. Augustine and to Father Coleman at Pensacola, who were to be his vicarios in East and West Florida, respectively. Although canon lawyers today would dispute the bishop's contention that the Diocese of Louisiana had been extinguished, Espada proceeded boldly on his course as though the right were firmly on his side. Interestingly, neither Bishop Carroll at Baltimore nor the first two administrators appointed by Carroll at New Orleans contested his jurisdiction in the Floridas. At New Orleans, Father Walsh died on August 22, 1806, the only man who was certain that the Floridas belonged to Louisiana. Not until 1812, when Father Louis-Guillaume-Valentin DuBourg was appointed administrator of Louisiana and the Floridas, did a new challenge come from New Orleans. The challenge was renewed, and with greater vigor, after DuBourg was consecrated Bishop of Louisiana and the Floridas in 1815. However, rumor of the impending sale of the Floridas to the United States caused the Sacred Congregation of Propaganda Fide to table Bishop DuBourg's case until such time as the sale was officially confirmed or denied.

Bishop Espada was widely acclaimed in Cuba for his learning, organizational genius, and Christian zeal, but it must be said that none of these qualities led him to success in the Floridas. The vigorous impetus expected there from his takeover never materialized. Espada slowly came to know what many other men, ecclesiastical and lay, had discovered before him: the Church in the Floridas was so closely bounden to the disintegrating provincial governments, it was not in a position to act independently of the weakened societies that those governments produced. Every disruptive force affecting the Crown or the local governors inevitably had a disorganizing effect on the Church. When, for example, the king, Ferdinand VII, was imprisoned by Napoleon from 1808 to 1814, the keystone of the arch of the patronato real was removed, and the Church in the distant frontier provinces tottered and swayed, bereft of financial support and legal redress. Internally, during such crises, the attention of civil officials was diverted from Church support and missionary undertakings to the more immediate problems of unemployment or commercial stagnation. Even when the crisis was of lesser magnitude, the inviolable rule imposed by the patronato—do nothing without State approval—tended to destroy initiative in the pastors, and held them to outmoded methods or to inaction, when the occasion demanded swift, decisive, *ad hoc* measures.

The last fifteen years of Spanish administration in the Floridas were particularly trying to both Church and State. Money was in short supply, food stocks were continually low. No answers came in response to letters to Cuba for help. The people grew increasingly bitter and despondent. They also grew fearful, since Spain had only 2,000 soldiers in both Floridas to ward off attacks from the restless Americans in the north and west. Their situation was particularly vulnerable in the years after 1810 when insurgent American and English settlers seized the portion of West Florida that lay west of the Perdido River and declared it a constitutional republic. This area as far as the Pearl River was annexed by the United States fifty-eight days later, and the remainder as far as the Perdido was added in 1813. More trouble came to the Floridas as a consequence of Spain's alliance with England in the War of 1812. The United States provoked rebellion, though unsuccessfully, in East Florida, and sent General Andrew Jackson to destroy the fort at Pensacola in 1814. Jackson returned in 1818 and ravaged the interior of north Florida, capturing Pensacola in the process. By this date Spain was convinced that she could no longer stay the attacks and depredations of her unfriendly neighbor, and she began to explore the possibilities of withdrawing with honor from her exposed and unproductive colonies.

In the area now known as Florida there were only two parishes after 1812. They were the same two parishes that had stood alone since the Spanish restoration. In their solitude and bare subsistence they perfectly symbolized the sad state of the fortunes of Catholicity in the Floridas. At war-ravaged Pensacola six hundred inhabitants, 40 per cent of whom were Negroes, eked out a difficult living. Low-class American frontiersmen predominated among the whites, thus the Catholics of the town became submerged in an alien environment. The best efforts of the vicario, Father Coleman, continued to be frustrated by flagging spirits and spiritual indifference. Mass was still celebrated in the old, leaky *almacén*, or warehouse, that served for a church. No school had yet been built, despite a royal order of 1796. And Father Coleman saw no prospects for better times. In St. Augustine, Father O'Reilly was vicario, and Father Crosby was assistant vicario. Two other priests served in the ancient parish, Father Gómez, the schoolmaster, and Father Cardoso, O.F.M., the chaplain at the garrison. Father O'Reilly was beset by continuing illness, and could not handle any but the lighter duties of the parish. His parishioners, now grown testy at the gloomy prospects for East Florida, rebuked their pastor for his failure to give the sermons at Mass. As for Father Crosby, they complained, he was too taken up with the Irish members of the parish and not sufficiently solicitous for the well-being of the Spaniards and Minorcans. In 1812 Father O'Reilly's health deteriorated rapidly, and on September 13, after twenty-eight years in the old presidio, he died. Father Crosby was impaired in health himself, but he took over the reins as vicario of the province. In 1815 Father Gómez was appointed assistant vicario. Together the two priests sought another priest from Cuba to serve the growing settlement of Fernandina in the northern district. But no priest would go to Florida. It was perhaps more plain to those outside Florida than it was to the colonists who lived there, that the days of Florida's Spanish and Catholic supremacy were numbered.

A picture of St. Augustine in 1819 has been left us by an English visitor: "The town was a great military station and beyond this, nothing. In one way or other the people were all engaged in servicing the king. They kept the king's accounts, labored at the king's fort, wrought in the king's forge, manned the king's pilot boats. . . . A guard of soldiers kept watch over the great treasure chest in the fort; a guard watched at the powder house in the plain south of the barracks; a guard noted the marking of high noon on the sun dial and, by the flowing of the sands in the hour glass on the plaza all day and all night, recorded the passing of time by strokes of a bell. . . .

"Funeral processions through the streets were led by the Padre in his robes and by acolytes in surplices bearing a crucifix, candles and aspersorium. Feast days and festivals were scrupulously observed. The massacre of Madrid *Dos de Mayo* was commemorated by the solemn celebration of High Mass and the flags throughout the city were displayed in mourning. With Carnival time came mirth and merry making; harlequins, dominoes and punchinellos held high revel and gay companies of maskers went about the streets. Among them, taking the part of St. Peter, went one clad in the ragged dress of a fisherman and equipped with a mullet cast net which he dexterously threw over the heads of the not unwilling children, by such rude travesty setting forth the Apostolic fishing for men.

"In the afternoon of Palm Sunday priest and people marched in procession from the church, south to the convent where on its platform in the open air stood an altar. . . . Then all repaired in procession to Ft. San Marco where, at a second altar, the rites were repeated. On Easter eve the waifs went about the streets, singing beneath the windows to the accompaniment of violin and guitar, their Minorcan hymn of praise to the Virgin:

> *Ended the days of sadness,*
> *Grief gives way to singing,*
> *We come with joy and gladness*
> *Our gifts to Mary bringing.*

In this very year 1819 the long-dreaded news reached the peninsula: by the Adams-Onís treaty, Spain and the United States had negotiated the transfer of the Floridas. Two years later the pact was ratified, and amid appropriate ceremonies the Spanish flag came off the masts from the Atlantic to the Perdido River. The Spanish era was done forever. And the Catholic Church, which had learned to live with so many governments in Europe and Asia, now had to live with another one in Florida.

VIII

Rise of the Church Wardens

1821-1827

ASAD GLOAMING now supervened for Catholic St. Augustine. In quick order following the day, July 10, 1821, when Colonel Robert Butler, United States Commissioner, marched into the courtyard of the old Castillo de San Marcos to receive the protocols of transfer of East Florida to the fast-fledging American Eagle, the Catholics of the oldest and only parish in the province were summarily dispossessed of their church buildings, their priests, their bishop, and, in great part, their livelihood. Once again, as had happened in 1763, the change of national allegiance worked serious prejudice to their religion. The decades that followed can only be described as a sea of troubles. The Church in East Florida found herself adrift, without moorings, without captains, without much more than a star to go by. She would not reach safe harbor for another thirty-seven years.

First to go were the Church buildings: the parish church, the burying ground, the bishop's residence, the Mission of Nombre de Dios (more frequently called at this time the hermitage of Nuestra Señora de la Leche), and the old Franciscan Convent of the Immaculate Conception, in long use by this date as a military barracks. Under the plea that it was not the Church but the King of Spain who held title to these structures and lots, they were appropriated by the United States as public property and assigned to be administered by the new Territorial government. The next loss was Father Michael Crosby. Disheartened by the change of flags, and fretful about his chances of maintaining Catholicity in the midst of a swelling population of Protestant immigrants, Father Crosby thought at first of abandoning the parish and of persuading his Spanish and Minorcan people to do the same. American Colonel Butler urged him otherwise: "The Rev. Mr. Crosby . . . was urged by me to remain in charge of the church and take care of his flock, assuring him that the government would never disturb them in their occupancy; and, after considering the subject, he said he would take my advice and remain." One year later, however, Father Crosby died. His assistant, Father Juan Nepomuceno Gómez, stayed on alone for another year, and then he, too, was gone as ill health forced his return to Cuba. For the second time in 256 years, and for the first time since 1768, East Florida was without a single priest.

Added to these losses, East Florida was also without a bishop. Since 1806 jurisdiction had been exercised over the Spanish province by the Bishop of Havana. Now that political communications between Florida and the Spanish islands had been severed, the Bishop of Havana petitioned Rome for the severance also of ecclesiastical ties between Florida and the Spanish hierarchy. Before hearing an answer, and while still unaware to which American diocese Florida might belong, the Bishop of Havana thrust the problem province into the hands of young Irish-born John England (1786-1842), Bishop of the newly erected (1820) Diocese of Charleston, in South Carolina. Bishop England recorded the news in his "Diurnal," or diary, under the date July 10, 1822: "I received a letter from the Bishop of Havannah, stating it to be out of his power to attend to East Florida, and requiring me to look after it, as being the nearest Bishop." For the next fifteen years, off and on, Bishop England, already hard pressed with the care of Georgia and the Carolinas, would find himself "looking after" Florida, although it would never be his proper charge. The firm decisions expected from

Rome did not arrive for many years. Florida, with more Catholics than could be found in many states of the Union, became caught in a tangle of jurisdictional disputes, as the prelates in the southern United States grew unsure how far their jurisdictions actually ranged, and none, with the notable exception of John England, showed any special desire to have Florida added to his responsibilities. The zeal shown by Bishop England in the exercise of his temporary stewardship adds the only luster to the story of Florida's otherwise anomalous position at this time in the scale of ecclesiastical administrations. Meanwhile the old Catholic center of St. Augustine went months, sometimes years, without seeing a priest. And the faith and morals of the people suffered as a consequence.

Unlike the period following the change of governments in 1763, when the Catholic population evacuated en masse to Cuba, the Catholics of East Florida generally remained after 1821. Spanish officials and soldiers, with their families, had been departing in groups since 1819, but some remained, and practically all of the Minorcan, Italian, and Greek refugees from New Smyrna held fast to their new roots. Through emissaries, Bishop England counted 300 to 400 Catholics at St. Augustine, perhaps 100 on the St. Johns River, and 100 to 200, mainly fishermen and descendants of Mexican immigrants, at Amelia Island and its vicinity. Although stricken by the loss of their priests, and deprived of the long-standing alliance of their church with the civil power, the Catholic population nonetheless took heart from assurances of protection given them by United States officials, and from the fifth article of the treaty of transfer, which guaranteed: "The inhabitants of the ceded territories shall be secured in the free exercise of their religion, without any restriction."

These assurances constituted about their only reason for hope, however. Politically and economically their position was exposed and precarious. As one-time "foreigners" and enemies, they were regarded with suspicion by the Americans who now poured south across the Florida frontier. Officially the inhabitants of Spanish and Minorcan descent were equal citizens with the American immigrants, possessing the same claims as any settlers from Georgia or Carolina on the shield of the young republic. Still, they knew that they had to prove their loyalty, and over a long period of time. In the matter of their livelihoods, they also had to learn to prove themselves, now that the controlled Spanish economy, with its subsidies and special privileges, had yielded to the laissez-faire competitive system of the Americans. It was a rare family that did not see hard times ahead.

St. Augustine was particularly vulnerable. The town's assets were few, its needs many. Surrounded by swamp and marsh, it had little agriculture and meager pasturage. Its harbor was good, but the narrow and treacherous entry made it unlikely that the town would become a stop on the coastal trade route. Its climate was salubrious, but the American had not yet became a vacationer, and there was no Chamber of Commerce to lure him into becoming one. Save for the fish in its surrounding waters, St. Augustine was unable to feed itself, and it had precious little in other resources to exchange for food from the outside. Left by both Spain and the United States to fend for itself, the little colony soon found itself hungry and diseased, trading fish for meat with the Indians whom it feared, and gazing wistfully to sea in the hope of sighting a food-laden ship from Charleston.

In June, 1822, Bishop England received a letter from Alexander Hamilton, United States Commissioner in residence at St. Augustine (and not to be confused with a more famous American of the same name). In it Hamilton advised the prelate of the death of Father Crosby and went on to mention the state of the Catholic Church properties: "I have been given to understand that the Church property belonged to the King of Spain, & by relation it has become that of the United States. Of course, whenever the United States shall act, they will dispose of it in such manner as will be adapted to the political changes of this country." Bishop England's reaction to this news, which he seems not to have learned before, was swift and direct. He dispatched a letter to James Monroe, President of the United States, in which he represented the nature of Church property ownership quite differently. He argued that "when the King of Spain or any other Sovereign power gives property to any corporation, such as under Spain the Roman Catholic Church of St. Augustine was, the sovereign divests

himself thereof & vests it in the corporation to whom it is given."
Acquitting Mr. Hamilton personally of any sinister intentions, the
bishop felt it necessary to add that there were "teachers of another
religious body," according to information that he had received,
who "wish to deprive the Roman Catholics who are the principal &
most numerous body of inhabitants of their property." (He probably was referring to the Episcopalians and to their newly arrived
minister, Andrew Fowler, whom Bishop England judged in a letter to Rome the month before as "a man of keen judgment, who is
now secretly trying to secure the Catholic Church property." In
1825 the Episcopalians of the city did succeed in obtaining title to
the old bishop's residence and lot, on the corner of King and St.
George Streets.) The bishop's letter to the President concluded:
"The Roman Catholics claim no privileges to which their fellow
Citizens are not entitled—they claim no favor or affection in the
eye of the State, but they do expect that by becoming Citizens of
the United States they shall not lose the property which they previously possessed & held until now."

This letter was forwarded to William Wirt, Attorney General
of the United States (and later the founder of Wirtland, Florida),
who communicated his opinion of its contents to Secretary of State
John Quincy Adams. Mr. Wirt wrote that, "Doctor England states
the law correctly. . . . The only question in this case is a question
of fact." Did the king of Spain actually grant these lands to the
Church? Mr. Wirt was unable to say because he lacked the pertinent documents. Secretary Adams, who as one of the chief ne-
gotiators for the purchase of Florida from Spain was acquainted
with the spirit of that agreement as it affected the Church, wrote
to Mr. Hamilton in St. Augustine, acknowledging that if the facts
in the case were as stated by Bishop England, "the property in question belongs to the Roman Catholic Congregation at St. Augustine;
and it is very desirable that the use of it should be effectually secured to them." Hamilton was not in possession of all the facts
himself, but he decided it the best course, in view of Adams' letter,
to hand over provisionally at least the parish church and burying
ground, as subsequently was done sometime early in 1823. The congregation would later be confirmed officially in its possession by

Acts of Congress on February 8, 1827, and June 28, 1832. About the other unclaimed Church holdings, namely, Nombre de Dios and the Franciscan convent, there seems not to have been any special concern in the Catholic community of St. Augustine at this date, and there would be no final disposition of them by the United States until 1849.

Without priests, the condition of the congregation at St. Augustine was not appreciably improved by the property decision. Bishop England assigned Father Simon Felix Gallagher to the town in late 1822, but that cleric, not satisfied with his salary, left Florida for Havana some months later, in January, 1823. The parishioners were no better situated in an empty church than they were in no church at all. Some parishioners wondered how they could legally administer the church that had come suddenly into their lay hands, but most looked to the example of certain similarly situated Catholic parishes in the northern states, where itinerant priests offered Mass only from time to time, and to the example of Protestant denominations generally. In these churches ecclesiastical properties were vested in the names of the congregations, and were administered by boards of wardens, or trustees, elected from the general memberships. Since the United States had conferred provisional ownership of the Church of St. Augustine on its congregation, and not on any particular diocese, bishop, or pastor, the parishioners felt justified in following the precedent established by Catholics in the North. On July 2, 1823, against a background of poverty, lack of priests, and confusion of ecclesiastical jurisdiction, the "Board of Wardens of the Catholic Congregation of St. Augustine" was born. Its birth was attended by an unhappy portent.

Before rehearsing the story of the wardens and their church, it will be appropriate at this point to trace the measures taken after 1822 in this country and in Rome to place Florida under definite episcopal direction. The first decisions in the matter were made in Rome by the Sacred Congregation of Propaganda Fide, which had general charge of the missionary Church in the United States. After reviewing communications that it had received from the Bishops of Havana and Charleston, Propaganda put forward the discomposing conclusion that the Bishop of Havana's canonical jurisdiction over Florida had ceased according to a decree dated April 25, 1793. The case argued by Bishop DuBourg of Louisiana and the Floridas in 1812, and again in 1815, had been, it turned out, substantially correct. Effectively Florida had been without a bishop for longer than she knew. Propaganda now recommended that East and West Florida be joined temporarily to a new Vicariate-Apostolic of Alabama-Mississippi, which was created on August 13, 1822. Father Joseph Rosati, C.M., of St. Louis, was nominated vicar-apostolic.

When the news of this decision reached St. Louis, Father Rosati wrote straightway to Rome stating his intention not to accept the mitre. He was supported in this refusal by his ordinary, Bishop DuBourg, who told him: "Truth to tell, I do not understand the decisions of Propaganda. To them it seems only necessary to appoint bishops and to send them, without inquiring whether there are any parishes to receive and support them and without providing any means for them for their work." Bishop DuBourg was aware, however, that some episcopal control was needed over Florida, and he considered that the matter was properly his own responsibility. In early 1823, therefore, he wrote Bishop England asking him, as had the Bishop of Havana, to look after Florida as his vicar-general. The Church in Florida came up again in a general meeting on American affairs at Propaganda on June 9, 1823. As a result of that meeting, the brief creating the vicariate of Alabama-Mississippi was revoked, Father Rosati was pressed to accept the episcopate as coadjutor to Bishop DuBourg, and Florida was allowed to revert formally to the administration of DuBourg until such time as a diocese comprising Alabama and Florida could be formed. On June 10, the day after the Rome decisions, Bishop England was writing to the Archbishop of Baltimore: "St. Augustine has been now four months without a Priest, overrun with Methodists and Presbyterians. I of course have no charge there, which is a calm to my conscience."

Eventually, on August 26, 1825, Propaganda erected Florida and Alabama into a vicariate-apostolic with Father Michael Portier (1795-1859), of New Orleans, as bishop. Like Rosati before him, the thirty-year-old Portier attempted to decline the mitre, but without success. At the time of his consecration, on November 5, 1826, he could count only two clergymen besides himself in the new vicariate, and only three congregations with churches, at St. Augustine, Pensacola, and Mobile, Alabama. He entered on his new duties with much energy, but without, apparently, having notified Bishop England of his accession, since on December 29 of that year, England wrote a puzzled letter to Bishop Rosati: "The departure of Dr. Du Bourg [to Europe] has placed me in some difficulty as to the exercise of jurisdiction. He requested of me to act as his Vicar-General *in spiritualibus* for East Florida. . . . I am at a loss to know whether you have succeeded to the See of New Orleans, & whether I have lost my delegated jurisdiction over East Florida. . . . I want six or seven priests for my own diocese, & must naturally give a preference thereto, & if Florida is neglected, the people will, as many have done, fall into other hands than ours." Rosati wrote to advise England of the changes that had taken place, and of Bishop Portier's assumption of responsibility for Florida. Not long afterwards, Bishop Portier would be writing England to ask him to "look after" Florida once more.

It is the place in our narrative now to return to St. Augustine, and to the first measures taken by that parish's Church Wardens. The Legislative Council of the Territory of Florida, like the Department of State in Washington, was pleased to have itself divested of title to the Church at St. Augustine, since it was contrary to the tenets of the Republic that the civil authority should either hinder or act as patron of a religious body. Accordingly, the Council approved the action of the Catholic congregation in forming themselves into Church Wardens, and incorporated the congregation by an Act dated July 2, 1823. The terms of incorporation stipulated that six wardens should be elected annually by the congregation to act as directors of the corporation, which itself was vested with legal personality as owner of the church's goods. Except for the church building and the cemetery, the corporation came into actual possession of little more than a long list of disputed claims on realty once associated with the church. The only other property to which they held clear title was a house and lot on Hospital Street that had been willed to the parish by one of its former pastors, Father Michael O'Reilly. On October 12, badly in need of cash, the wardens commissioned a parishioner, Carlos Robiou, to auction the property for not less than two-thirds of its appraised value (420 pesos). On October 16, Robiou reported that he had made the sale, at 371 pesos, to one Rafael Fontane, who presented one-half the price in cash and promised to pay the rest in two installments of 90 and 120 days. The Church of St. Augustine now had 185 pesos to its name. Three days later, word came that it was to have a priest as well.

Father John McEncroe, of Cashel, Tipperary, newly ordained for the Diocese of Charleston, arrived on board ship at St. Augustine on October 21, 1823. Sent by Bishop England with faculties of one month's duration, he was maintained without salary in a private home. The wardens were delighted to have a priest, their first since Father Gallagher ten months before. Apparently, during his short stay Father McEncroe made a favorable impression, as evidenced by this labored entry of November 13 in the Spanish language minutes of the wardens: "The Presbiter Don Juan McEncroe, having shown the wardens of this parish church his desire to purchase the silver cup, or ciborium, which is found deposited in the Chest of Jewels, because the Church at Charleston lacked such a piece, the Corporation, in virtue of this, full of gratitude for the effectiveness and good services of the said priest . . . agreed that they would give it to him, and he accepted it with the greatest pleasure, offering to give it to the Most Illustrious Bishop [England] in the name of the faithful Catholics of this parish as a gift to the City of Charleston."

That entry was the last recorded act of St. Augustine's first Board of Wardens. When the records were resumed a year and four months later, the old corporation was defunct and a new one had been established. What happened in the interim is not clear. In all events, a more rigid corporate structure was organized and given legal status by the Territory of Florida on December 30, 1824. The new terms of incorporation defined with greater precision than before the various duties and tenures in office of the Board of Wardens, and stipulated that elections to the six-member board should be held each year on or near April 1. Also in 1824 St. Augustine was visited by another newly ordained Irish priest from Charleston, Father

Francis Boland. Of his ministry there we learn very little from the existing records, particularly since no minutes were kept by the wardens during his stay. Bishop England recorded in his diocesan paper, the *United States Catholic Miscellany*, that Father Boland left Charleston for East Florida on January 26, 1824. Our next news of him comes from the same organ in the September following, when the bishop commented on attacks made in St. Augustine against Father Boland and his "Romish practices" by Eleazer Lathrop, a Presbyterian minister newly arrived in the town. "Mr. Lathrop," wrote England "looks upon the Roman Catholic Church in St. Augustine to be a Temple of Idolatry, and considers Mr. Boland as not one whit more pure in his Christianity than a Priest of Apollo."

The same issue of the *Miscellany* carried an open letter to Mr. Lathrop received from an anonymous "Friend to Candour" in St. Augustine. In its defense of Father Boland and the parish, the letter revealed the sensitivity of the Catholic inhabitants to moral preachments from Protestant newcomers: "Any one who knew St. Augustine previous to the change of governments, would have informed you that there were few places, if any, on the continent of America, where there was more order, more upright morals, and more comparative happiness than in St. Augustine. It was not then, indeed, a refuge for bankrupts in fame and fortune; it was not a mart for place-hunters; it did not exhibit a scene of fraud and chicanery; justice was not expensive and unattainable—yet it was all that time under the influence of a religion which keeps the people in ignorance and which inculcated superstitious and demoralizing principles!!! . . . One fact is unquestionable, that St. Augustine is now ten degrees lower in every point of view, both religious and political, than it was whilst under a Catholic government and under a Catholic priesthood." Father Boland was recalled to Charleston in February, 1825, because of increasing demands in Bishop England's own diocese. Like Father McEncroe before him, he left with the encomiums of the Church Wardens. And East Florida settled back into another spiritual interregnum.

The first election under their new constitution was held by the wardens on February 18, 1825. It resulted in the selection of the

Plaza of St. Augustine in 1857. To the left is the Catholic Church. To the right is the Episcopal Church—on grounds once called the "Episcopal lot" and used as the residence of auxiliary bishops from Cuba during Spanish times.

"Plaza de la Constitución," St. Augustine, showing the old Spanish Government House, monument, and the parish church.

Catholic Vestry room Monday, 7th March 1831

The Board of Church Wardens met this day

Present   Charles Robiou   President
Peter Benet
Bernardo Segui
Antonio Alvarez   } Wardens
Anacleto Llambias
Jos: Simeon Sanchez

The minutes of the last meeting were read and approved.

The Committee to whom was refered Sundry accounts presented by Francis Gue against the Catholic Church Report. That they have examined the said accounts and find a charge of Six Dollars for repairs put upon the house of O'Reillys (Est) unauthorised which Sum they have deducted and recommend the ballance for paym't

The report of the Committee is received and the ballan. due Mr Francis Gue is passed for payment

Mr Robiou as Auctionier Presented an acct amounting Seven Dollars Seventy Cents Commissions, for selling the Lease of the Church Property, which was passed for paym't

Mr A Alvarez Presented an account amounting to One Dollar advanced for the Church by him to the Clerk of the Superior Court for a Copy of the Mandamus awarded to the Rev'd Edward Mayne against the Wardens of the Roman Catholic Church. Which is passed for paym't

Antelm Gue Presented an account amounting to Four Dollars for Translations made by him of certain Documents in the case of the Rev'd Edward Mayne vs The Wardens of the Roman Catholic Church, which was passed for paym

Page from the March 7, 1831 Minutes of the Board of Church Wardens of St. Augustine. The last two paragraphs refer to the pastor, long-suffering Father Edward Francis Mayne.

following men: Bernardo Segui, who was appointed to serve as president until the regular elections could be held in April; William Travers; Peter Miranda; Eusebio M. Gomez; Joseph B. Lancaster; and Francis J. Fatio. In its lame-duck capacity this first board accomplished little else than the composition of letters to Rafael Fontane, asking him kindly to pay the money that he still owed the congregation on his purchase of the Father O'Reilly property on Hospital Street. The regular elections of April were scheduled for the fourth day of that month, but not a single member of the priestless congregation showed up at the vestry room to cast a ballot. On the following Sunday a quorum was secured, and a new board was chosen. Bernardo Segui was re-elected president; Thomas Murphy and G. W. Perpall replaced Lancaster and Gomez.

For years the wills of Fathers O'Reilly and Crosby had gathered dust, while their extensive properties in St. Augustine had sprouted weeds. Although the wills stated that the properties were left to the church, in their language they had bequeathed them specifically to Spanish church societies which no longer existed. Now, with a sudden show of energy, the newly elected wardens posted claims on these properties and hired an attorney to circumvent the legal obstacles involved. The determination displayed by the wardens had happy results at once in another direction. Señor Fontane presented half of his long-overdue payment, and promised to satisfy the balance promptly. A sense of prosperity prevailed among the congregation for the first time in several years. Some needed repairs could now be undertaken. The wardens decided to "put a saddle on the roof of the church." And about this same time news arrived that another priest was on his way from Charleston.

Father Timothy McCarthy sailed into St. Augustine on June 20, 1825. Immediately the wardens assembled to greet him, and, with an air of authority, carefully examined his credentials. Apparently finding them in good order, and pleased with the new priest's bearing and manner, they arranged for his lodging at the home of Mr. James Cashen, and insisted that he accept the price of his passage from Charleston. For nearly a year St. Augustine and Father McCarthy got along very well together. The faith and morals of the people were strengthened, minor improvements were

129

carried through on the church, and large crowds attended the venerable building to avail themselves of Mass and the sacraments. One young artillery officer from the north noted that "it was not an uninteresting spectacle to see the veiled Spanish Minorcan beauties gracefully kneel upon the hard stone floor during Mass, and they were not so devout as to preclude the telegraphic sign sub rosa between lovers." On July 4 the church was the scene of a civic Independence Day ceremony, in which the Declaration of Independence was read and an oration was delivered. During this same period the wardens succeeded in gaining title to the properties of Father O'Reilly and began to realize some income from them. They also secured clear possession to the school building adjoining the church, and were in a position to present a bill to the city council for rental of the property, which the city fathers had commandeered some years earlier as a meeting chamber. In the course of Father McCarthy's first year, only one untoward incident was recorded in the minutes: the sacristan got drunk and had to be fired. A few weeks later, however, he was back on the payroll, and the work of the parish hummed along smoothly as before.

Trouble came in July, 1826. Father McCarthy appeared before the wardens with a complaint that he was no longer able to get along without a salary. He appreciated the payments made for his lodging, but he needed money to pay for indispensible requirements of the liturgy, and asked if he might not have permission to collect stole fees for marriages and funerals. The wardens, apparently jealous of their prerogatives, refused to grant this permission, but promised to take under consideration the question of a regular salary. At their next meeting they agreed to set the priest a salary of $300 annually, and appointed a committee to collect a subscription. Trouble now bred more trouble. The city fathers decided that they were paying too much rent on the schoolhouse, and threatened to move unless the rate was lowered. Fontane, still owing money on his 1823 purchase, presented a bill amounting to more than his indebtedness. The sacristan went on another spree, and ran up a bill for which the wardens were held responsible. And, to add bad news to bad, the subscription committee reported that there was no money to be raised in St. Augustine.

In August matters reached a head, as Father McCarthy found it necessary to rebuke the wardens for allowing one of their number to interfere with his spiritual jurisdiction. The exact nature of the interference is not recorded, but on the twenty-seventh of that month the priest demanded to know "if the faculties of this body extend to mixing into his attributes," adding, as the wardens' secretary recorded defensively, "other unfounded and insignificant expressions." The unhappy confrontation between priest and wardens led to a decision, made reluctantly by the wardens on September 13, to surrender a portion of their legally constituted proprietorship over the parish. In the interests of maintaining peace, of providing for the legitimate needs of their pastor, and—what may have been their principal interest—of unloading their indebtedness on someone else, the wardens resolved that, "from the 16th of the present month, [Father McCarthy] is given charge of collecting, for his own benefit, all that the parishioners wish voluntarily to contribute," and that from these funds "it will be his obligation to pay the small expenses that originate in the church."

This was in September. By the following January Father McCarthy realized that, no matter what system of financial control might prevail, the congregation of St. Augustine was unwilling to support its church and its pastor. He had tried to collect a subscription, and had failed; he had asked for offerings at Mass, and had been met with empty hands; he had even been arrested by the civil authorities for nonpayment of parish debts. On February 1, 1827, the priest wrote to the Board of Wardens, explaining the "impossibility he finds of being able to exist longer in this city because of lack of means for his most necessary food, and the necessity in which he sees himself of returning to Charleston." On February 10 a chastened congregation stood on the wharf at St. Augustine, watching as Father McCarthy's ship sailed out of Matanzas Bay. The parish had had its second opportunity to hold a resident priest, and had not been equal to it. The properties of the church were in no better position than they had been months before; if anything, they were in worse position. Several bills were read at the next meeting of the wardens, and the members dutifully voted to pay them "as soon as there might be funds."

Ralph Waldo Emerson visited the old Spanish town in the winter of 1827. He found the living costs "intolerably dear," the people "lazy," and the parish church "full of coarse toys." But St. Augustine gave him back his health, and he spoke more kindly about the place on his leaving:

Farewell; & fair befall thee, gentle town!
The prayer of those who thank thee for their life. . . .

In 1827 also St. Augustine and Florida received an episcopal visitation. Bishop Michael Portier, newly consecrated for the Vicariate of Florida and Alabama, arrived at Pensacola in January to examine at first hand what remained of Catholic life in Florida. From the records of his visit we learn our first information in several years about the state of Catholicity in West Florida. Although Pensacola was the oldest of the Gulf Coast settlements, geography and history had conspired to prevent its growth, and it was the least developed of the three centers of Catholic population within the vicariate, the other two being Mobile and St. Augustine. A haphazard municipal administration and periodic ravages of yellow fever compounded the town's difficulties. About 1,500 Catholics could be counted there at the time of Bishop Portier's arrival. They still had no church, but worshipped in the same wooden almacén of Spanish times. The congregation had incorporated themselves under the territorial laws of Florida in July, 1823, and they annually elected nine wardens to represent them legally. More fortunate than the congregation at St. Augustine, the Pensacola Catholics had a resident priest, Father Constantine Maenhaut, who was described by a French visitor to the town as "universally esteemed and loved on account of his exemplary conduct and learning." Bishop Portier also had high praise for the priest, and did all he could to keep him in the vicariate. Only months later, however, Pensacola's good fortune would run out, when Father Maenhaut decided to transfer his labors to New Orleans.

Bishop Portier left Pensacola for St. Augustine on June 12, 1827. He had written to Propaganda in Rome the previous month: "There is but one way to establish religion and that is to be campaigning always in the field, to preach everywhere, to destroy the prejudices of Protestants, to confirm Catholics in their faith, and to render respectable the august [episcopal] character in which we are vested by word, example, and independence." Later he would send a richly detailed journal of his first campaign in the field to the *Annales de l' Association de la Propagation de la Foi* in Lyons, France, the publication of a missionary body that disbursed assistance funds to a number of American dioceses and vicariates. Portier wrote that he set out from Pensacola along the dirt paths that led eastward into the old Apalache Indian country, accompanied by "my guardian angel," a farmer, and a mail carrier. The latter two companions soon reached their destinations, but the bishop shortly afterwards met a young Scotch traveler whose goal was also St. Augustine, and the two men agreed to remain together, pledging "in case of accident or sickness to help one another mutually." As the travelers passed the springtime scenes of flora and fauna that lay along their route, Portier recorded them in minute detail. One such scene, discovered after crossing the Chipola River near present-day Marianna, the bishop described in these words:

"We climbed up a small sloping hill on the left bank, enjoying at our ease the most beautiful and varied spectacle. Everywhere we heard the murmur of deep brooks with steep banks. Some rocks rose as high as the trees, all around flowers had been able to flourish and presented an agreeable border, while small odoriferous trees grew out of the sides and along the tops of little hills. Natural springs, subterranean caves, oaks torn by lightning or felled by hurricanes, like artificial bridges crossed our path—nothing was missing to render the tableau perfect. I narrate what I saw, I describe my sensations, and yet must confess that my expressions fall far short of reality."

Sometimes the bishop would pause a while to meditate amid the splendors that Providence had lavished on the Florida landscape, as he did one day where a majestic "fountain" poured forth from a basin in the deep forest, and "my soul, charmed also by the religious silence that then reigned there, paid, with a new sentiment of gratitude, the daily tribute of prayer it had vowed to God." Even where the walking was hard, and the surrounding scenes were less agreeable, the bishop's journal relates that he found reasons

133

for gratification: missionaries, he wrote, should be grateful for such a lonely task where "we walk with Jesus Christ, we share the work of the founders of the Faith; we are happy to suffer as they for the same cause, and especially to offer, as they did, a frail existence into the hands of Him who gave it to us."

One night the bishop sought hospitality in a Presbyterian household, where he was carefully examined from head to foot, with the result that, "My glasses, my ring, my watch, my breviary, and particularly my cross drew to my arms all the children." An elderly lady seated near the fire watched this scene with mounting displeasure. "After holding back for some time," Portier wrote, "a sacrifice that cost her much, she began to lecture me on religion, and suddenly surrendered herself in a violent tirade to all the rage of a repressed fanaticism. We [Catholics] were worse than idolators; we adored the Saints, and even their images; we had our golden calf and we made a shameful traffic out of the sacrament of Penance to permit all sorts of crime. You are *Roman*, she said to me, it is you who persecuted the first Christians, and who, along with the other powers of hell, tried to wipe out the Religion of salvation in the blood of the first faithful. . . . I answered categorically her every objection, I cursed with a great anathema all the doctrines that had so well stirred her bile. My anathemas had a more happy effect on her than the best arguments. They gave me for breakfast an old piece of fat and some corn bread, still warm. I then left, and the old lady bade me farewell in a very friendly tone, which led me to understand that she had been at least a little reconciled to Catholics."

The bishop's journal contains many gracious words about the Protestant settlers. He respected sincerity of belief wherever he found it, as in one large household where the Methodist father "night and morning gathered his children and domestics, read to them some chapter of the Scriptures, which were heard with respect, gave his advice or explained some obscure passage. . . ." During his odyssey Portier met many more Protestants than he did Catholics. He records only one occasion when he celebrated Mass, June 23, at Tallahassee, which was at that time a city of a hundred houses, "very clean and built on a regular plan." Hardly had he begun Mass for the few Catholics of the place when the hall filled with Protestant spectators. The bishop improvised a sermon on salvation through good works, and "these good people," he said, "listened with attention and stayed until the end of Mass."

The remainder of Portier's trek overland was marked by incessant physical hardships and dangers. The frontier people who lived along the route from Tallahassee to the Atlantic were not prodigal in their hospitality, and it was a rare night when the bishop and his Scotch companion had decent beds and more for their stomachs than fat meat and corn bread and stagnant water from a ditch. The sticky heat of mid-June was always with them in the day, and clouds of mosquitoes aggravated their sleeping hours at night. The bishop worried constantly about alligators, which he incorrectly called crocodiles, and about snakes and other dangerous animals that moved about in the woods after dark.

Finally, on July 4, the bishop and his companion arrived at Jacksonville, and, after a fast march, managed to reach St. Augustine on the following day. His welcome there was warm and friendly beyond his expectations. The Church Wardens placed a house at Portier's disposal and offered to provide for any other of his needs. The congregation completely filled the Church on the following Sunday when the bishop sang a High Mass and preached in English. A number of Protestants also attended, including several ministers who had postponed their own services. For the next two weeks Portier administered baptisms, instructed children for first Holy Communion, visited the sick, and officiated at a funeral. Then suddenly he was struck down by a fever, which threatened at one point to carry off his life and did not break for twelve days. It was near the end of August before the bishop could resume his normal duties. The number of baptisms increased; they would reach sixty before his departure. He preached now in Spanish as well as English, and to Bishop Rosati he wrote about the experience: "They tell me that I pronounced this language like a Castillian, but believe none of it, for I do not believe it myself."

The bishop concluded his visitation in September with a two-week retreat, or parish mission. He spoke each morning and evening to large crowds, and on the last day he gave fifty first

Communions and confirmed ninety persons. On September 19 he decided that it was time to start his return to Pensacola and Mobile. St. Augustine was in better spiritual condition that it had been in several years, and Portier was satisfied that most of the ravages which long neglect and scandals had brought on the parish had been healed as a result of his visit. The local *Florida Herald* of September 22 editorialized that the prelate had succeeded in restoring the fervor not only of his Catholic people, but of "all denominations, who seemed to forget their sectarian differences in listening to the pure and unadultered truths of christianity. . . ." A hint of the separatist cast that still surrounded the Spanish-Minorcan element at this date came in the same paper's statement that Portier had won "the favor and esteem of the American portion of our population, as well as of his Catholic congregation."

On September 22 Portier began the long trek westward. He walked toward bad news. At Pensacola he learned that the two priests stationed at Pensacola and Mobile had given up their posts and returned to New Orleans. Bishop Portier was now alone in his vast vicariate. In desperation he wrote to Bishop England at Charleston, asking him to look after East Florida again as his vicar-general. England's diocesan organ, the *Miscellany*, observed the change of fortunes resignedly: "Doctor England is disposed to do what he can in the case, but his own difficulties are extremely pressing."

IX

Church and State

1827-1857

I N AUGUST, 1835, Bishop England wrote some words of his own
about East Florida for the pages of the *Miscellany*. They were
grave words, about the "spiritual destitution" of that place,
and about the "foolish pretensions of a few men in whom confidence was thoughtlessly placed." In those several words the
bishop adequately stated the condition of the Parish of St. Augustine, still the only parish in East Florida, during the intervening
eight years since Bishop Portier's first visitation. England went
on: "We have for some time back had lying by us a melancholy
history of the church in this place; which we once thought of
placing in our columns. We should, however, hope from recent
indications, that this shall be forever buried in oblivion."

Unfortunately, so important a series of events as occurred at
St. Augustine during those eight years could not be buried, as
Bishop England wished. The events attracted too much notice in
their own time, and they have been recounted in bits and pieces
ever since, as one of the classic episodes of "lay trusteeism" in the
American Church. What happened at St. Augustine can best be

described as a schism: a defiance by the congregation of legitimately appointed episcopal and pastoral authority. The whole story can now be put together from the original records, some of which, the minutes of Church Warden meetings, have only recently come to light. The story provides one of the principal reasons why the fortunes of Catholicity in East Florida continued to fare ill during most of the first half of the nineteenth century, and it supplies as well the background to later events at St. Augustine, in 1848, when the pastor and Catholic congregation made separate and independent petitions to the federal government for restitution of church properties lost at the time of cession in 1821.

There was nothing in the provisions of canon law, as the legislation of the world-wide Church was called, that expressly forbade the system of lay trustees or wardens. That system, whereby the temporalities of parochial administration were left to the hands of the laity, had by 1827 become common practice in many sections of the American Church. As Archbishop John Hughes of New York would state later, in 1853, "Regarded *a priori*, no system could appear to be less objectionable, or more likely, both to secure advantages to those congregations, and at the same time to recommend the Catholic religion to the liberal consideration of the Protestant sentiment of the country." What the prelates of the twenties could not foresee, however, was that lay control over the finances of parishes all too easily led to attempts by the laity to exercise control over the appointment and dismissal of pastors as well. And this was a right that canon law vested solely in the bishops. Attempts by laymen in various parishes, northern and southern, to usurp this right would become one of the most vexing problems that faced the American bishops in the decades prior to the Civil War, and in some congregations around the country, notably at New Orleans, Charleston, Norfolk, and Buffalo, the conflicts resulted in open schisms that lasted several years.

One of the first great crises took place at St. Augustine. There in April, 1827, an important election took place in the Board of Wardens of the nation's oldest parish. An entirely new slate of wardens was chosen, and two men came forward who were to dominate the board's actions for several years to come. One, Pedro Benét, was 29 years old, a son of Estevan Benét (also variously spelled Baineto or Beneto in early documents), one of the original Minorcan colonists. Two distinguished descendants would come from this family, both named Stephen Vincent: the first, born in this same year of 1827, would rise to be Chief of Ordnance of the United States Army; the second, born 1898, died 1943, was the celebrated poet, novelist, and short story writer. With Pedro Benét was elected an ex-mayor of the city, Geronimo Alvarez. A strong personality and a man of proved executive ability, Alvarez enjoyed a considerable stature in the Catholic community. He had come to St. Augustine with Governor Zéspedes in 1784 as a baker for the troops. Later he had served as a member, and then the head, of the Spanish city council. It was he who had erected the obelisk still standing in the city's plaza to commemorate the abortive Spanish Constitution of 1812. Another Alvarez gift was the bell that still occupies the uppermost niche in the parish church façade. Warden Alvarez entered upon his new duties with an air of efficiency and authority. On April 8 he was unanimously elected president of the board. Only a year later, after the elections of April 21, 1828, Alvarez and Benét held all the board's offices between them. The two men took over direct administration of the houses and lots and orange groves left to the parish by Father O'Reilly, and they seem to have put them in better order than they had enjoyed in many years.

In the fall of 1828 news came from Charleston that Bishop England, acting again for Bishop Portier, had found a permanent pastor for St. Augustine, the first such regularly assigned priest for the city since the withdrawal of the Spanish clergy nearly a decade before. He was Father Edward Francis Mayne, born in County Antrim, Ireland, in 1802. As a youth he had come with his parents to Philadelphia, and he received his education at Mount St. Mary's Seminary in Emmitsburg, Maryland. Father Mayne was stationed at St. Augustine's Church at Philadelphia in 1827, but left for Charleston in the following year on the advice of his physician, who thought that the warmer climate would better suit the priest's fragile health. Mayne arrived at Charleston on November 26, 1828, and Bishop England sent him on by ship the next day to St. Augustine, where he arrived on the twenty-ninth and was courteously greeted by the wardens. During the days that followed, Father Mayne celebrated Mass, heard confessions, officiated at marriages, buried the dead, and otherwise settled peaceably into the round of spiritual duties to which he had been assigned. To most of the congregation the future of the parish looked bright. But if there were some who expected an eventual confrontation between the priest and Warden Alvarez, they were not long disappointed.

A funeral took place on January 5, 1829, from which date we can place the beginning of Father Mayne's troubles. The deceased was José M. Sanchez, a former treasurer of the Board of Wardens. The year before, he had defeated Geronimo Alvarez in a municipal election. Now, as the Sanchez funeral cortege was about to enter the parish church, Alvarez locked the doors and blocked its entrance. To Father Mayne's objections Alvarez answered with the assertion that Sanchez had been a member of the Free Masons, and as such was not entitled to Christian burial. Father Mayne proceeded with the burial at a graveside service, and the whole affair was scheduled to be discussed at the next meeting of the wardens, two days later. On that occasion Mayne condemned the action of the president, and stated that he would carry his complaints to the bishop if such an incident occurred again. Alvarez replied, with what was described in the minutes as "insulting expressions," that he would do the same again if ever the priest "should try to violate the church as he did in the funeral of José M. Sanchez, whose cortege bore insignia not corresponding to the religion. . . ." Father Mayne then stated that he had not come to that meeting to learn from Alvarez what were his obligations as a priest, or what were the proper insignia belonging to religion; he concluded by saying that he would not thereafter enter that church building until he was certain that he would not be molested in the performance of his spiritual duties.

The board was now plainly on the spot. The next day, January 8, its members asked Alvarez to give assurance that he would not interfere with Father Mayne, and to make an apology to the priest. Alvarez refused both requests. As a result, on the following day the board met again and passed a series of resolutions. It declared its deep regret at the "outrage" committed on January 5, and stated that its members were "without any power whatever in spiritual things or in the ceremonies of religion, where sole competence belongs to the clergy." The zeal, talent, and virtue of Father Mayne were noted and approved. Finally, the board resolved: "That Geronimo Alvarez, one of the members of this body, having opposed its deliberations, is considered from this day to be excluded from this board as a member."

There the matter might have ended had it not been for the political adroitness of Alvarez, and the reluctance of Antonio Triay, who was named on April 6 to replace him on the board. Triay, apparently, was a popular member of the Minorcan community, since in almost every election he was given a place on the board, from which he invariably resigned at the first opportunity. True to form, at the first meeting following his latest election Triay handed in his resignation. The popular support built up by the deposed Alvarez during many years of campaigning for municipal office now revealed itself in the voting for a replacement to Triay. Under the date June 14 the minutes recorded: "Conforming to the notice given, various persons of the Catholic congregation gathered, and, having proceeded to the election of a warden in the place of Antonio Triay, it resulted in Geronimo Alvarez being elected." Only two months later, on August 17, 1829, Alvarez was reinstalled as president! And at the first subsequent meeting, on August 31, a vindictive president directed the board's secretary to "write a letter to Father Edward Mayne making him understand that the Church is deeply in debt and cannot support any Minister because of lack of funds." Within the space of eight months the Mayne-Alvarez contest had come full circle, and Father Mayne was suddenly a priest without a parish.

Meanwhile Bishop Portier was in Rome reporting to the Congregation of Propaganda Fide on his far-flung responsibilities. The Catholic population of Florida was numbered by him at 4,000, that of Alabama at 3,000. On May 6, 1829, at Portier's urging, Rome elevated the Vicariate of Florida and Alabama to the dignity of a diocese, with an episcopal see at Mobile. Armed with new stature as Bishop of Mobile, and not aware that in his absence Bishop England had stationed Father Mayne as pastor of St. Augustine, Portier succeeded in recruiting a young French priest, Joseph Nicholas Bourdet, to serve in that post. He also found an assistant pastor in Frederick Rost, a German priest from Propaganda's Urban College in Rome. The two clerics sailed from Europe toward the close of the summer, and paused briefly at Bishop England's See of Charleston to give news of their appointments before proceeding on to St. Augustine. Bishop England wrote to the beleaguered Father Mayne to explain the situation, and as the bishop later remembered it, Mayne "immediately acquiesced, and though he remained in the place, assumed no powers, and did no duties but with the full approbation of the new incumbent Mr. Bourdet to whom he rendered every assistance." Bourdet had been designated by Portier to be vicar-general as well as pastor, but England, while acknowledging this, did not resign his own commission to act in that capacity. To England it must have seemed a fortunate coincidence, if not a divine retribution, that two priests should arrive for St. Augustine just as that city's lone pastor was declared *persona non grata*. This was "coals of fire," indeed! But what was to be the fate of Fathers Bourdet and Rost?

As it happened, the two new priests decided their own fates. Unaccountably the Church Wardens found funds with which to support the priests, and they entered without incident on their new labors. Bourdet, however, understood neither English nor Spanish, and conditions in the parish were such that he quickly became discouraged and returned to France in March, 1830. On his way through Charleston, Bourdet gave, as the *Miscellany* noted, "excellent testimonials in favour of Mr. Mayne." Father Rost succeeded to the office of pastor, but the latter's opinion of Father Mayne was not so generous, perhaps for the reason that Mayne enjoyed faculties directly from Bishop England, hence was not subject to Rost's jurisdiction. In all events, Rost sided with the wardens in their complaints against Mayne, and got himself so entangled in parochial intrigues that England was forced to revoke his faculties, acting under the vicarial powers that he had retained.

On May 2, 1830, the Board of Wardens learned by letter from Bishop England that Father Mayne had been appointed to supersede Rost as pastor. The wardens' reaction was instant and defiant. They answered that they did not recognize any authority in the Bishop of Charleston to make such an appointment. The board considered that the vicarial powers that had been given him by Bishop Portier had been revoked by the subsequent appointment of Father Bourdet as Vicar-General of East Florida. On the same day what the minutes called a "Public Meeting of the Majority of the members of the Roman Catholic Church" was held on the same subject, and a number of resolutions were adopted, among which were the following: "That the Revd. Mr. Mayne be notified . . . that he is not hereafter to interfere in any manner with the Curateship of this Parish. . . . That our Pastor the Revd. Mr. Rost be [sic] and continue to exercise his ecclesiastical functions within this Parish untill [sic] the Board shall receive orders to the contrary from the proper authority, the Bishop Mr. Portier." On May 9 the resolutions were transmitted to Father Mayne. The secretary was instructed that he was to have nothing more to do with the priest after his delivery of the message.

The wardens were not to have matters arranged as they would have liked, however. Father Rost suddenly departed the city sometime in the middle of May, sailing to New York, and thence to Cuba. Father Mayne was once again the sole priest in East Florida. Rost's departure was attended by regret among the Minorcan and other older families, whose part he had taken in the local squabbles. The newer and younger members of the congregation seem to have sided with Mayne, although that was little consolation to the latter, who was greatly saddened by the controversies, and, despite his worsening health, would have returned to Philadelphia had he not been urged to remain by Bishop England. All the while since the doors of the parish church had been closed to him, Mayne had celebrated Mass in a private home for those of the congregation who wished to attend, and he continued to do so now after Rost's departure. His hand was appreciably strengthened on June 5 with the arrival of a communication from Bishop Portier to the wardens confirming England's appointment of Mayne as pastor.

As late as December of the same year, however, the doors of the parish church were still locked against the pastor, and Mayne began to consider the advisability of seeking a solution through civil process. In this he was influenced by England, who had posed the possibility of a suit in a stinging letter to the wardens on August 24: "Gentlemen, this is not intended as a threat, God forbid it should be necessary to have recourse to lay tribunals for the purpose of religion. It is intended merely to convey to you my opinion that you are not only acting against the laws of the church and the principles of religion, if you persevere in excluding Mr. Mayne from the church, or in annoying him therein, but that you are . . . exposing yourselves to the consequences should any of the Catholics of St. Augustine determine to bring process against you for the violation of his rights." Why did the wardens, and many of the congregation, persist in their recalcitrance? It is hard today to find a satisfactory answer. It was hard even for Bishop England, who rehearsed the whole affair later in the *Miscellany* (December 17, 1831). The original culprit, England saw, was Geronimo Alvarez. "We are told," he wrote, "that the majority of the wardens disapproved of the conduct of this man, but were too supine to act against him. . . ." In a still later issue (April 28, 1832), after the wardens' resistance had finally broken down, England noted their curious admission that, "the opposition [to Father Mayne] was upon caprice and dislike, for which they could not account."

Whatever the reason, the wardens still guarded a locked church door as December came and the unhappy year neared its close. Abandoning hope of an amicable settlement of the dispute, Father Mayne finally appealed to the civil courts for a mandamus ordering the wardens to allow him entry into the church. The Board of Wardens at once secured the services of two attorneys to contest the action. Thus, what Bishop England had dreaded now came to pass, and it was left to a civil tribunal to decide whether the spiritual or the temporal should reign supreme in the Parish of St. Augustine. Not surprisingly, the courts were no less reluctant to see this turn of events, and delayed a hearing on the case as long as possible. Sometime before March 7, 1831, Father Mayne was awarded the mandamus that he sought, but on tenuous grounds, and the wardens'

(Right) *Bishop John England of Charleston.* (Below) *His letter of February 10, 1836, toward the start of the Seminole war, to the Wardens of the Church of St. Augustine stated that because of "the peculiar circumstances and extraordinary assemblage of military and others in and about your city," he was sending them a priest, Father John Barry, pastor of Augusta, Georgia, later Second Bishop of Savannah.*

JOHN ENGLAND,   **BY THE GRACE OF** GOD

AND WITH THE APPROBATION   OF THE HOLY APOSTOLIC SEE

PRO RELIGIONE

BISHOP OF CHARLESTON,

Vicar General of East Florida in the Diocess of Mobile

To all who may see these presents, health and blessing.

especially to the Wardens of the R. C Church of St Augustine—

Know ye, that by reason of the absence of your regular pastor, and the peculiar circumstances and extra-ordinary assemblage of military and others in and about your city, we have to our own great inconvenience and the bereaving of our own Diocess appointed the Reverend John Barry, Pastor of Augusta (Geo) to proceed to your city and to remain there and in its vicinity until the arrival of your pastor, unless sooner recalled by us, he is charged by us to give the aid of his ministry not only to you but to the troops that may need and desire the same; And we, having on a former occasion experienced your kindness and generosity to the Rev Philip Gillick, have been thereby the more encouraged to send you a clergyman on the present occasion in whom we have the greatest confidence trusting that he will receive from you every protection solace, and aid which his station may require. We also pray that God may protect and preserve you in happiness upon earth and bring you to glory in Heaven, through the merits of our Lord, Jesus Christ.—

Given at Charleston, (S. C.)

under our hand and Seal of our Diocess, on

this **tenth** day of **February**

in the year of our Lord, one thousand eight

hundred and thirty **six**

✠ John, Bishop of Charleston

By order of the Bishop,

R. S. Baker

SECRETARY.

(Upper) *The first church building of St. Mary Star of the Sea in Key West. Dedicated by Bishop Gartland of Savannah in 1852, the church stood on the west side of Duval Street, between Fleming and Eaton Streets.*

(Left) *Father William J. Hamilton, first pastor of the Church of the Immaculate Conception in Jacksonville and hero of Andersonville.*

attorneys immediately appealed for a reversal of the order. Another long delay ensued, as the courts hesitated again to make a final settlement of the matter.

On August 14 the wardens received a lengthy letter from Joseph L. Smith, Judge of the Superior Court, who explained his "serious reluctance to approach a subject, wherein I might be liable unintentionally to trespass on sacred rights of conscience and on spiritual things, which no secular judge has a right to do. . . ." He expressed surprise that Catholics should seek an ecclesiastical decision "from one who, according to your belief, is a heretic from the true faith." Reporting his first impressions of the division of authority between wardens and pastor, Smith stated: "I now find, as I anticipated, that the question is perplexed with difficulties, and involved in doubts, which to my mind, uninformed as I am of the prerogatives, rights and usages of the Roman Catholic Church, are serious causes for hesitation in passing a judgment upon it. The peculiar circumstances of your Church, situated in a Province lately transferred from the King of Spain, under whose authority it was erected and established, add, in my opinion, materially to these embarrassments. . . ." Smith urged the wardens to reconsider the whole matter and to reconcile the differences that led to the present impasse, or, at least, to submit the whole matter again to the bishop and abide by his award. Fearing that a decision by him would "rather be a brand of discord, than the seal of peace among you," he nonetheless advised that, all attempts at arbitration failing, he would "interpose and juridically decide the question submitted."

The wardens rejected Judge Smith's conciliatory letter and continued the case in court, where they entered a brief declaring: "That the church or church property cannot be appropriated to the use and support of a priest or pastor contrary to the will of the corporation of said church." Father Mayne, supported by Thomas Murphy, one of the newer members of the parish, countered with an affidavit stating that he had been duly appointed as pastor of the parish by Bishop England, and again later by Bishop Portier, and that he had been prevented by the wardens from exercising his parochial duties "for no just cause known to the deponent." Further arguments were heard on both sides, and Judge Smith handed down a decision in December, 1831. His opinion took an hour and a half to read, and at its conclusion, Father Mayne learned that he and his episcopal superiors had been handed a stunning defeat.

The court reasoned that the *jus patronatus* possessed by the Spanish crown and exercised "independently of the Pope or of the Bishops" was among the proprietary interests that were transferred to the United States at the time of cession, and that the new government had transferred all the rights in question to the Catholic congregation of St. Augustine, and not to any specified bishops or pastors. The common law of England, which had been adopted in Florida, also vested the right of presentation of pastors in the congregation, not in bishops or other spiritual rulers. And finally, by the common law that existed in the United States itself, the founders of churches possessed the right of deciding who should preside over their spiritual interests. Such were the reasons given by Judge Smith. News of them spread rapidly. The *Florida Herald* published at St. Augustine approved them as sound, and editorialized that the rights sought by Father Mayne could not be conceded to the ministers of any denomination, "without weakening the value of our free institutions." Bishop England, for his part, saw the dangers to free institutions in another light and coming from another direction entirely: "The decision," he wrote in the *Miscellany* soon after reading about it in the *Charleston Mercury*, "is totally at variance with the canon law of the Catholic Church, and . . . that church cannot continue to exist freely in any place where the tribunals of the country subvert the discipline which her canons enact."

A schism was now in full bloom. The wardens had repudiated their pastor and had defied their bishop. Now they had enlisted the sanction of the secular arm against the spiritual order. Bishop Portier realized that he had no alternative but to visit St. Augustine himself and speak to the rebels in language that they would understand. Accordingly, he left Mobile in January, 1832, accompanied by Jules Massip, a subdeacon preparing for the priesthood. He paused briefly at Charleston to discuss the schism with Bishop England, then took a schooner for St. Augustine, which he reached on February 14. The showdown between bishop and wardens did not come right away; several of the wardens were out of town, and Portier decided to put off the confrontation until all the board members were present. In the meantime he declined the wardens' offer to place the church at his disposal, and celebrated Mass in a private home instead. After two weeks the full Board of Wardens and the entire congregation met in solemn session with the bishop. Portier demanded to know the nature of the charges raised against their pastor, Father Mayne. He advised them that, unless their charges could be substantiated before his scrutiny, he was prepared to place that parish under interdict and to excommunicate the "authors, abettors, and promoters of the little schism."

The parishioners conceded to the bishop that there were no serious grounds for the accusations that had been brought against Father Mayne, and that opposition to him was based mostly upon simple dislike for the man. On the following day in another assembly the congregation voted by an overwhelming majority to instruct the wardens to submit to Portier unconditionally. Within twenty-four hours the wardens did so, acknowledged all the bishop's rights, and placed him in possession of the parish church. A reconciliation then followed before the altar. Portier reinstalled Mayne formally as pastor and vicar-general, a *Te Deum* was chanted, and on March 18 the bishop gave Communion to 120 persons and confirmed 130 others. The following resolutions were then agreed to and adopted by both bishop and people: that the church should never again be closed against a priest sent by diocesan authority; that in the case of any complaint against a priest, the decision of the bishop should be final; and that, thenceforth, the income of the parish should be given to the stewardship of the regularly appointed pastor. In Charleston a relieved Bishop England noted in the pages of the *Miscellany*, "the termination of this miserable and unfortunate little schism."

At Pensacola, also, wardens controlled the finances of the sole parish of that town, St. Michael's, but the church properties supplied very little income, and the wardens consequently never assumed the same importance as their counterparts at St. Augustine. St. Michael's grew hardly at all in the years from 1830 forward, and in that it reflected the troubles of the city which it served. Although Pensacola possessed one of the best harbors in the South, and was in an admirable position to benefit from coastwise commerce, it lacked the one geographic feature needed to insure rapid growth in Territorial days, namely, a navigable river connection with the interior. Commerce languished in the 1830's, and two other towns, Apalachicola and St. Joseph, soon loomed as formidable rivals for the Gulf trade. The number of Catholics in West Florida as a whole (the panhandle between the Suwannee and Perdido Rivers) was very small in these years—about 2000 in all—and they do not seem to have had any appreciable influence on the development of laws and culture in the frontier towns.

The Catholics of Pensacola were served from 1830 to 1832 by a Mexican priest, Canon Matías Monteagudo. Father Andrew Poujade, newly ordained from France, came to assist in the parish briefly during 1831. At the beginning of that year the old warehouse-church that had been used since Spanish times finally collapsed, and the congregation, though hindered by poverty, resolved to build a new one. Bishop Portier gave what assistance he could from funds disbursed by the Society for the Propagation of the Faith at Lyons. Just as the new structure neared completion, it was totally wrecked by a hurricane. A new start was made, and new and serious debts incurred. At last, by 1833, the building was successfully completed, and Pensacola Catholics had a suitable place of worship for the first time in their history. In the same year, Father John Symphorian Guinand, another newly ordained priest from France, was assigned to the church as permanent pastor.

In East Florida, St. Augustine was not the only town to see priests during these years. The much-harassed Father Mayne made several mission trips to the commercial and plantation villages that were sprouting along the St. Johns River and the Atlantic shore. Among these were Pilatka (Palatka), Jacksonville (the Cowford of English times), Pablo (Jacksonville Beach), and Fernandina. In April, 1832, Jules Massip was ordained at Charleston by Bishop England and sent to assist Mayne at St. Augustine and in the surrounding mission stations. A common school which Bishop Portier hopefully called the "beginning of a college" was organized at St. Augustine by the two priests, who worked together until March, 1833, when Massip was reassigned to north Alabama. Mayne himself seems to have done well in St. Augustine after 1832, save for one final, futile gesture on the part of the wardens to regain control over the right of presentation. Upon Massip's departure, Portier wrote the wardens to inform them that Mayne would continue alone in the parish. Under the date July 1, 1833, the wardens replied that they had been "invested by law with the right of designating the pastor," and that it was their respectful but unequivocal duty to declare that "the Rev. Mr. Mayne has never been received, considered, or presented by us as such pastor, and that it is our decided and deliberate determination, founded on mature reflection, and on an ardent and sincere desire to promote the best spiritual and temporal interests of this Church, *never* so to *present or receive him.*" Bishop Portier ignored this last gasp of bravado, and Mayne continued to function as pastor with no further obstacles, other than the burden of his lingering unpopularity. The resolute Irishman yielded only to death, which finally overcame his frail body on December 21, 1834, in the thirty-second year of his life. The *Miscellany* reported his passing, and added this consoling note: "His body was followed to the grave prepared for it in [St. Augustine] by a numerous and mourning train."

Bishop England was able to send Father Andrew Byrne of his diocese (later First Bishop of Little Rock) to reside at St. Augustine in January and February, 1835. In the latter month, England expressed surprise that Bishop Portier had not yet sent a priest to take Mayne's place. "His best city, St. Augustine, within a day's sail of me, is unprovided, though in it is a fine Church and property to support a priest. I have written to him that it is vacant and cannot get an answer." In August, still lacking any word from Portier, England sent another priest of his own diocese, Father Philip Gillick, to take charge of St. Augustine until October. When Gillick arrived, he found Portier's "best city" in a state of economic collapse. A freeze of extended duration during the previous February had destroyed St. Augustine's orange groves, the principal source of livelihood for many of the city's people. Another disaster followed closely on the heels of the freeze. In December, after Gillick's departure from the city, war broke out with the Seminole Indians. Plantations in the vicinity of St. Augustine were attacked and burned, and refugees arrived in the city with gory tales of Indian atrocities. On January 16, 1836, a number of Catholics in the city sent a desperate letter to the Bishop of Havana—unknown to them, the see was at that time under the charge of an administrator apostolic—declaring their "total ruin" and asking for financial assistance.

Seventy-five heads of families, all Spaniards and Minorcans by name, signed the letter, which read in part: "Since this poverty-stricken town was ceded to the United States, we have experienced nothing but ill fortune and disgraces. The severe freeze of the winter just past destroyed entirely our abundant orange groves, the produce of which was the only resource that some of us possessed. . . . In this general disgrace, our church has been affected, as it has suffered the loss of approximately 400 pesos annually, which was the only source of income that it possessed. . . . And on top of our ruin and everything, we find ourselves under arms day and night protecting our lives and homes against the Indian savages that have revolted in a body against the government, burning and committing all kinds of hostilities, plunder, and murder in the countryside, and even to the very limits of the city. . . ." It is not recorded that this appeal met with any success in Cuba. As usual, it was the solicitous Bishop England who proved to be the parish's best friend. In February, England sent another priest of his diocese to care temporarily for the distressed congregation and for the federal troops who were now garrisoned in the city to protect it against rampaging Seminoles. The priest was Father John Barry, pastor of Holy Trinity Church in Augusta, Georgia, and future Second Bishop of Savannah (1857-1859). After Barry's departure in the following spring, Bishop Portier finally decided to send another permanent pastor, Father Claude M. Rampon, a French recruit ordained in 1832. Rampon arrived in the summer of 1836. He would stay for seven years—the longest reign of any pastor since Spanish times, and certainly the calmest. During his tenure the Board of Wardens, now bereft of its incomes, became quiescent. Father Ram-

pon went the round of his duties unhindered in his actions and undisputed in his authority. For a time, he had the help of a newly
ordained priest from Charleston, Father Patrick Hackett. New mission stations were established at Black Creek (Middleburg), Mandarin, St. Johns Bar, Picolata, and as far away as Tampa. (From
1840 to 1841 the mission at Jacksonville was looked after by
Father Andrew Doyle, pastor of St. Marys, Georgia.) In St. Augustine itself the faith of the people waxed strong once more, and the
long-dampered spiritual life of the nation's first parish took fire and
began to glow again as it had in the best years under Spain. Numerous families enrolled their boys in the parish school. By 1843, the
year of Father Rampon's departure from the city, the parishioners
had become so assiduous in the practice of their faith that even
the prejudiced visitor to the city, such as a young Protestant from
New York, Henry Benjamin Whipple, future Episcopal Bishop of
Minnesota, found his bias against Roman Catholicism yielding ever
so slightly in the face of their example. The Catholics of the city,
Whipple recorded in his diary, worship in a church "with one of
the most quaint looking fronts I have ever seen . . . & nothing can
equal their strict attendance upon the ordinances of their religion.
They put to shame too often the less rigid followers of a pure religion. Would their quiet zeal and devoted lives were spent in
spreading the glorious gospel of Christ unshackled by monkish superstitions" (!)

In 1844 Bishop Portier placed the Parish of St. Augustine and
the missions of East Florida in the charge of two French Fathers
of Mercy, Benedict Madeore and Edmond Aubril, who were seeking assignments after their Order had given up an attempt to man-
age Portier's Spring Hill College near Mobile. Father Madeore,
the older of the two, was appointed pastor of St. Augustine and
Vicar-General of East Florida; Father Aubril took up residence on
Amelia Island, at the northernmost point of East Florida. Small
mission churches were soon afterwards built at Fernandina, Jacksonville, Mandarin, and Black Creek. Meanwhile at the extreme
southern end of the peninsula, on the island of Key West, a small
Catholic colony was forming around the Mallory family.
Stephen R. Mallory, an Episcopalian, and his Catholic wife Ellen

had settled there in 1820, and Mallory had died shortly after their arrival. His widow raised their son, Stephen Russell Mallory, in the Catholic faith. The youth was educated at Spring Hill College and served later as United States Senator from Florida, and, during the Civil War, as Secretary of the Navy in the Confederacy. In 1845 Bishop Portier recognized the need for a church and priest on the island, which, owing to the presence of a federal military installation, now counted an unusual number of Catholics. The next year, he was able to send Father Peter Corcoran, an Irishman in the first year of his priesthood, who remained on the island for several years.

On July 4, 1845, Florida was admitted to the Union. The young city of Tallahassee, which had served since 1824 as a compromise Territorial capital between the major East and West Florida population centers, now graduated to the status of capital of the nation's twenty-seventh state. In St. Augustine, the old seat of government in Spanish days, the advent of statehood produced little rejoicing. As the *Pensacola Gazette* had complained five years before, "Instead of rejoicing in the prosperity and increasing population of Florida, and the near approach of that day when she may assume the position of an independent state—St. Augustine sighs for the return of those days when she was all of Florida, and all of Florida was comprised in her." Another reason for St. Augustine's uneasiness at this time was the realization by her large Catholic community (probably two-thirds of the total population) that the city was an island of Catholicism in a spreading sea of Protestantism. Figures compiled five years later, in 1850, reveal that at that time there were 170 Protestant churches in the state as compared with 5 Catholic churches (only one a parish), and that Protestant property valuation exceeded the Catholic by $151,800 to $13,600. Fortunately for the Catholics, however, the continuing migration of southern planters and yeomen to Florida brought with it no overt hostility to Catholics, and even the American Party, the politically organized nativists of Florida, showed little more than the usual Protestant suspicion of the Church, and it never made Catholicism an issue. Only one instance of friction can be found during these years, and it was precipitated by a non-Floridian.

In the summer of 1848 a Presbyterian minister from Philadelphia, Rufus K. Sewall, published a small book, *Sketches of St. Augustine,* in which he referred to the Catholic Minorcans there as being "of servile extraction." He added: "They lack enterprise. Most of them are without education." When the book appeared in St. Augustine, on October 21, 1848, the page containing the derogatory sentences was ripped from almost every copy before sale was permitted. When the author, who was in town, protested, a mob of Minorcans gathered in front of his house and threatened to do him personal injury. Sewall managed to engineer his escape with the help of a band of Protestant "Anglo-American citizens," who exchanged blows with the Minorcans in the street. A few injuries and minor property damage resulted. The incident was over almost as soon as it began, and it was the only one of its kind to occur in Florida. Even at the height of the nativist movement in the 1850's, when the so-called "Know-Nothing" movement was spreading anti-Catholic venom in the northern states, Florida nativists held themselves apart from that bigotry. An American Party meeting at Quincy on September 8, 1855, adopted a resolution typical of those voted for elsewhere in Florida at the grassroots level: "We do not entertain the opinion that Roman Catholicism or any other religious creed must necessarily convert a native born American into a Benedict Arnold."

In 1848 the Catholic congregation of the city petitioned Congress for redress of certain grievances dating from the year 1821, when Florida became a United States possession. The Church Wardens demanded restitution (in realty or equity) of three properties once occupied and used by Catholics in the city. These were the hermitage of Nuestra Señora de la Leche (on the mission site, Nombre de Dios, north of the city gate); the "old Episcopal church lot," or "bishop's house" (on the southeast corner of King and St. George Streets); and the Franciscan convent of the Immaculate Conception (at the south end of the city). In 1848 the hermitage was being used as farmland; the "Episcopal church lot" was in the hands of the Episcopalians; and the Franciscan convent was in use as a military barracks, as it had been since the British occupation. The wardens claimed these properties for themselves in their

153

capacity as the legally incorporated trustees of the parish, and thus the legally recognized successors to the Florida church of Spanish times. Father Madeore, pastor and vicar-general, immediately countered the wardens' claim with one of his own, as representative of the bishop, in whose name, under canon law, church property was generally held.

The two claims were similar in the arguments that they adduced. Both rested fundamentally on the assertion that the properties in question were possessed by the Catholic Church for many years prior to the cession of Florida to the United States, and that the favors of the patronato real, or royal patronage, accorded Spain by the Holy See were given in order to secure the rights of the Church in the new world, and not in contravention of those rights. Differences came in the manner in which the Church's prior ownership was expressed. Father Madeore argued that the properties were owned by the ruling Spanish bishop, as a corporation sole. The wardens avoided a direct opinion of the precise mode of ownership, but by stressing their present legal control over the church building itself, they left the implication that it was the parishioners, not the bishops, who owned property in Spanish times. The wardens were particularly incensed over the manner in which La Leche had been given "on simple application" to a Protestant resident, and over the disposition of the "old Episcopal church lot," which they described in this fashion: "In 1821, it had the fate of all the other property belonging to the Catholics, and in 1822 or 3, the Episcopalian congregation built a church on a part of that lot, and claimed the balance as their own, stating that it was the site of the ancient Episcopal church, and Congress granted it to them."

Father Madeore's brief was the more knowledgeable and competent of the two. He argued that the right of the Church to retain and hold property designated for religious purposes was a counterpart to the freedom of worship guaranteed to the Catholic citizens of Florida by the United States at the time of cession. The properties in question, Madeore said, were delivered to the new government by oversight as public property, and Spain had no more right to give the properties than the United States had to receive them, since the Church held property independently of any civil power.

In support of this last assertion, he produced citations from ecclesiastical history and canon law, documents from various Spanish
archives relating to the Florida church, and testimonials from the
Minister Plenipotentiary of Spain and from an attorney of the
Spanish royal council at Havana. He stated in conclusion: "Our
constitution gives no right to Congress to legislate on church matters, so that here all denominations necessarily stand in the same
light; every one of them is allowed to make her regulations concerning the management of her funds, and, provided they do nothing
against the law of the country, the government never interferes
with them. We hope that no exception will be made for us, who
are directed by a law as ancient as our Church."

Under a joint resolution of Congress dated August 11, 1848,
and with the approval of President James K. Polk, the questions
arising from these claims were submitted to arbitration. Both parties,
the United States as owner, and Father Madeore and the Church
Wardens jointly as claimants, agreed on Stephen R. Mallory, then
a Key West attorney, as arbitrator. Accordingly, the Catholic Mallory visited St. Augustine and Havana in September, October, and
November, examined the archives of Spanish East Florida, and took
the depositions of a "great number" of persons. "It would appear
somewhat surprising," Mallory wrote, "that but little is known relative the oldest religious establishment in the Floridas, and one of
the oldest in the new world; and one, too, that must have exercised so decided an influence upon the civilization and settlement
of the country, were we not aware of the fact that portions of the
records of the Floridas, have at various times been lost or destroyed." Still, he was able to accumulate sufficient evidence on
which to base a decision, which he rendered on January 27, 1849.

Mallory found that the original owner of the three properties
in question was the Spanish Crown. Under the privilege of the patronato real the Crown acquired and held these properties in its
own name, and had the right to dispose of them without ecclesiastical approbation. In 1763, when Florida was ceded to England, the
Crown chose to convey these as public properties to the new British government (despite a local effort to block the conveyance
through a private sale of the three properties in trust to John Gor-

don and Jesse Fish), and they were transferred back to Spain under the same title at the time of retrocession in 1783. At neither date did the Holy See or the ruling bishop interpose any objections to the manner in which the properties were transferred. Furthermore, Mallory found no proof that the contested properties were included in the private properties which Spain directed should be returned to their rightful owners by a royal decree of 1791. Although the arbitrator granted the contention of Father Madeore that in certain documented instances, the Church in Florida did hold property independently of the crown (e.g., thirty-one and a half acres of land at Esperanza, a subdivision of St. Augustine), these were exceptions to the general rule and did not apply to the properties in question. The Church, he said, had been unaccountably silent since 1783 in claiming her own property, if indeed it was hers to claim, and now any clouds on the title of the United States to these properties seemed to have been removed by prescription.

As for the parish church, here Mallory conceded that for the United States to assert ownership over that building would be to frustrate the guarantees of religious freedom included in the treaty of transfer in 1819. In this instance, the arbitrator said, it must surely have been an oversight that Spain, after solemnly securing for her people in Florida the "free exercise of their religion," should then "deprive them of the very temples and altars essential to the performance of many of these exercises." The matter must be considered, he said, "as if no such transfer had ever been made." He then confirmed the congregation and the Church Wardens in their ownership of the building, which had been granted earlier by Acts of Congress in 1827 and 1832. Thus, as a result of the arbitrator's labors—and Mallory confessed that "I would have been pleased if they had conducted me to a different conclusion"—nothing changed at St. Augustine: no real estate bonanza came into the congregation's hands, and no progress was achieved by the clergy in their long struggle to regain control from the wardens over administration of the parish.

Three important names were associated with St. Augustine's Catholic community at mid-century. The first two names belonged to native sons, residents of the city until their early teens. Anthony Dominic Pellicer (1824-1880) and Dominic Manucy (1823-1885) were first cousins. Their grandfather, Francisco Pellicer, had led the Minorcans from New Smyrna to St. Augustine in 1777. By a strange series of coincidences, their careers were linked together throughout most of their lives. In 1837, at the urging of their pastor, Father Rampon, the two youths entered Spring Hill College. They were ordained together to the priesthood for the Diocese of Mobile on August 15, 1850, by Bishop Portier, and twenty-four years later, on December 8, 1874, the two St. Augustine natives were consecrated bishops together at Mobile by Archbishop Napoléon Joseph Perché, of New Orleans. Both were first appointed to Texas, Bishop Pellicer to the Diocese of San Antonio, Bishop Manucy to the Vicariate of Brownsville; Manucy was elevated afterwards (1884) to the Diocese of Mobile. Their deaths came five years apart.

The third distinguished name associated with St. Augustine belonged to a Cuban priest, Félix Francisco José María de la Concepción Varela y Morales. Father Varela was born in Havana in 1788. When six years old, he was taken to St. Augustine by his father, a captain in the Cuban regiment stationed there. Later, he was given to the care of his maternal grandfather, Don Bartolomé de Morales, who commanded the troops of the St. Augustine garrison. He was taken back to Havana at fourteen to complete his education, and in 1811 was ordained to the priesthood. Subsequently he was appointed professor of philosophy, law, and science at the episcopal college of San Carlos, where his lectures attracted a wide following. In 1821 Varela was elected one of three Cuban representatives to the Spanish Cortes, or parliament. His advocacy of Cuban rights in that body angered Spanish King Ferdinand VII. In 1823 French armies aided Ferdinand in overthrowing the Cortes, and Varela and the other members of the assembly were driven into exile. The priest arrived in New York on December 17, 1823, and not long afterwards was named pastor of the Church of the Transfiguration and vicar-general of the Diocese of New York. His writings and other scholarly attainments quickly established him here as a national Catholic figure. During the course of the next thirty years, Father

Varela frequently visited St. Augustine, the home of his youth. In 1850 ill health forced him to retire there, where he assisted the priests of the parish until his death on February 25, 1853. He was buried at Tolomato Cemetery on the following day. One month later a commemorative service was held, at which Father James H. O'Neill of Savannah preached the sermon, and Don José María Casal, Cuban scholar and disciple of Varela, gave a eulogy in Spanish. Two years later Cuban admirers erected a mortuary chapel to enclose his remains. In 1911 the remains were removed to Cuba and enshrined in a monument that acclaimed the patriot-priest as a national hero.

Bishop England, Catholic Florida's long-time friend, had died in 1842, and had been succeeded at Charleston by Bishop Ignatius A. Reynolds. The latter seems not to have had much interest in Florida, and peninsular Catholics lived out the rest of the decade under the sole care of Bishop Portier. Then in 1850 the state of Florida east of the Apalachicola River was transferred from the Diocese of Mobile to a newly erected Diocese of Savannah, and Francis X. Gartland, vicar-general of the Diocese of Philadelphia, was consecrated for the new see, on November 10 of that year. No one greeted this news with more enthusiasm than Michael Portier at Mobile: the remote reaches of Florida had too long given his diocese a grotesque shape, and made it difficult for him to maintain contact with such areas as the extreme south end of the peninsula. Bishop Gartland had much the same problem, since his new diocese comprised all of Georgia as well as most of Florida. Yet Gartland was more sanguine about the chances of doing something for south Florida, and soon after taking canonical possession of Savannah, he gave his attention to the needs of the Catholic community at Key West. Father John F. Kirby was sent to the island from Savannah early in 1851, and within a year's time the priest built a parish church on the west side of Duval Street, between Fleming and Eaton Streets. Bishop Gartland came from Savannah to dedicate the building on February 28, 1852. It marked the first time a bishop had visited the Keys. Because the boundaries of the parish were formed by the Atlantic Ocean and the Gulf of Mexico,

Gartland dedicated the church under the title Saint Mary Star of the Sea.

The total population of Key West at the time was about 2,000; of this number some 300 were Catholics. During the bishop's stay he confirmed two groups of children, on February 9 and March 14, and from the records of the ceremonies we learn some of the Catholic names on the island: Mallory, Wall, Baldwin, Gunn, Alderslade, Bowyer, Gandolfo, Whatton, Fagan, Cook, Mead, Clark, English, Logan, Mulherin, Madden, Noonan, Driscoll, Connell, Savelli, Haley, and Grillon. The presence of Negro Catholics—most of them slaves—was also noted at this time. The Negroes occupied a separate section of pews in the church during Mass and other services. (This was also the practice at St. Augustine, Pensacola, and the various mission churches of the state.) Father Kirby was recalled to Savannah in November, 1852, and Father Joseph N. Brogard was sent to replace him. The new pastor was given charge over the Catholics of Tampa and Tallahassee as well—a feat made possible by the Gulf Coast schooner traffic. Father James H. O'Neill took over the parish in 1853, and he was followed by Fathers Edward Quigley (1854), Edward Murphy (1855), John Barry (1855), Kirby and Clemens C. Prendergast (1856), and Barry (1856-1857). Under the Diocese of Savannah, Key West saw more different priests than any other community in Florida, including that part of the state that lay west of the Apalachicola and remained under the Diocese of Mobile. Bishop Gartland died on September 20, 1854, and Father John Barry served as administrator of the diocese, *sede vacante*, from 1855 to 1857. In the latter year, on January 9, Barry was elected Second Bishop of Savannah. He was consecrated on the following August 2, and shortly afterwards, accompanied by Father Prendergast of Savannah and Father Aubril of the St. Augustine missions, he journeyed by ship to Key West, where he conferred Confirmation on a small group of children and appointed Aubril to remain temporarily as pastor.

Father Madeore remained at St. Augustine, where parochial life, like that of the city itself, proceeded during most of the 1850's at a business-like, uneventful pace. Neither the parish nor the city showed any marked growth. Although Father Madeore had the care of several outlying missions as well as St. Augustine itself, he found leisure to pursue his academic interests, and in 1856 he became one of the founding members of the Florida Historical Society. Father James H. O'Neill of Savannah was a frequent visitor to the city. In 1853 O'Neill wrote a melancholy letter to a Sister of Mercy in Savannah about the "monuments—though in ruins—of our holy faith" that he had found in St. Augustine. Of one such monument, he wrote: "The old Franciscan convent facing a beautiful beach which confines a lovely bay, is seen in the skirts of the old city. The remains of the chapel and choir can be traced by a discerning eye. That once sacred building is now a military barrack, the choir a banquetting hall, the once silent dormitories of the monks a sleeping place for soldiers, and the belfry whence sounded the call for mattins [*sic*] has given way to the American flagstaff. Attached to the premises are extensive lots with orange groves, which in days long gone by were a source of revenue to the original owners. This is the property wh[ich] Rev. Mr. Madiore [*sic*] labored so long to get back, or its equivalent, from the government, for the benefit of the church of St. Augustine, but which he failed to obtain."

At Jacksonville, thirty-five miles to the north, a lot for a church had been purchased sometime in the 1840's—the records of the sale are lacking—from Isaiah D. Hart, founder of the city. The property stood at the northwest corner of Duval and Newnan Streets. Father Aubril built a small church on the site sometime before 1847, when it appeared on a map of the city. A frame structure, it was dedicated under the title, Church of the Immaculate Conception (of the Blessed Virgin Mary), thus anticipating the definition of that dogma as an Article of Faith by Pope Pius IX in 1854. Over the altar Father Aubril placed a large painting of Mary that had been presented to the church by the French government. The circumstances of the gift are not recorded. In 1857 the church was formally erected into a parish, and Father William J. Hamilton was appointed as first pastor. Born in Ireland and educated at All Hallows College at Dublin, Father Hamilton had been ordained there by dispensation before he reached his twenty-fourth year, the minimum age under canon law. Soon afterwards

Mother Marie Sidonie Rascle, superior of the first group of Sisters of St. Joseph to arrive in Florida from Le Puy, France, in 1866.

Bishop Augustin Verot, Vicar Apostolic of Florida (1858-1870) and First Bishop of St. Augustine (1870-1876).

Father Peter Dufau, French-born Florida missionary and vicar-general of Bishop Verot.

Father Henry Peter Clavreul, long-time Florida missionary, recruited by Bishop Verot in 1859.

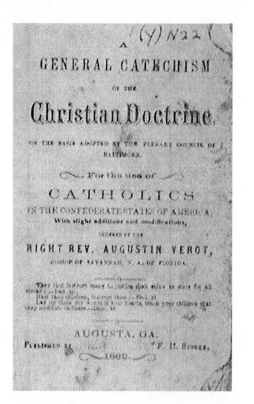

Catechism published by Bishop Verot for Catholics in the Confederacy during the Civil War. The text gave a summary of Catholic teaching in question-and-answer form and made no mention of the war.

In the 1860's the sacristan of th. Church of St. Augustine rang th church bells by hitting them with hammer. The oldest bell was cast 1682.

Civil War engraving shows Union occupation troops in formation before the parish church of St. Augustine shortly after capture of the city in 1862.

he came to this country to serve in the Diocese of Savannah. Under his care the pioneer parish of Jacksonville was soon self-supporting, and showing signs of growth. Another and larger church would be necessary only four years later.

Catholics in Florida's capital city of Tallahassee had a small church as early as 1846, named in honor of the Sorrowful Mother. Mass was celebrated there occasionally by priests from St. Augustine or Apalachicola. In January, 1847, the church was destroyed by fire, and the local newspaper, the *Sentinel,* commiserated: "The church just destroyed was a more than ordinary achievement of the handful of Catholics in Tallahassee. They are few and generally poor. The building was of brick, neatly stuccoed and beautifully finished throughout. . . . We are sorry to learn that a small debt yet remains to be paid." In 1853 the congregation was able to begin construction of a second church on the site of the first. It was completed in the following year and named St. Mary's, although it was not formally dedicated as such. By 1857 this second building was in a dilapidated state, and the city still did not have a resident priest.

In the western reaches of the panhandle, where Bishop Portier still ruled, Pensacola continued to be the leading Catholic settlement. Although the 1,500 Catholics found in St. Michael's Parish in 1850 showed no growth over the same number reported to Rome in 1828, there was a substantial increase during the following year, owing to the presence of a naval yard at Warrington, a suburb to the southwest of the city. The installation drew enough Catholics to that vicinity in 1851 to permit the founding of a separate parish, St. John the Evangelist, to which the young Father Dominic Manucy was assigned as first pastor. Catholics were not sufficiently numerous in Apalachicola to justify a resident priest until 1853. Prior to that date the Catholics of the one-time boomtown, now a cotton export center, were visited by priests from Mobile and Columbus, Georgia. In 1851 Father Patrick J. Coffey, of Columbus, persuaded the Catholic families to form themselves into a parish, called St. Patrick's. A board of trustees was organized and Father Coffey began construction of a church. Bishop Portier blessed the cornerstone in May, 1851, and despite damages suffered

161

in a hurricane of that summer, the building was ready for use in the middle of 1852. Father Manucy moved from Warrington to take up pastoral duties there in 1853, and two years later, in 1855, he persuaded the trustees to dissolve their body and to invest Bishop Portier and his successors in office with authority as the sole trustees of all ecclesiastical property.

Thus, St. Augustine and Pensacola remained the only Catholic parishes in Florida under lay trustee administration, and in both places the system was weakening as, on the one hand, parochial properties produced less and less revenue, and on the other, Florida's two bishops strengthened their control over parish activities. By 1857 it was clear that a bishop actually residing in Florida could successfully force the issue, separate Church from State, and bring the last stages of lay trusteeism to a close. By that year it was also clear that Florida needed a resident bishop for other reasons as well.

X

War and Reconstruction

1858-1870

LTHOUGH THE CHURCH in the Florida panhandle west of the Apalachicola was adequately governed by the nearby episcopal See of Mobile, by 1857 it was clear that the greater part of Florida, the peninsula proper, was too large an ecclesiastical district to permit efficient control by a see as distant as Savannah. Not only did the material state of the Florida Church suffer, but spiritual fervor lagged as well, and the obedience given by the people to ecclesiastical laws and counsels was less than the norm. The Mother Church of the nation needed nothing so much as a bishop of her own. Recognizing this, the Holy See at Rome in 1857 erected Florida east of the Apalachicola into a Vicariate Apostolic. As a vicariate, Florida was separated from the Diocese of Savannah and given a more or less independent character, although it remained a missionary district under the final supervision of the Congregation of Propaganda Fide. Florida was in a position at last to receive a resident bishop with powers and faculties roughly the same as those possessed by bishops in dioceses. On March 7, 1857, the new vicariate was offered by Rome to Francis Patrick McFarland, a priest of the Diocese of Albany in New York. McFarland declined the honor only to be appointed Bishop of Hartford the following year. On February 1, 1858, a letter from Archbishop Francis Patrick Kenrick of Baltimore arrived at the rectory of St. Paul's Church in the modest village of Ellicott's City, Maryland, where it was opened by the pastor, Father Augustin Verot. The letter read: "I feel great pleasure in informing you that the Bulls of your appointment to the Vicariate of Florida are in my possession. The Cardinal Prefect of the Congregation of the Propagation of the Faith urges dispatch. I trust that you will recognize the divine will in this matter."

Jean-Pierre Augustin Marcellin Vérot was born in Le Puy, France, on May 23, 1805. He studied for the priesthood under priests of the Society of St. Sulpice at Issy, outside Paris, and joined the Society after his ordination on September 20, 1828. In 1830 young Father Verot came to this country to teach in St. Mary's College conducted by the Sulpician Fathers at Baltimore, Maryland. For twenty-two years he served there as a professor of mathematics and the physical sciences, and gained for himself a distinguished name in several of the fields in which he specialized. Verot was not altogether happy as a teacher, however, and in 1852, when the college closed its doors, he asked permission from his Sulpician superiors in Paris to undertake pastoral work at nearby St. Paul's Church in Ellicott's City, with its missions at Sykesville, Clarksville, and Doughoregan Manor. His success as a pastor soon rivaled his reputation as a teacher, and with the work he found a contentment that he had never enjoyed before. To a colleague in Paris he wrote in 1854 that he was "very happy and busy in good works, above all for the poor Negroes." His letters for the next three years expressed the same themes. It was, then, with full hope of spending the rest of his life at Ellicott's City that Father Verot opened the mail on February 1, 1858.

The news struck him, he said, "like a bolt of thunder." He used every available excuse to refuse the appointment to Florida. He wanted to live and die a Sulpician, he said—accepting the episcopacy meant resigning from the Society—he felt that he was doing good enough in his present post; at fifty-three he was getting old; he had lost all his upper teeth and the tympanum of his right ear was torn. And besides all that, "The heat bothers me terribly here during the month of July, when I have some difficulty in handling my affairs. What will it be like in Florida?" Archbishop Kenrick and Verot's superiors in Paris prevailed, however, and the reluctant bishop received the mitre and the powers of his office in April 25 in an elaborate ceremony at the Cathedral of Baltimore. On the twenty-second of the following month, accompanied by Father Madeore who had come up from St. Augustine, Bishop Verot left for Florida and a new life. The words of his parishioners on the wharf at Baltimore followed after his southbound vessel: "Go forth out of thy country, and from thy kindred, and out of thy father's house, and come into the land which I shall shew thee" (Genesis 12:1).

It was a happy throng that gathered on another wharf, at St. Augustine, on the evening of June 1. Things had gone well for the "Ancient City" as the century neared its median. The city had become a celebrated tourist resort, and two new hotels, the Magnolia House and the Florida House, were drawing large numbers of invalids and wealthy northerners to luxuriate in the sunshine and Old World atmosphere. The city's 952 white and 376 Negro Catholics were sharing in the new-found prosperity, the former a great deal more than the latter, of course. Now as the Spanish bells in the belfry of the parish church sounded the arrival of Florida's first bishop, the general rejoicing seemed to presage a new age for the peninsular Church. A correspondent for the *Catholic Mirror* of Baltimore wrote: "Men, women, and children, white and colored, old and young, all joyfully flocked toward the church to see the Bishop and kiss his ring, the emblem of the solemn covenant which he has made with the Church in Florida."

Bishop Verot was formally installed in his vicariate by Bishop John Barry of Savannah, and immediately afterwards he set out to learn as much as he could about the country and the people he had come to serve. "The country is poor," he wrote Archbishop Kenrick, "& the people are not like the North, fond of giving to the

Church, even out of their poverty." Doubtless Verot had learned of
the reluctance of St. Augustine's Catholics to support the priests
sent to them by Bishops England and Portier. And certainly he
learned from study and investigation how far the fortunes of the
Church had fallen since Spanish days, for on the occasion of his
first pastoral letter, dated August 28, he addressed these melancholy
words to his people: "Over an immense region including more than
six degrees of latitude we have but three clergymen, but three missionaries to act as the co-operators of our ministry. How strange!
How desolating is this statement for such a country as Florida . . .
Florida which bears almost everywhere marks, remembrances and
tokens of its Catholic institutions—Florida which two hundred
years ago possessed so many convents, in which men were trained
in study and austerity for the labor of evangelizing the poor and
the ignorant—Florida which abounded with devoted and self-deny-
ing missionaries who had set at nought everything that the world
holds dear, for the sake of diffusing the light of heaven among
those who were sitting in the shadow of death—Florida which has
been bedewed in the East and the West, in the North and in the
South with the purest blood of martyrs! O the dreadful effect of
human vicissitudes! O the desolating proof of the instability of
every thing here below!"

In early 1859 Verot called together the Church Wardens and
117 members of the congregation of St. Augustine and announced
that he desired to have them "lease the Parochial Church and Burying Ground, all other property real and personal belonging to said
Church and also resign and depute the right of presentation or appointment of Pastor, and management of the said Church, and said
property unto Augustin Verot, Roman Catholic Bishop of Florida,
and his successors in office. . . ." The congregation complied without an argument. An era had come to an end. With the filing of
the deed in Circuit Court on February 20, the lay-trustee system
at St. Augustine receded into history, and with it, the last faint
traces of the Spanish patronato real. The two priests in the parish,
Fathers Madeore and Aubril, were confirmed in their authority
over the church, and the Board of Church Wardens, long quiescent,
now disappeared finally as a public body. (The board would not

foregather again until March 28, 1943, when at the request of Bishop Joseph P. Hurley, and by their own unanimous consent, they conveyed in perpetuity all properties possessed in their name to Bishop Hurley and his successors in office.)

Verot now made a swing around the state to examine the few resources, mostly small mission chapels, that belonged to the vicariate elsewhere. Jacksonville boasted both a parish church, named in honor of the Immaculate Conception, and a pastor, Father William J. Hamilton. The mission at nearby Black Creek (Middleburg) was visited from Jacksonville, but the other missions of northeast Florida were visited from St. Augustine: Old Town (Fernandina), St. Johns Bar (Mayport), Mandarin, Palatka, and Ocala. Fathers Madeore and Aubril also had to care for Tallahassee, which was reached by a long and arduous overland trip. Coastal schooners enabled the two priests to visit the Church of St. Mary Star of the Sea at Key West, which was without a pastor at this time, and new missions at Tortugas Island, Fort Myers, and Tampa. The *Catholic Mirror* correspondent wrote: "The Bishop stated the regret and inexpressible grief he had felt on being unable to grant a resident pastor to many places which asked for one with such earnestness, such as Key-West, Tampa, and Tallahassee."

On May 14, 1859, Verot sailed for France—his first visit home in twenty-nine years—in order to seek priests for the vicariate. In Le Puy, Paris, and several other places in his native country he succeeded in recruiting seven secular priests. Their anglicized names were: Peter Dufau, Henry Peter Clavreul, Emile Hillaire, Charles A. Mailley, John Bernard Aulance, John Francis R. Chambon, and Silvain Joseph Hunincq. All except Father Clavreul accompanied the bishop on his return to Florida in October; Clavreul followed a year later. The bishop personally instructed the priests in the English language, and with such success that three of them were preaching at St. Augustine three months later. After being satisfied that they could handle themselves in the Florida countryside, Verot assigned them to the mission chapels. Father Hillaire was stationed at Old Town (Fernandina); Father Chambon at the Church of St. Joseph in Josephstown, the settlement of Mandarin; Father Dufau at St. Peter's Church, Tallahassee; Father Mailley at the

Church of St. Louis, Tampa; and Father Hunincq at St. Mary Star of the Sea, Key West (where that young priest would soon lose his life in the yellow fever epidemic of 1862). At St. Augustine Father Aulance was assigned as assistant to Father Aubril, who had succeeded Father Madeore as pastor and vicar-general of the vicariate after the latter was recalled to France by his Order in 1859. New mission stations were now established in the areas where there were resident priests. Moccasin Branch, Pellicer's Creek, and Roger's Settlement were added to the responsibilities of St. Augustine. Samsonville (Samson) and Diego (Palm Valley) were attended from Josephstown. Amelia Island was given to the care of Old Town, as also were Starke, Gainesville, and Newnansville which lay along the route of the Florida Transit Railroad from Fernandina to Cedar Key. Monticello, St. Mark, and Newport were now visited from Tallahassee. Cedar Key and Manatee were served from Tampa. Miami, at the southern extremity of the east coast, was only sparsely settled, but in 1860 Bishop Verot observed in a report to *The Metropolitan Catholic Almanac and Laity's Directory* that: "This is a post where the few Indians left in Florida can be visited by the missionary. It is believed that they show a preference for the Catholic worship, as they have lately rejected the teachings of a Methodist preacher. Efforts will be made to visit them soon from Key West."

In 1859 Bishop Verot succeeded also in recruiting five sisters of the Order of Mercy from the Diocese of Hartford in Connecticut and three Christian Brothers from Canada to open, respectively, a girls' academy and a boys' day school. The schools got under way in modest quarters in early 1860, but unexpectedly met some civic resistance. The local St. Augustine *Examiner* charged: "The moment our schools erect fortifications of *sect* and *ism* around them, from that moment, we honestly believe, they strike the first blow at their own ruin." But two visiting American prelates, Archbishop John Hughes of New York and Bishop Patrick Neison Lynch of Charleston, encouraged Verot to keep the schools open, and in April, 1861, after the academies had been in operation a year, and two free schools had been opened in conjunction with them, the *Examiner* spoke a different language: "Too much gratitude cannot be felt by the Citizens of St. Augustine, to the Catholic Bishop and Priests, under whose auspices the schools connected with that Church have been established."

In 1859 the western panhandle of Florida that remained in the Diocese of Mobile received a new ordinary. Bishop Portier died on May 14, 1859, and on the following August 1 the Congregation of Propaganda Fide in Rome chose to succeed him Father John Quinlan, rector of Mount Saint Mary's of the West, major seminary for the Province of Cincinnati, at Cincinnati. The new bishop was born at Cloyne in County Cork, Ireland, on October 19, 1826, and emigrated to the United States at the age of eighteen. He studied for the priesthood at Cincinnati and at Mount St. Mary's in Emmitsburg, Maryland, and was ordained at Cincinnati on August 30, 1852. After serving for two years in parishes at Cincinnati and Piqua, Ohio, he was named rector of the provincial seminary. He was consecrated for the See of Mobile on December 4, 1859, in ceremonies at the Cathedral of St. Louis in New Orleans. Six days later he was installed in his diocese. After a warm Mobile welcome, which included the gift of a $700 horse and buggy, Bishop Quinlan began to take stock of his new charge. Alabama and west Florida together counted about 10,000 Catholics. Of that number it is not recorded how many lived in the Florida portion of the diocese, though the percentage likely was small. The west Florida counties under Quinlan had a total population at that time of 30,456, and of these, 1,037 were Irish, German, English, French, and Scottish aliens. St. Michael's Church in Pensacola was in the care of Father Patrick Francis Coyle, who also served St. John the Evangelist in Warrington and the missions at Barrancas and Perdido. Father Dominic Gibbons was stationed at St. Patrick's in Apalachicola. Neither parish had grown much in the preceding decade, but the outlook of the people was optimistic, even in the face of clouds that now hung threateningly over everyone's horizon.

The clouds of war boiled over the entire nation as 1860 drew to a close. On December 3 President James Buchanan, having despaired of all other means to prevent North and South from rushing headlong toward a fatal collision on the slavery issue, proclaimed

Friday January 4, 1861, as a day "set apart for Humiliation, Fasting and Prayer." In St. Augustine Bishop Verot chose that occasion to deliver a remarkable sermon in defense of Southern rights. Standing in the pulpit of the old Spanish church, Verot excoriated the "false and unjust principles of Abolitionism." The institution of slavery, he said, did not offend any of the sanctions of natural law, divine positive law, ecclesiastical law, or civil law. Granted that slavery was not an ideal form of life, and it ought to be abolished gradually, by careful stages, it was no worse a form of life than that of the average wage earner in the industries of the North. "It is truly remarkable how gay, cheerful, and sprightly are the slaves of the South. I do not hesitate to say that they seem to be better contented than their masters; assuredly more so than the sullen and gloomy population found in the work shops and factories of large cities." Indeed, the bishop argued, "A man may sell his labor and work for a day, a week, a month, or a year: why may he not sell it for all his life?" What particularly nettled Verot was the fact that many of the abolitionist voices belonged to Know-Nothing bigots whose "unholy attacks" had only recently been directed toward the Catholic Church. "But the South," he warned, "has not been, and will not, as a Nation, be as patient as the Catholic Church." These words electrified his audience, and were afterwards published and disseminated throughout the South as a Confederate tract. In the North they earned for Augustin Verot the opprobrium of being a "rebel bishop." What very few remarked at this time, either North or South, was the second half of the sermon. By 1865, less sure of the moral grounds on which the Confederacy fought, Southern newspapers would be quoting that second half rather than the first.

What Bishop Verot went on to say was that slaveholders had certain duties as well as rights, and that not all had observed those duties. Some masters had cruelly abused their slaves, treating them as animals instead of as their fellow human beings. Thus they had proven themselves unworthy of their own rights; they had abjured human nature and made themselves liable to expulsion from human society itself. He gave a number of examples, in the course of which he made this eloquent condemnation: "I am a sincere and devoted friend of the South, to which Divine Providence sent me, and I am ready to undergo any hardship—to make any sacrifice—for the true welfare of the people among whom I live; still I must say it for conscience sake—who knows whether the Almighty does not design to use the present disturbances for the destruction of frequent occasions of immorality, which the subservient and degraded position of the slave offers to the lewd. I hope I am a false prophet: but at the same time, I must admonish my countrymen that obscure, secret, and hidden crimes often call for an open, public, and solemn chastisement at the hands of the Supreme Moderator of events. . . . The Southern Confederacy, if it should exist, must rest on morality and justice, and it could never be entitled to a special protection from above, unless it professes to surround Slavery with the guarantees that will secure its morality and virtue." The bishop then proposed that a "servile code" be adopted that would (a) repudiate the international slave trade; (b) protect the liberty of free Negroes; (c) require masters to treat their slaves with justice, fairness, and morality; (d) allow slaves freedom to choose partners of their own liking and to remain joined together with them; (e) compel delinquent masters to provide their slaves with adequate food, clothing, and shelter; and finally (f) to provide that slaves be given the means of knowing and practicing religion. On this last point Verot argued that to deny Negroes religious instruction "would be the sure way to render slavery an untenable and ruinous institution, deserving the contempt of men, and the malediction of God." This was the first such servile code proposed in the South. As the Civil War ran its course, similar demands for slavery reform were heard in other quarters of the Confederacy. By 1865 the Protestant and secular press alike was supporting all the same conditions that Bishop Verot had laid down in 1861 as necessary for a just and lawful slavery.

Florida's dynamic bishop surprised everyone, possibly himself included, with the vigor and the depth of his involvement with the political controversies of 1861. He was the first Catholic prelate, North or South, to commit himself on the social principles at stake in that controversy, and he seems to have been the first bishop since the establishment of the American episcopate in 1790 to enter national politics on an issue not directly affecting Catholicism as such.

171

Other bishops soon followed, however, and when on April 12, 1861, the guns at last began to roar at Fort Sumter, the bishops of the country lined up along geographical lines as everyone else was doing. Bishop Quinlan of Mobile was an early and militant supporter of secession, as were his Catholic people in Florida and Alabama. The majority of Catholics in Florida lived, of course, within the confines of Bishop Verot's vicariate, and encouraged by their outspoken spiritual leader, they too warmly embraced the Confederate cause and prepared to defend it on the field of honor. The struggle now joined between North and South would prove that, if there had ever been any question that Florida Catholics made good Americans, there could be no question after 1861 that they certainly made good Confederates.

The Diocese of Savannah had been vacant since the death of Bishop John Barry on November 21, 1859. Now that war was beginning in the American states, it was imperative that a bishop be named to the see. On July 22, 1861, Pope Pius IX named Augustin Verot to be Third Bishop of Savannah. Thus in addition to Florida which he retained, Verot had also to care for the entire state of Georgia with its 8,000 Catholics. On September 1 he took possession of the see. The installation occurred at a time when the war was about to touch Florida and Georgia directly. Only two months later, Union troops landed at Port Royal, South Carolina, and the residents of Savannah, Catholics with the rest, fled the city in panic. Verot wrote to a colleague in New Orleans: "It is a veritable 'stampede.' The Yankees are only a day's march from Savannah. I must not leave my post. . . ."

Florida experienced panics of its own in 1862. Union troops landed with ease at Fernandina (March 2), Jacksonville (March 12), and St. Augustine (March 11). Fernandina and St. Augustine would remain in Federal hands for the duration of the war. Jacksonville would be occupied off and on four separate times. Father Clavreul, newly arrived from France, was serving at Fernandina, Amelia Island, when Federal gunboats appeared there on March 2. "It was garrisoned by a force of 2,000 men," he wrote, "recruits from all parts of the State, who at the first appearance of the Federal gunboats, abandoned the island to take refuge on the mainland." Two months later Clavreul managed to cross the lines to Savannah and to bring Bishop Verot news of desecrations committed by the invaders. Some of the landing troops, he reported, had broken open the church and stolen its vestments and chalice. Outraged, Verot sent a strong protest to the nearest Union general officer, who dispatched equally strong orders to Colonel Richard Rich, commanding the troops in the city: "Such an act of sacrilege must be detected and punished. . . . If necessary open every knapsack in your command and examine every house in the city." There is no record that the stolen articles were recovered.

Panic and retreat also greeted the appearance of Federal gunboats off St. Augustine on March 10. A Confederate soldier attending Mass celebrated by Father Aulance in the parish church was handed a message reading, "The Yankees are landing." The report passed from pew to pew, and soon the church was in a state of pandemonium. The congregation poured out of the doors, raced to their homes to gather a few belongings, and fled from the city. A letter writer said: "The Catholic congregation left en'masse [*sic*], not heeding the remonstrance of Father Lance [*sic*]." The Confederate troops were not far behind them. The next day Union forces landed against no resistance. News of St. Augustine's capture greatly saddened Bishop Verot in Savannah. When fears of invasion of his own city had subsided, on July 2, he left Savannah to see what he could do for the Sisters of Mercy who remained in the "Ancient City." The Christian Brothers had closed their boys' academy at the beginning of the war, and now that many Catholic families of the city had fled into the interior, St. Mary's Academy conducted by the sisters was virtually deprived of its student body. Reluctantly the sisters closed the doors of their own school in May. Bishop Verot successfully passed through the Union lines and made arrangements to take out seven of the eleven sisters to Columbus, Georgia. He was ready to depart with the sisters on August 7, but Federal officers refused him a pass for ten days, during which Verot described himself as "a prisoner of the Yankees." Finally allowed to leave on August 17, the bishop and the sisters with their baggage passed through the north picket posts toward Jacksonville. Their transportation consisted of an old wagon drawn by a mule recently broken, a horse-drawn tent wagon covered by a ragged carpet, and two dump carts drawn by mules in rope harness. Before this unlikely procession reached Jacksonville the next evening, the bishop lived through a number of extraordinary experiences, some comic, some grave. A short distance north of St. Augustine, he was pursued and stopped by Union cavalry after a rumor spread through the countryside that he was transporting slaves into Georgia in the guise of Sisters of Mercy! During the first night, spent in a deserted house along the roadway twenty miles short of Jacksonville, the bishop tried sleeping on boards placed between two stools, but a loud crash halfway through the night announced to the sisters in the next room that the device did not work. A fall of a different kind occurred the next morning when Verot tried leaping over a good-sized waterhole; this time the travelers had to interrupt their journey while the bishop's clothes dried. Reaching the St. Johns River shortly after dark, the party crossed over to Jacksonville by raft. Halfway across, the raft was struck by a volley of rifle balls fired by rebel infantry. No one was injured, and after a lantern signal from the boatman, the firing ceased. From Jacksonville the only open route to Savannah was circuitous: first by rail to Lake City on the Florida, Atlantic and Gulf Central Line, then by stagecoach to the railhead at the Georgia border, finally by rail to Savannah. Only one incident occurred on these three legs of the journey, but it was memorable. Three hours west of Jacksonville, the bishop's train was stopped and boarded by Confederate Partisan Rangers under Captain John Westcot. The Rangers were a newly organized guerrilla band, "wild-looking fellows in bandit costume," one of the sisters remembered later, "red shirts, black pantaloons, leathern belts with huge daggers and pistols stuck in them, and broad-brimmed straw hats." The bishop was taken off the train and questioned for an hour by Westcot, then he returned to his seat, and the train was allowed to go on. The party reached Savannah safely on the evening of August 23. Several weeks later the bishop ordered a *Te Deum* of thanksgiving for Confederate victories of that summer to be sung in all the Catholic Churches of Florida and Georgia, "with the exception of St. Augustine."

The Catholics who lived under Bishop Quinlan in west Florida had also tasted war as the year 1862 drew to a close. In January of that year, only five months after Quinlan had dedicated a new church at Apalachicola, the state troops defending that city were disbanded and the city was left defenseless against Union blockaders. In consequence, most of the population fled to Ricco's Bluff on the Apalachicola River about ninety miles inland. A detachment of Union soldiers and marines landed at Apalachicola on April 2, but left shortly after ceremonies marking the city's surrender. Union forces did not reoccupy the city during the rest of the war, but neither did most of the inhabitants, and the Catholic parish languished as a result. At Pensacola Father Patrick F. Coyle of St. Michael's was commissioned a Confederate chaplain in May, 1861, to care for the Southern garrisons at Forts McRee and Barrancas, which had been abandoned by Federal troops early in the war. When the Pensacola navy yard at Warrington was surrendered on January 12, 1861 to a combined force of Florida and Alabama troops, the Union held only Fort Pickens. The latter installation stood on Santa Rosa Island, where it commanded the entrance to Pensacola Bay. It would remain in Federal hands during the entire course of the war.

In the summer of 1861 Brigadier General Braxton Bragg, commanding the Confederate troops at Pensacola, sent a request to Mobile for Catholic sisters to treat the many diseased men in his command. Bishop Quinlan sent six Daughters of Charity of St. Vincent de Paul, whose Order staffed two hospitals and one orphanage in his diocese. The sisters left Mobile on August 12 and arrived at Warrington two days later after a difficult journey. General Bragg at once placed them in charge of his hospital, which stood on a rise overlooking Pensacola Bay in full view of the Federal lines around Fort Pickens on Santa Rosa Island. There were two wards, one for Floridians, the other for Alabamians. Most of the patients had what the doctors called "tropical fever." Soon after the sisters' arrival, an epidemic of measles caused the hospitalization of over 800 men, and for lack of beds most of the men had to lie on the floor with knapsacks under their heads. The sisters were shocked to find that the physicians took an indifferent attitude toward their patients, and that many cases had serious bed sores, some had gangrene, and at least two had their bedclothes grown into their backs. "On investigation," one of the sisters wrote, "I found for seven weeks they had been lying in [the] same position and without a change of clothing and owing to the fetid smell, when [the clothing was] removed, we could not induce one of the men to assist in cleansing or purifying their sores." What most startled the sisters, however, was the fear that their presence seemed to induce in the patients: many soldiers were seeing a religious habit for the first time in their lives, and the spread-eagled *cornette* of the seventeenth-century French peasant worn by the Daughters of Charity was not exactly a reassuring sign to fever-stricken youths from the piney woods of Florida or the cotton fields of Alabama. One of the nuns, obviously not very literate, described the reaction of one group of soldiers toward the sisters: "On one occasion there were quite a number come to the hospital sick, and when we went into the wards they covered their heads with the blankets and nothing would induce them to uncover them while we were in the wards for three or four days, as they were so frightened at our appearance or so 'skerte' as they used to say, they were anxious to know to what regiment we belonged to [sic] or if we had been engaged in any battles for if ever we were the 'Yankeese' [sic] would be more afraid of us than any gun the boys could show them. . . ."

In the early fall of 1861 three of the sisters and the seriously ill men were evacuated two miles to the rear. A bombardment was expected from Fort Pickens. The three sisters left behind paraded back and forth in front of the hospital to let the enemy know that it had not been deserted. In the rear the evacuated cases were placed in hastily constructed open sheds where many of them died from exposure. When the expected Union attack failed to materialize, the evacuees were moved back to the hospital. Then, on November 22, as one of the returning sisters wrote, "We were merely settled when too [sic] our astonishment they [Union troops] opened fire on the hospital without the least warning." While the sisters worked to remove the patients, three shells crashed into the building. One entered a clothes room where one of the sisters narrowly escaped death. The Confederate batteries answered

Original frame building of the Church of St. Louis in Tampa, built in 1859 on Florida Avenue and Madison Street. Father Charles A. Mailley, 27-year-old priest from France, was stationed there as Tampa's first pastor in 1860.

Earliest known view, dated 1863, of the barracks in St. Augustine. Portions of the building were once a part of the Franciscan Convent of the Immaculate Conception. The convent was remodeled to serve as a barracks during the British period (1763-1783), and was used for the same purpose by the subsequent Spanish and American governments.

St. Mary's Convent and Academy in St. Augustine. The first convent school in Florida, it opened in 1860 and stood near the corner of St. George Street and what is now Cathedral Place.

Two-story coquina building, south on St. George Street, was used by Father Juan Nepomuceno Gómez as a parish school in 1816 and for several years thereafter. In 1866 the Sisters of St. Joseph opened it as a free school for Negroes. No longer standing, the building was located close to the present entrance to St. Joseph's Academy.

St. George Street entrance to St. Mary's Convent of the Sisters of Mercy during the 1860's. The sisters served in St. Augustine from 1859 until 1870.

Fort Pickens' fire, and an intense, though inconsequential, artillery duel lasted until dark of the following day. In the course of the Union shelling, the village of Warrington was struck by hot shot and the Catholic Church of St. John the Evangelist went up in the resulting flames. When a short time later St. Michael's in Pensacola was destroyed by a blaze that had no connection with the war, west Florida was left with only one church, and it was deserted, St. Patrick's at Apalachicola. In May, 1862, the Confederate forces at Pensacola abandoned their positions as no longer tenable. Ninety per cent of the population fled into the interior, and the sisters returned to Mobile.

On the morning of March 29, 1863, a "fine south wind" was blowing over the city of Jacksonville, Florida. The city had not proven to be the best point from which Union troops might raid the Confederate interior, and now it was being abandoned for the third time. As units of the Eighth Maine and Sixth Connecticut regiments marched toward their vessels, a number of men broke ranks to loot private dwellings, business offices, and stores. Soon a section of the downtown area was in flames and the looters, now an uncontrolled mob, swept toward the Church of the Immaculate Conception. What happened next was described the following day by a correspondent of the New York *Tribune:* "Yesterday the beautiful little cottage used as the Catholic parsonage, together with the church, was fired by some of the soldiers, and in a short time burned to the ground. Before the flames had fairly reached the church, the soldiers had burst open the doors and commenced sacking it of everything of value. The organ was in a moment torn to strips and almost every soldier who came out seemed to be celebrating the occasion by blowing through an organ pipe." Bishop Verot, who was in Savannah, learned of this act of desecration several days later. He would grieve over it all the rest of his life.

By 1863 many of the Catholic bishops in the country had taken positions on the justice of the Confederate war cause. Bishops Verot and Quinlan were both staunch advocates of the Confederate philosophy, and Verot was particularly outspoken. On November 22, 1863, Verot issued a pastoral letter to his Catholic people in

177

Florida and Georgia in which he assured them that "the justice of our cause is clear; clear enough to admit of no doubts in our mind." In answer to charges published by Archbishop Hughes of New York that the secession of the Southern states was in contravention of the Constitution of the United States and therefore illegal, Verot answered in his pastoral letter that it was not the South but the North that had violated the Constitution, when many of the Northern states enacted "personal liberty laws" nullifying the provisions for pursuit of runaway slaves contained in the Fugitive Slave Act (part of the famous Compromise of 1850). "These enactments of State Legislatures against the law of Congress constituted a true rebellion," the bishop argued, "which was, however, unchecked, either by armies or by blockades . . . and the Northern States having thus themselves broken the Union, the Southern States were not bound to stand by it, and they vindicated only their plain right when they formally abjured a Union which had already been virtually dissolved." In October, 1864, the bishop elaborated on these views in the first three issues of the *Pacificator*, "A Journal Dedicated to the Interests of the Catholic Church in the Confederate States," which he helped found at Augusta, Georgia. But it was the necessity of peace, a peace with honor, a peace that guaranteed Southern independence, that was Verot's overriding concern. In October, 1863, he called on all the bishops of the South to set aside a certain period of prayers to that end, as subsequently was done in the first three weeks of the following December. To his own people in Florida and Georgia he addressed a fervent appeal for such prayers—"to arrest the further effusion of blood which has already deluged our land, and rescue thousands from grief, distress, privations and sufferings which language is inadequate to describe."

On April 11, 1864, while Union General William Tecumseh Sherman was preparing to invade Georgia from Chattanooga, Bishop Verot set out from Columbus to visit the war-contested flatlands of Florida. "I started for Florida down the Chatta[h]oochee [River]," he recorded in his diary, "and preached in a meeting house to a pretty good audience; went to Quincy, where I found a few Catholics but could not say Mass for want of baggage, and arrived at Tallahassee for the third Sunday after Easter." The next day he left for Jacksonville, now occupied again by Union troops, and arrived there on April 21. Just two months before, the Federals had suffered their worst defeat of the Florida campaign at nearby Olustee. "On Sunday, the 24th Ap[ril]," Verot wrote, "I preached in [a] shanty converted into a church, and gave confirmation to a dozen of workmen and Yankee soldiers. The next day, 25th Ap[ril], started for St. Augustine by land in [a] buggy with Father [John Francis R.] Chambon, went to Mandarin and from there to Diego, where I confirmed 5 or 6 children; the next day at [the house of] James Mickler I confirmed half a dozen of persons, some colored. I arrived safely in St. Augustine for the end of April." The bishop remained in the old city, now a Union rest camp, until the first week in June. On June 5, "after great difficulty passing the lines," he made his way to Lake City by rail and preached there in the city hall on the twelfth. On June 14 he arrived safely back in Savannah, completing his second and last wartime visit to Florida.

Two Florida priests spent much of the summer of 1864 in the unfortunate Confederate prison camp (Camp Sumter) at Andersonville, Georgia. The prison was an open pen bordered by a double stockade. Between February, 1864, and April, 1865, some 50,000 Federal soldiers were incarcerated there. During the summer of 1864, 10,187 prisoners died from disease or malnutrition; 2,989 died under the broiling sun of August alone. Bishop Verot visited the place on two occasions, July 18 and 25, and estimated that 30,000 men were imprisoned at that time, "one-fifth perhaps being Catholics." The quality of the bishop's mercy was not strained by the less important imperatives of political conviction, and, full of compassion for the unhappy Yankees, he stationed priests in the camp to care for their spiritual wants. Five priests in all served in the prison that summer. They were the only representatives of religion to enter the compound and to minister among its horrors. Two of the priests were from Florida parishes originally. Father William J. Hamilton had been transferred to Macon after his Church of the Immaculate Conception at Jacksonville was burned by rampaging Union troops in 1863. The other, Father Henry Peter Clavreul, had been serving in Savannah following the Union capture of Fernandina in 1862. Both priests left detailed descriptions of their spiritual ministrations at Andersonville, and the following words from Father Hamilton suggest the agonies that they endured along with the prisoners: "The priests who went there after me, while administering the sacrament to the dying, had to use an umbrella, the heat was so intense. Some of them broke down in consequence of their services there. . . . One of the priests from Savannah [Clavreul] came to Macon, where I reside, completely prostrated, and was sick at my house for several days. . . . I was kept so busily engaged in giving the sacrament to the dying men that I could not observe much; but of course I could not keep my eyes closed as to what I saw there. I saw a great many men perfectly naked, walking about through the stockade perfectly nude; they seemed to have lost all regard for delicacy, shame, morality, or anything else. I would frequently have to creep on my hands and knees into the holes that the men had burrowed into the ground and stretch myself out alongside of them to hear their confessions." It would not be extravagant to say that these two Florida priests, Fathers Hamilton and Clavreul, wrote one of the great stories of charity in the history of the American Church.

On December 21, 1864, Savannah fell to the Union as General Sherman's troops completed their march from Atlanta to the sea. Bishop Verot heard "their yells and hurrahs" as he was saying Mass in the city. Four months later at Appomattox Court House, Virginia, the war ended for everyone. The Confederate flag was furled forever. Its empty flagstaffs looked out on a wrecked Southland—what Verot called "a heap of smoking ruins." The Church of Florida shared in the general devastation and poverty. Not since the time of James Moore's raids in 1702-1704 had the Mother Church of the nation faced such a calamity. Indeed, it is doubtful that the Church anywhere else in the South experienced a setback equal to that which faced Bishops Verot and Quinlan in Florida as the era of Civil War yielded to the era of Reconstruction.

The church at St. Johns Bar (Mayport) lay in ruins. Pillaging Union soldiers had carried away its sacred vessels and had paraded about in its vestments. The church at Fernandina had also been sacked. So had Immaculate Conception at Jacksonville before being burned to the ground. "The officers of the [Federal] Government," Bishop Verot wrote in the 1866 *Catholic Almanac*, "regretting this sad occurrence, have given boards to put up a temporary shelter to assemble the Catholics of the place. They are unable to rebuild the church and the house. . . ." In west Florida under Bishop Quinlan's jurisdiction, St. Michael's at Pensacola had been lost to a fire unconnected with the war, but St. John the Evangelist at Warrington had been destroyed in a Union bombardment. Worse than the physical destruction was the appalling poverty and demoralization of the Catholic people. Bishop Verot wrote to a missionary aid society in France that the people of his vicariate were so desperate that, without help, "many will have to abandon their homes and flee elsewhere lest they die of hunger." When Archbishop Martin J. Spalding of Baltimore sent $1,200 in October, 1865, and another $800 in February, 1866, Verot thanked him from his heart: "Your people have done indeed a noble thing in behalf of the South. May it be returned to them a thousand fold!"

Other than this welcome gift, about the only resources Bishop Verot possessed at this time were his written and spoken words, and these he offered wherever he went, to assuage grief, to mitigate hardship, and to draw what blessings he could from the "Lost Cause": "The war has left you poor, distressed, and reduced to beggary," he told his people. "Be not dismayed: this state of things so untoward in the eyes of the world is full of hope, of consolation, and of spiritual treasures in the eyes of faith and religion. Worldly prosperity is not always a blessing. . . . It makes men live and die as if there was no reality but this earth, and no other world beyond the grave." There were other consolations as well, he said. The Church had come out of the war much richer than she was before in reputation and esteem. The people of the South "have heard the preaching of our missionaries; they have seen them in the hospitals and in the camps; they have witnessed their zeal and their devoutness. A good number of *crackers* have seen our priests and our Sisters of Charity for the first time in their lives, in the towns and in the camps where conscription called them, and they could not but carry away a very favorable impression of what they saw with their own eyes." Besides that, the Catholics of Florida could take justifiable pride in the fact that the Church had vigorously and steadfastly supported their legitimate political aspirations, and that the patriotism of their two bishops and of their all too few priests, having been weighed in the scale, had proven to be second to that of no other group of leaders in the state.

Bishop Quinlan had not visited west Florida during the course of the war, owing to his refusal to take an oath of allegiance to the United States, an oath which he understood was a prerequisite for obtaining a pass to cross the Union lines around Pensacola. At war's end Quinlan took stock of his resources in the western panhandle. The church at Apalachicola still stood. Deserted by its congregation in 1862, it now filled again and took on new life. But the churches at Pensacola and Warrington lay in ruins. In August, 1866, the bishop wrote Archbishop John Purcell of Cincinnati: "The two burnt churches of Pensacola and Warrington Navy-Yard I have made contracts for the building of. In the Navy-Yard the Catholics will be able, I think, to pay for their church, owing to the generous cooperation of the Navy officers and seamen; but the Pensacolans, in consequence of the burning of their property are utterly unable of themselves to erect anything in the shape of a building at all large enough for their accommodation." Quinlan went ahead nevertheless with a contract for a new church at Pensacola—"it had to be done or the people must spiritually suffer." Within the year both Pensacola and Warrington had churches again, and a succession of young priests during the remainder of the 1860's effected a marked renewal in the material and spiritual welfare of the two congregations. By 1870 Pensacola boasted a parish school and academy conducted by the Sisters of the Holy Cross with one hundred pupils enrolled.

Teaching sisters were also at work in Bishop Verot's vicariate during the immediate postwar years. In 1865 the Sisters of Mercy reopened St. Mary's Academy at St. Augustine, and in 1866 the Sisters of St. Joseph, a French order from Le Puy, arrived in the same city to open a school for freed Negroes.

The entrance of the French nuns into Florida came at a time when Bishop Verot was working to make the overthrow of slavery both meaningful and beneficial for the Negro people of Florida and

Georgia. At war's end the bishop had laid aside his proslavery doctrine as though he had never believed it true, and during the years from 1865 forward what reservations he may have maintained about the sudden emancipation of four million slaves was successfully hidden behind his genuine heartfelt concern for the freedmen's welfare. He was confident that the Catholic Church would win the Negroes to her elevating influence, in Verot's words "enlightening, civilizing, and ennobling a race that has suddenly emerged from bondage to the enjoyment of civil rights and the blessings of liberty." The education and Christian instruction of a people who heretofore had been denied those rights of the human mind Verot judged to be the greatest challenge ever to face Catholicism in the South. In two important and widely noted pastoral letters, dated October 4, 1865, and August 1, 1866, he proclaimed a new social order for the Negroes, but cautioned them at the same time that their freedom was all in vain if they now gave themselves over to practices that violated law and order; there was a slavery worse than the one from which they had just emerged, he said: "It is the slavery of sin, the slavery of wicked and criminal passions, the slavery of bad habits and evil practices." To the white population Verot addressed these words: "We exhort all to put away all prejudice, all dislike, all antipathy, all bitterness against their former servants. Away with all feelings of bickerings, envy or jealousy which would only bespeak a narrow mind and the lack of noble and elevated feelings. The golden rule, *love thy neighbor as thy self*, must not admit of any exception."

In June, 1865, the bishop sailed for Europe to obtain teaching sisters for the Negro children in Florida and Georgia. At his native city of Le Puy he asked for eight nuns from the Congrégation de St. Joseph (Sisters of St. Joseph). Sixty volunteered, from whom eight were chosen: Sisters Marie Sidonie Rascle, Marie Julie Roussel, Joséphine Déléage, Saint Pierre Borie, Clémence Freycenon, Marie-Joseph Cortial, Marie Célenie Joubert, and Julie Clotilde Arsac. To their mother superior, Léocadie Broc, the bishop said: "I want you to understand fully and clearly that it is for the Negroes and for them almost exclusively that I have arranged for the daughters of your Order to come into my diocese. I have five or six hundred thousand Negroes without any education or religion . . . for whom I wish to do something." The sisters took ship at Le Havre in August, 1866, and one month later, after brief stops at New York and Savannah, they landed in Florida at Picolata, the mail station for St. Augustine on the St. Johns River. A stagecoach took them the rest of the way to St. Augustine, where the Sisters of Mercy gave them temporary lodging at St. Mary's Convent, on the northwest corner of St. George Street and what is now Cathedral Place. Bishop Verot arrived in St. Augustine shortly afterwards and placed the nuns under his personal instruction in the English language.

Only five months later, in February, 1867, the sisters were able to open a school for Negro children in a small building that stood on the east side of St. George Street, near the present gate of St. Joseph's Academy. About the same time they moved their residence to the former house of Father Michael O'Reilly on Hospital (now Aviles) Street. Toward the end of the year Father Dufau moved them again, this time to the former residence of the Christian Brothers on South Charlotte Street, where they remained for the remainder of Bishop Verot's episcopate. More sisters arrived from Le Puy in 1867 and 1868. By May of the latter year, the Sisters of St. Joseph had sixty Negro pupils in their school at St. Augustine, and had begun two new schools for the children of former slaves at Jacksonville and Savannah. In 1870 they opened still another school at Fernandina. To Bishop Verot the sisters' success seemed to presage a new age for the Negroes of Florida, and for the Church who sought to win the freedmen to her creed and altar. Neither hope would be realized, however, as the freedom of the Negro was gradually circumscribed by successive state legislatures, and the Catholic Faith proved to be less attractive to the Negro than Verot had anticipated. By the end of the century most Negroes in the state would belong to Negro-run evangelical groups that bore little resemblance to the pioneer religion of Florida. In the long run Bishop Verot failed. But he remains the first great figure in the first great social enterprise to occupy the interests and energies of American Catholics.

From 1866 forward, missionary aid funds came to Bishop Verot from the Society for the Propagation of the Faith in France. These funds, together with the receipts from two begging tours of the North made by Verot in 1866 and 1867, enabled him to undertake the reconstruction or enlargement of several churches in the vicariate. The entries in his diary during the years 1865 to 1870 record seven extended trips through the mission fields of Florida. His itineraries carried him to all the prewar stations, and to new stations at Lake City, Madison, Monticello, St. Mark's, Newport, Quincy, and Chattahoochee, all attended from the handsome brick Church of Mater Dolorosa at Tallahassee; Starke and Cedar Key, attended from Fernandina; New Smyrna, Orange Springs, and Ocala, attended from St. Monica's Church at Pilatka (Palatka); and Miami, "where a remnant of Seminole Indians can be seen occasionally," Verot said, attended from St. Mary Star of the Sea at Key West. Verot visited Key West three different times between 1865 and 1870. Since the death of Father Hunincq in 1862, the parish had seen a succession of priests: Felix Ciampi, S.J., and Joseph M. Encisio, S.J. (both from Havana), 1862; James Hasson, 1862-63; James O'Hara, 1863-66; and Henry Peter Clavreul, 1866. Father J. B. Allard served as pastor for the rest of the decade, and for a time, 1869-70, he had the assistance of Father Paul La Roque, future Second Bishop of Sherbrooke in Canada. In 1868 Bishop Verot secured five Sisters of the Holy Names of Jesus and Mary from Montreal to open a school at Key West. The sisters arrived in the latter part of that year and established a convent in the abandoned Union officers' quarters of the late war. Within a short time their school was under way.

The bishop also found more priests for his vicariate in the years from 1865 through 1870. Through intermediaries he recruited a number from France, Italy, and Canada. Several more came to Florida for reasons of health. And another group, members of the Congregation of the Most Holy Redeemer (Redemptorists), came on special invitation to give missions, or revivals, at Jacksonville and St. Augustine. Fathers Joseph Wissel, Nicholas Jaeckel, Timothy Enright, and William H. Gross (future Fifth Bishop of Savannah) arrived in Florida at the start of 1868. The Jacksonville mission took place in the makeshift board church that had been put up by

Federal occupation troops. "Our mission was a perfect jubilee," Father Gross recorded. "The Protestants even attended in such glee that balls and parties were deferred until after the Mission. . . ." In St. Augustine the *Examiner* remarked the extraordinary crowds that attended the lectures of Fathers Wissel and Jaeckel and expressed its hope "that our City will long remember the present occurrence, and that the Mission will banish many vices from our midst, and will give a tone of morality, honesty and industry that will be more creditable to our City than the empty privilege of being the Oldest City in the Country." Redemptorist missionaries returned to give missions at Jacksonville and St. Augustine in 1869, and in 1870 a final Redemptorist campaign took two priests on a restricted mission to Key West and Dry Tortugas Islands.

Bishop Verot thought that the whole of Florida, including the counties west of the Apalachicola, deserved to be erected to the dignity of a separate diocese, with St. Augustine as see city. As early as 1866 he communicated this view to Archbishop Spalding at Baltimore: "St. Augustine has many titles to the honor of being an episcopal city. It is the oldest City of the United States; the population is almost exclusively Catholic . . . and there are more antiquities & precious reminiscences in St. Augustine than in any other church of the United States. . . . The only reason I know against the expediency of raising St. Augustine to an Episcopal See is that the City is not populous, having only two thousand inhabitants, & that Florida is exceedingly poor; if not assisted by the French Propagation of Faith, it could scarcely support one priest; things however may improve."

Things did improve. As the decade neared its close the Church at St. Augustine was enjoying a modest prosperity and the vicariate of Florida as a whole could count nineteen churches and chapels, seven schools, twelve priests, and about 10,000 Catholics. Out of the "heap of smoking ruins" left by the Civil War, Bishop Verot with his priests and people had reconstructed and even surpassed the ante-bellum Church. It was an accomplishment quite out of proportion to their numbers and resources, and it marked the peninsular Church with a merit that, Verot thought, deserved recognition from bishops elsewhere in the country. That recognition came, finally, during the Tenth Provincial Council of Baltimore in 1869. (The ecclesiastical Province of Baltimore included the Archdiocese of Baltimore and the following dioceses: Wheeling, Richmond, Charleston, Savannah, and St. Augustine.) On April 26 at ten-thirty in the morning, Bishop Verot described the great improvement of the Church in Florida to Archbishop Spalding and the other prelates of the province. Bishops Richard Whelan of Wheeling and Patrick Neison Lynch of Charleston moved that the new diocese be erected. The resulting vote was unanimous in favor, but the bishops placed the western limits of the diocese at the Apalachicola River, instead of at the Perdido, as Verot had wished. Whelan proposed that Jacksonville be selected as the see city because of its growing importance as a port and commercial center. The other bishops, however, joined Verot in choosing St. Augustine. Several days later a letter was sent to Rome requesting the new jurisdiction. The Holy See wrote back on February 25, 1870, announcing its approval.

On March 11, 1870, during the course of the First Ecumenical Council of the Vatican at Rome, the Diocese of St. Augustine was formally erected, and Augustin Verot, at his own request, was transferred from Savannah to St. Augustine as first bishop of the new diocese. Verot was in Rome at the time attending the Council, where he distinguished himself by the learned and trenchant speeches that he made on matters that came before that assembly of the world's bishops. He wrote at the conclusion of the council to the superior of the Sisters of St. Joseph at Le Puy: "I have chosen St. Augustine in preference to Savannah, principally because St. Augustine and Florida are the place where I was first sent, and also because in Florida there is more holy poverty as well as more good to be done in building churches and founding schools." In St. Augustine, observing that the old parish church was now a cathedral, the local *Examiner* exulted: "Everywhere in this new land the erection of a City into a bishopric has been the signal of immense material improvement. . . . Beyond a doubt the population of the Ancient City will double in the next ten years."

Bishop Verot's outlook was more reserved. On taking possession of the Diocese of St. Augustine on October 23, 1870, he cautioned his people not to expect a more rapid growth of the Church than their few material resources would permit. The events bore him out. Just as the subsequent growth of the see city failed to match the expectations of the *Examiner*, so the subsequent expansion of the Church in Florida proceeded at a slower pace than that predicted by the more sanguine of the bishop's subjects. Still, it was hard to temper the optimism of Florida Catholics. For everyone sensed, and rightly we may say, that the early history of the Catholic Church in Florida was ended, and a new and larger history had begun.

EPILOGUE

The diocese of st. augustine remained under Augustin Verot until the bishop's death on June 10, 1876. His successor, John Moore (1834-1901), born at Rossmead, Ireland, was consecrated May 13, 1877. Through the introduction of Jesuits to the Tampa area and Benedictines to Pasco County, Bishop Moore could count thirty-two priests in the diocese by the turn of the century. Three of his diocesan priests, Fathers Charles Peterman, Felix Swemberg, and Denis O'Sullivan, died at Tampa fighting the yellow fever epidemic that swept much of Florida in 1887-88. In Jacksonville the burden of caring for victims of the fever fell upon Father William J. Kenny (1853-1913), pastor of Immaculate Conception, who in 1902 succeeded Moore and was the first native American bishop of the diocese.

From Delhi, New York, originally, Father Kenny grew up in Scranton, Pennsylvania, and was ordained a priest in 1879 at the Cathedral of St. Augustine. His consecration as bishop, on May 18, 1902, also took place in the cathedral and was the first such event in the history of the city. During Bishop Kenny's administration, the Church experienced a steady growth and a number of important parishes were established in the south of the peninsula.

Father Michael J. Curley (1879-1947), a priest of the diocese stationed in DeLand, was named to succeed Bishop Kenny, who died in 1913. Born in Athlone, Ireland, Father Curley was ordained at Rome in 1903. In DeLand his powerful sermons and attractive personality drew as many Protestants as Catholics to his Masses. When he was consecrated in the Cathedral of St. Augustine on

189

June 30, 1914, he was, at thirty-six, the youngest bishop in the country. In 1915 and 1916 Bishop Curley had to face a swelling tide of anti-Catholicism in the state, which at one point caused three Sisters of St. Joseph in St. Augustine to be arrested on the charge of teaching Negro children. The bigotry reached a climax in 1916 when Sidney J. Catts was elected governor of Florida on an anti-Catholic platform. Bishop Curley's reasoned and eloquent defense of the Church during this period was widely noted in the country, and in 1922 he was named to succeed James Cardinal Gibbons as Archbishop of Baltimore.

His successor, the Fifth Bishop of St. Augustine, was Patrick Barry (1863-1940), born in County Clare, Ireland, and a priest of the diocese since 1895. Father Barry was founding pastor of the Church of the Assumption in South Jacksonville and later rector of the Cathedral and vicar-general of Bishop Curley. He was consecrated at St. Augustine on May 3, 1922. During the first ten years of his episcopate, which corresponded roughly with Florida's first boom, the Church in Florida experienced a phenomenal growth. Between 1922 and 1932, the number of diocesan priests increased from 29 to 72, parishes from 32 to 60, schools from 27 to 37, and the number of students in the Catholic school system from 4,000 to 8,000. Bishop Barry died on August 13, 1940, near the close of the depression which had temporarily slowed the Church's growth.

Bishop Joseph P. Hurley (born in 1894), a native of Cleveland, Ohio, acceded to the see in 1940; he received the personal title of archbishop in 1950. In 1958 the southern 16 counties of Florida were separated to form the new Diocese of Miami, and Bishop Coleman F. Carroll (born in 1905), a native of Pittsburgh, Pennsylvania, was appointed as first ordinary. The counties west of the Apalachicola River continued as part of the Diocese of Mobile-Birmingham. Originally suffragan sees of Baltimore, the Dioceses of St. Augustine and Miami were transferred to the Province of Atlanta when it was formed in 1962. The extraordinary growth of the Church in all parts of Florida since the end of the Second World War can be seen in the figures for priests, brothers, sisters, communicants, parishes, schools, and charitable institutions published annually in the *National Catholic Directory*.

THE SOURCES

T
HIS VOLUME was written in popular narrative form for the general reader. It anticipates a more detailed and documented study to follow later. For the benefit of students and professional historians, however, the principal sources for this narrative are given below.

MANUSCRIPT SOURCES

All the following manuscript collections are in the Mission of Nombre de Dios Library, St. Augustine, Florida.

(A) *Papeles de Pedro Menéndez de Avilés.*—(Microfilm.) These papers of the founder of Nombre de Dios and St. Augustine include cédulas, commissions, letters, reports, and memorials relating to Florida's infant colony from the period immediately prior to Menéndez' voyage in 1565 until his death at Santander in 1574. Photoduplicated for the first time in 1964 by the St. Augustine Foundation, the papers have been retained in the private possession of Alvaro Armada, el Conde de Revillagigedo, a direct descendent of Menéndez, and present holder of the title Adelantado de la Florida. The papers are stored in the Count's archives at Gijón under the designation, Casa de Canalejas, Legajo 2.

(B) *St. Augustine Parish Registers.*—(Original.) The oldest written records of American origin in the United States, these registers of the Spanish Parish of St. Augustine comprise 1,340 pages in fifteen folio volumes. From the first entry, dated June 25, 1594 (registers for the first 29 years of the parish were lost or destroyed), the registers form a continuous record to 1763, when Florida was ceded by Spain to England. The registers were removed by the departing Spanish population to Cuba, where they remained in the archives of the Cathedral of Havana for the next 143 years. Bishop Augustin Verot, first bishop of the Diocese of Saint Augustine (erected 1870), discovered the registers at Havana in 1871. They were finally returned to their proper parish church, then a cathedral, in 1906. In 1939, at the instance of Bishop Patrick Barry (1922-40), the register pages were laminated in protective sheaths of cellulose acetate foil under a cooperative program with the Carnegie Institute and the National Archives.

For historians of early Spanish St. Augustine, the registers form a valuable parochial and genealogical record. They indicate the origin of many of the Spanish families, as well as of the Negroes, Indians, and mixed racial groups of colonial Florida, and they include as well certain marginal data that will be of interest to the student of social history. A description of the contents follows:

GROUP I

Volume I: Baptisms, Marriages, Burials, 1594-1638 (184 pages).
II: Confirmations, 1735-1755 (65 pp.).

GROUP II: MARRIAGES

I: 1643-1725 (159 pp.).
II: 1720-1756 (171 pp.).
III: 1735-1756 (97 pp. with blanks).

GROUP III: BURIALS

I: 1720-1743 (148 pp.).
II: 1745-1765 (162 pp. with blanks).
III: 1736-1763 (129 pp. with blanks).

GROUP IV: BAPTISMS

I: 1675-1694 (194 pp.).
II: 1695-1720 (184 pp.).
III: 1720-1737 (193 pp.).
IV: 1735-1763 (186 pp. with blanks).
V: 1737-1751 (198 pp.).
VI: 1751-1760 (188 pp.).
VII: 1760-1763 (73 pp.).

(C) *The Stetson Collection.*—(Microfilm.). This exceptionally valuable collection consists of 100,000 pages of photostats taken from the colonial archives of Spain, particularly the Archivo General de Indias at Seville. It includes official correspondence between Spain and Florida for a period of more than three centuries (that is, from 1518 to 1821). Without question it is the most comprehensive collection of its kind outside Spain itself. The great majority of the documents deal with the first period of the Spanish occupancy of Florida (1565-1763). The collection was amassed in the late 1920's under the patronage of John Batterson Stetson, Jr., and the direction of James Alexander Robertson, and originally was known as the Florida State Historical Collection. In 1929 the collection was stored at Tocoma Park, Maryland, and later was placed on sealed loan to the Library of Congress. In 1954 it was returned to Florida and stored in the P. K. Yonge Library of Florida History of the University of Florida at Gainesville. An index of the documents was prepared by William B. Griffen in 1959. Realizing that this collection contained a large number of untapped sources for Florida's mission period, 1565-1704, the St. Augustine Foundation established a Graduate Research Assistantship at the University of Florida, in 1963, for the purpose of indexing and calendaring all the materials in the collection that dealt with the Parish of St. Augustine and the interior and coastal missions. This program, which occupied the labor of three graduate historians, was successfully completed in the spring of 1965. In the same year the Mission of Nombre de Dios secured the entire collection itself on microfilm, under a cooperative program with the University of Florida.

(D) *"Golden Book of the Minorcans."*—(Original.) This one-volume register began as the parish record of Father Pedro Camps, pastor of the ill-fated Minorcan colony at New Smyrna in 1768. The priest and his parishioners took refuge at St. Augustine in 1777, and the register came with them. Although the Minorcans (who numbered among them many of Greek and Italian origin) were later absorbed into the Parish of St. Augustine following the retrocession of Florida to Spain in 1783, they continued to record in their "Golden Book" the principal ecclesiastical events of their lives. When Florida became a territory of the United States in 1821, most of the Minorcans remained and formed themselves into Church Wardens for the administration of the church building. The minutes of the wardens' meetings over the stormy next thirty-seven years comprise the greater part of the volume, which is 140 pages in length. Recently, a separate 24-page volume of wardens' minutes for the years 1831-33 was discovered in St. Augustine, and added to the above collection.

(E) *The East Florida Papers.*—(Microfilm.) These papers constitute the archives of the Spanish government of East Florida between the years 1783, when England retroceded the area to Spain, and 1821, when the young United States took possession. East Florida was the name given during most of this period to the entire peninsula exclusive of the panhandle. Fully as important to historical scholarship as the Stetson Collection, these documents, 65,000 in number, are an indispensable source for Florida's second Spanish period, which has too long been neglected in the accounts written of the later colonial history of the Spanish empire, the background history of the North American border states, and the history of Florida itself. The larger features of Florida policy during the last generation of Spanish control are revealed in such series as the correspondence between the governors of Florida and the captains general of Cuba; correspondence of the governors with the Spanish departments of the Indies, state, war, grace and justice, and the exchequer; various correspondence with ministers and consuls of the United States; relations with the trading house of Panton, Leslie & Company; and relations with the Indians. In addition, there are various documents from the first Spanish period, including correspondence to and from Governor Manuel de Montiano in the years 1737-41, and an index to all royal decrees and letters relating to Florida from 1595 to 1762. The original papers are preserved at the Library of Congress, where they fill 749 manuscript boxes, 119 volumes of laminated pages, one folder, and two bundle boxes. Federal officials directed their removal from St. Augustine to the state capital of Tallahassee in 1869, and thence to the Library of Congress in 1905. Thanks to a grant from the St. Augustine Foundation, the papers are now home again by film in St. Augustine, where most of them were datelined a century and a half ago.

(F) *Archives of the Diocese of St. Augustine.*—(Original.) The entire extant archives of the diocese prior to 1940 have been boxed, calendared, cross-indexed, and microfilmed under a program inaugurated at the Mission by Archbishop Joseph P. Hurley in 1962. The archives begin with a box containing property deeds, acts of incorporation, parish records, and miscellaneous correspondence from the period 1821-57, when East Florida was governed ecclesiastically by the Diocese of Louisiana and the Floridas (1793-1825), the Vicariate of Alabama and the Floridas (1825-29), the Diocese of Mobile (1829-50), and the Diocese of Savannah (1850-57). As the single box of papers indicates, not much remains from that period. It was a time when East Florida was often without a single priest and more official documents relating to Florida passed between Charleston and Mobile than arrived in Florida itself. With the coming of Bishop Augustin Verot in 1858 as Vicar Apostolic of Florida, the number of ecclesiastical documents increases. Fortunately all the documents of erection and appointment that arrived from the Holy See at that time have survived, as have also the documents for the erection of the Diocese of St. Augustine in 1870 and the appointment of Bishop Verot as first ordinary. Most of the first bishop's own manuscripts and letters received have been either lost or destroyed. However, a large number of his published writings and letters sent have been photoduplicated or transcribed from other archival and library holdings, and these fill two boxes in the present collection.

PRINTED SOURCES

There is an abundant literature on early Florida, much of it rich in detail on the activities of the Catholic Church. In composing the present narrative the following works have been found to be the most helpful. The indispensable study of the early periods of exploration and settlement is still Woodbury Lowery, *The Spanish Settlements Within the Present Limits of the United States, 1513-1574* (2 vols.; New York, 1911). Other valuable general histories for these periods are Andrés Gonzáles de Barcia Carballido y Zúñiga, *Ensayo Cronológico para la Historia General de la Florida* (Madrid, 1723), recently translated by Anthony Kerrigan, *Barcia's Chronological History of the Continent of Florida* (Gainesville, 1951); and Antonio Herrera y Tordesillas, *Historia general de los hechos de los Castellanos en las islas y tierra firme del mar oceano* (6 vols.; Madrid, 1727).

For the expeditions of Ponce de León there is, in addition to Lowery, T. Frederick Davis, "Juan Ponce de León's Voyages to Florida," *Florida Historical Quarterly*, XIV (July, 1935). The classic source for the Pánfilo de Narváez expedition is *La Relación que dio Aluar nuñez cabeça de vaca de lo acaescido en las Indias en la armada donde yua por gouernador Pamphilo de narbaez desde el año de veynte y siete hasta el año de treynta y seys que boluio a Seuilla con tres de su compañia* (Zamora, 1542). The Hernando De Soto expedition was related by an anonymous companion, the "Gentlemen of Elvas," *Relaçam verdadeira dos trabalhos que ho governador Don Fernando de Souto y certos fidalgos portugueses passarom no descobrimento da provinçia de Florida. Agora nouamente feita per hun fidalgo de Eluas* (Évora, Portugal, 1557). Another detailed account was written by Garcilaso de la Vega, "The Inca," *La Florida del Ynca. Historia Adelantado, Hernando de Soto, Gouernador, y Capitain General del Reyno de la Florida y de Otros Heroicos Caualleros, Españoles e Indios* (Lisbon, 1601). The Elvas work was published in facsimile with an English translation by James Alexander Robertson, *True Relation of the Hardships Suffered by Governor Fernando de Soto & Certain Portuguese Gentlemen During the Discovery of the Province of Florida. Now newly set forth by a Gentleman of Elvas* (2 vols.; DeLand, 1933). The most recent and best translation of "The Inca" is John Grier Varner and Jeannette Johnson Varner, *The Florida of the Inca* (Austin, Texas, 1951). Another original account of the De Soto expedition is by Luis Hernández de Biedma, "Relación de la isla de la Florida," in Buckingham Smith (ed.), *Colección de varios Documentos para la Historia de la Florida y Tierras adyacentes (1516-1794)* (London, 1857). An original source for the Fray Luis Cáncer expedition is "Relación de la Florida para el Ilmo. Señor Visorrei de la Nueva Espana la qual trajo Fr. Gregorio de Beteta," in Smith (ed.), *Colección de varios Documentos;* the best secondary account is Victor Francis O'Daniel, O.P., *Dominicans in Early Florida* (New York, 1930). For the Tristán de Luna settlement there are Agustín Dávila y Padilla, O.P., *Historia de la Fundación y Discurso de la Provincia de Santiago de Mexico* (Mexico, 1596), and Herbert Ingram Priestly (ed.), *The Luna Papers, Documents Relating to the Expedition of Don Tristán de Luna y Arellano for the Conquest of La Florida in 1559-1561* (DeLand, 1928).

Many of the documents for Pedro Menéndez de Avilés were published by Eugenio Ruidíaz y Caravia, *La Florida: su conquista y colonización por Pedro Menéndez de Avilés* (2 vols.; Madrid, 1893). The memorial of Father López de Mendoza Grajales is in the Archivo General de Indias, Seville (cited hereafter as AGI), Estante 1, Cajón 1, Legajo 1-19. The memorial has been translated into French, and several times into English. In the present narrative the writer has followed the translation of B. F. French (ed.), *Historical Collections of Louisiana and Florida* (Second Series; New York, 1875). The Gonzalo Solís de Merás biography of Menéndez is part of the Revillagigedo Papers, legajo 2, document no. 2. In the present narrative the writer has followed the translation of Jeannette Thurber Connor (ed.), *Pedro Menéndez de Avilés, Adelantado, Governor and Captain-General of Florida. Memorial by Gonzalo Solís de Merás* (DeLand, Fla., 1923). There are two other sources for the voyage of Menéndez and the subsequent foundation of St. Augustine: (1) a letter from Menéndez to Philip II, St. Augustine, September 11, 1565, the original of which is in the AGI, 54-5-16, and (2) a biography of Menéndez completed in 1567 by Bartolomé Barrientos, professor in the University of Salamanca, "Vida y hechos de Pero Menéndez de Auiles, Cauallero de la Hordem de Sanctiago, Adelantado de la Florida: Do largamente se tratan las Conquistas y Poblaciones de la Prouincia de la Florida, y como fueron libradas de los Luteranos que dellas se auian apoderado." The Barrientos account was published by Genaro García (ed.), *Dos antiguas relaciones de la Florida* (Mexico, 1902).

The early Jesuit missions were treated in Felix Zubillaga, S.I., *La Florida, la Misión Jesuítica (1566-1572) y la Colonización Española* (Rome, 1941). Most of the pertinent Jesuit documents were published in Zubillaga (ed.), *Monumenta Antiquae Floridae (1566-1572)* (Rome, 1946). A popular account is Michael Kenny, *The Romance of the Floridas* (Milwaukee, 1934).

The first years of the Franciscan missions in Florida were the subject of a brilliant study by Maynard Geiger, O.F.M., *The Franciscan Conquest of Florida* (1573-1618) (Washington, D.C., 1937). The "Golden Age" as such has not been treated in any specialized way, although there are disparate materials from that era in Geiger, *Biographical Dictionary of the Franciscans in Spanish Florida and Cuba (1528-1841)* (Paterson, N.J., 1940); an excellent work by John Tate Lanning, *The Spanish Missions of Georgia* (Chapel Hill, N.C., 1935); Fr. Diomede Pohlkamp, O.F.M,, "Spanish Franciscans in the Southeast," *Franciscan History of North America* (Washington, D.C., 1936), pp. 124-50; Zelia Sweett and Mary H. Sheppy, *The Spanish Missions of Florida* (St. Augustine, 1940); Mark F. Boyd, Hale G. Smith, and John W. Griffin, *Here They Once Stood: The Tragic End of the Apalachee Missions* (Gainesville, Fla., 1951); and P. Gregory Joseph Keegan, M.M., y Leandro Tormo Sanz, *Experiencia Misionera en la Florida (Siglos XVI y XVI)* (Madrid, 1957). Most of the information on the "Golden Age" contained in the present narrative was gleaned by the late Father Charles W. Spellman from the Woodbury Lowery Transcripts (AGI papers) in the Library of Congress. The letter of Bishop Gabriel Díaz Vara Calderón on the Florida missions in 1574-75 can be found in Lucy L. Wenhold (ed.), *A 17th Century Letter of Gabriel Díaz Vara Calderón, Bishop of Cuba, Describing the Indians and Indian Missions of Florida* (Washington, D.C., 1936). For the geographic locations of the missions, the student will want to see Mark F. Boyd, "Mission Sites in Florida; An Attempt to Approximately Identify the Sites of Spanish Mission Settlements of the Seventeenth Century in Northern Florida," *Florida Historical Quarterly*, XVII (April, 1939), 254-80; and Boyd, Smith, Griffin, *Here They Once Stood*. Another enumeration of the Florida missions was submitted to Queen Mariana in 1675 by Don Pablo de Hita Salazar, Governor of Florida. Dated at St. Augustine, August 24, 1675, it is in the AGI, 58-1-26/38. Boyd has published a translation, "Enumeration of Florida Spanish Missions in 1675," *Florida Historical Quarterly*, XXVII (October, 1948), 181-88. An important evaluation of the Spanish mission system in Florida was published by Herbert E. Bolton, "The Mission as a Frontier Institution in the Spanish American Colonies," *American Historial Review*, XXIII (October, 1917), 42-61; see also Verner W. Crane, *The Southern Frontier, 1670-1732* (Durham, N.C., 1929), especially pp. 7, 23-27. Verne E. Chatelain has studied the missions in relation to the Spanish military operations in Florida, in *The Defenses of Spanish Florida, 1565 to 1763* (Washington, D.C., 1941). The destruction of the missions in the early eighteenth century is related, with translations of the pertinent documents, in the above cited work of Boyd, Smith, Griffin, *Here They Once Stood*. The subsequent decline of missionary activity as far as 1763 has recently been examined by John Jay TePaske, *The Governorship of Spanish Florida, 1700-1763* (Durham, N.C., 1964). The coming of the Minorcan colony to Florida during the British Period was the subject of a master's thesis by Kenneth H. Beeson, Jr., "Fromajadas and Indigo: The Minorcan Colony in Florida" (University of Florida, Gainesville, 1960). The formal reestablishment of the Church in Florida after the retrocession to Spain in 1783 is treated in Joseph Byrne Lockey (ed.), *East Florida, 1783-1785, A File of Documents Assembled, and Many of Them Translated* (Berkeley, Calif., 1949). The second Spanish period as such has been examined in a first-rate study by Michael J. Curley, C.SS.R., *Church and State in the Spanish Floridas (1783-1822)* (Washington, D.C., 1940).

The Territorial Church has not been treated as a unity prior to Chapter Nine of the present work. There are certain materials for the period published in Clarence Edwin Carter (ed.), *The Territorial Papers of the United States*, Vols. XXII-XXV (Washington, D.C., 1956); Peter Guilday, *The Life and Times of John England, First Bishop of Charleston, 1786-1842* (2 vols.; New York, 1927); and a doctoral dissertation by Oscar H. Lipscomb, "The Administration of Michael Portier, Vicar Apostolic of Alabama and the Floridas, 1825-1829, and First Bishop of Mobile, 1829-1859" (The Catholic University of America, Washington, D.C., 1963). A complete file of the issues of the *United States Catholic Miscellany* is preserved in the archives of the Diocese of Charleston.

The period immediately after statehood (1845) was marked by the property dispute at St. Augustine, for which there is a collection of documents, *Report of the Solicitor of the Treasury with documents in relation to the claims of the Catholic Church at St. Augustine to certain property held by the United States at that place*, 30th Congress, 2nd Session, Senate, Executive Document No. 21, January 30, 1849 (Washington, D.C., 1849); and a recent study: Ambrose B. De Paoli, *Property Laws of the State of Florida Affecting The Church* (Rome, 1965). For Father Varela, there is Joseph J. McCadden, "The New York-to-Cuba Axis of Father Varela," *The Americas*, XX (April, 1964).

The administration of Bishop Verot as Vicar Apostolic of Florida (1858-70) was examined by the present writer in *Rebel Bishop: The Life and Era of Augustin Verot* (Milwaukee, 1964). Other printed sources for Chapter Ten are: Henry Peter Clavreul, *Notes on the Catholic Church in Florida, 1565-1876* (St. Leo, Fla., 1910); Benedict Roth, O.S.B. (ed.), *Brief History of the Churches of the Diocese of Saint Augustine, Florida*, 10 parts (St. Leo, Fla., 1923-34); and a master's thesis by Oscar H. Lipscomb, "The Administration of John Quinlan, Bishop of Mobile, 1859-1883" (The Catholic University of America, Washington, D.C., 1959).

The serious student will want to see several other important secondary sources. Largely outdated now but still valuable for certain episodes is John

Gilmary Shea, *The History of the Catholic Church in the United States* (4 vols.; New York, 1886-92). Also outdated now, and less reliable than Shea, is Jeremiah J. O'Connell, *Catholicity in the Carolinas and Georgia, 1820-1878* (New York, 1879). A new review of the latest research on the early American Church has been published by the country's outstanding Catholic historian, John Tracy Ellis, *Catholics in Colonial America* (Baltimore, 1965). Still valuable, and suggestive of areas for further research, is an article by James A. Robertson, "Notes on the Early Church Government in Spanish Florida," *Catholic Historical Review*, XVII, 2 (July, 1931), 151-74. There is scattered information, particularly on the Church in Spanish times, in the volumes of the *Florida Historical Quarterly*.

INDEX

Printed in the United States
152528LV00005B/14/A